SECOND EDITION

Simon & Schuster

WORKBOOK
for WRITERS

Emily R. Gordon
and
Lynn Quitman Troyka

PRENTICE HALL
Englewood Cliffs, New Jersey   07632

Editorial/production supervision and
  interior design: Virginia Rubens
Cover design: Lorraine Mullaney
Manufacturing buyer: Mary Ann Gloriande

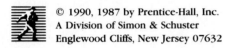
Printed in the United States of America

10 9 8 7 6 5 4 3

ISBN 0-13-808437-8

PRENTICE-HALL INTERNATIONAL (UK) LIMITED, *London*
PRENTICE-HALL OF AUSTRALIA PTY. LIMITED, *Sydney*
PRENTICE-HALL CANADA INC., *Toronto*
PRENTICE-HALL HISPANOAMERICANA, S.A., *Mexico*
PRENTICE-HALL OF INDIA PRIVATE LIMITED, *New Delhi*
PRENTICE-HALL OF JAPAN, INC., *Tokyo*
SIMON & SCHUSTER ASIA PTE. LTD., *Singapore*
EDITORA PRENTICE-HALL DO BRASIL, LTDA., *Rio de Janeiro*

Contents

Part Four

WRITING EFFECTIVE SENTENCES

Part Five

WRITING EFFECTIVE WORDS

Part Six

USING PUNCTUATION AND MECHANICS

Part Seven

WRITING RESEARCH

Preface

We have been deeply gratified by the warm reception of the *Simon & Schuster Workbook for Writers*. In preparing the second edition, we have retained the dual intentions of the original, so the book remains one that can be used as an adjunct to the *Simon & Schuster Handbook for Writers* or as a primary text. To accomplish this, we have carried over key aspects of the first edition:

- Charts and lists highlighting key points, writers' options, and sequences of activities.
- Matching section heads and section numbers for easy cross-reference to the *Simon & Schuster Handbook for Writers*.
- Definitions of technical terms in simple language to ease student understanding.
- Exercises using connected discourse about a variety of interesting subjects, to stimulate and maintain student interest.
- Exercises sequenced to lead to independent work: moving from simpler tasks, such as identifying sentence elements, to guided writing, such as sentence combining, and on to original sentences, paragraphs, and essays.
- Exercises keyed to the text, enabling students to locate material they may need to review.
- Exercises on perforated pages to simplify collection of assignments and to leave students with a usable, concise reference work at the end of the course.
- Complete coverage of all traditional issues in basic grammar and mechanics, as well as thorough discussion of idea-generating and organizing strategies and their place in the writing process.
- Discussion of paraphrasing, summarizing, and quotation—not usually covered in workbooks.
- Photographs as writing prompts to appeal to today's graphics-conscious students.

This second edition also features

- Expanded and simplified explanations to give students greater access to information.
- New exercises to offer fresh content and stimulate interest.
- Increased numbers of items in many exercises to provide students with more practice in key skills and concepts.
- An index to make it easier for students and teachers to locate desired information.

We were heartened during the revision of this text by the support of our colleagues at Prentice Hall. We thank Jane Baumann and Fran Falk, Assistants to Phil Miller, for their ability to cut through complicated problems, and we thank Ilene McGrath for once again exercising rare skill and good sense in copyediting the manuscript. We especially thank Virginia Rubens, Production Editor, for her thoughtful, caring supervision of the entire project, and Phil Miller, Editor in Chief for the Humanities, for his continued support. Finally, as always, we thank David Troyka for his unflagging moral support.

Emily R. Gordon
Lynn Quitman Troyka

1, 2, and 3 | Thinking about Purposes and Audiences; Planning and Shaping; Drafting and Revising

1: THINKING ABOUT PURPOSES AND AUDIENCES

Why write? In this age of telephones and tape recorders, television and film, why should you bother with writing? The answer has many parts.

Writing is a way of thinking and learning. Writing gives you opportunities to explore ideas and obtain information. By writing, you come to know subjects well and make them your own. When you write what you know, you are also teaching the reader.

Writing is a way of discovering. The act of writing allows you to make unexpected connections among ideas. As you write, thoughts develop and interconnect in new ways.

Writing creates reading. Writing creates a permanent record of your ideas for others to read and think about.

Writing ability is needed by educated people. College work demands that you write many different types of assignments. Most jobs require writing skills for preparing letters, memos, and reports. Throughout your life, your writing will reveal your ability to think clearly and use language to express ideas.

1a | Understanding the elements of writing

Writing is a way of communicating a message to a reader for a purpose.
Let us look at the key words in this definition. **Communication** means that a message has a destination, a reader. The **message** of writing is its content. You need a thesis, a central idea that unites your writing. You also need enough content to support that thesis. Finally, the **reader** of your writing is your audience.

1b | Understanding purposes for writing

Students often think their **purpose** for writing is to complete a class assignment. However, purpose means more than that: It refers to what the writing seeks to achieve. This workbook concentrates on the two purposes most frequently found in academic writing: **to provide information for your reader** and **to persuade your reader**.

Informative writing (also known as **expository writing**) seeks to give information and, when necessary, to explain it. Informative writing focuses on the subject being discussed. Informative writing includes reports of observations, ideas, scientific data, facts, and statistics. It can be found in textbooks, encyclopedias, technical and business reports, nonfiction books, newspapers, and magazines.

CHECKLIST FOR INFORMATIVE WRITING

1. Is its major focus the subject being discussed?
2. Is its primary purpose to inform rather than to persuade?
3. Is its information complete and accurate?
4. Is its information verifiable?
5. Is its information arranged for clarity?
6. Is it interesting to read?

Persuasive writing (also known as **argumentative writing**) seeks to convince the reader about a matter of opinion. Persuasive writing focuses on the reader whom the writer wants to influence. Examples of persuasive writing include editorials, letters to the editor, reviews, sermons, business or research proposals, opinion essays in magazines, and books that argue a point of view.

CHECKLIST FOR PERSUASIVE WRITING

1. Is its major focus the reader?
2. Is its primary purpose to convince?
3. Does it offer information or reasons to support its point of view?
4. Is its point of view based on sound reasoning and logic?
5. Are the points in the argument arranged clearly?
6. Does it move the reader to act or to think in the desired way?

1c Understanding audiences for writing

Good writing is often judged by its ability to reach its intended **audience**. The more information you have about your audience's background, beliefs, and concerns, the better you can think about how to reach that audience.

CHECKLIST OF AUDIENCE CHARACTERISTICS

WHO ARE THEY?

Age/sex/education?
Ethnic background/political philosophy/religious beliefs?
Role(s): student/veteran/parent/wage earner/voter/etc.?
Employment/economic status?
Interests/hobbies?

WHAT INFORMATION DO THEY HAVE?

Level of education?
Experience with reading academic or business writing?
Amount of general knowledge about the subject?
Amount of specialized knowledge about the subject?
Set ideas they bring to the material?

2: PLANNING AND SHAPING

Experienced writers know that **writing is a process**, a series of activities that starts the moment they begin thinking about a subject and ends when they complete a final draft. Experienced writers also know that good writing is rewriting. Their drafts are filled with additions, cuts, rearrangements, and rewordings.

2a Understanding the writing process

For the sake of explanation, the different parts of the writing process are discussed separately in this chapter. In real life, you will find that the steps loop back and forth as each piece of writing develops.

AN OVERVIEW OF THE WRITING PROCESS

Planning calls for you to gather ideas and think about a focus.

Shaping calls for you to consider ways to organize your material.

Drafting calls for you to write your ideas in sentences and paragraphs.

Revising calls for you to evaluate your draft and rewrite it by adding, deleting, changing, moving—and often totally working material.

Editing calls for you to check the correctness of your grammar, spelling, punctuation, and mechanics.

Proofreading calls for you to read your final copy for typing errors or handwriting legibility.

2b Thinking about writing

As you think through and gather ideas (2d) for your topic, your task is to establish a **focus**, or a point of view, about the topic, and **support** for that focus. You also need to think about the purpose for your writing (1b) and the audience (1c).

2c Choosing a topic for writing

Some assignments leave no room for making choices. You may be given very specific instructions, such as "Explain how plants produce oxygen." Your job with such assignments is to do exactly what is asked and not go off the topic.

Some instructors will ask you to write on whatever topic you wish. In such situations, you need to select a topic that is suitable for informative or persuasive writing in college, one that reflects your ability to think through ideas. You need to demonstrate that you can use specific, concrete details to support what you want to say. Be careful not to choose a topic that is too narrow, or you will not have enough to say.

When you choose or are assigned a topic that is very broad, you have to **narrow the subject**. To do this, you must think of different areas within the subject until you come to one that seems workable for an essay.

Any broad subject may contain hundreds of possible essay topics. Do not try to think of them all, but also do not jump on the first topic that occurs to you. Consider the purpose of the assignment, the audience, the word limit, the time available to you, and your own interests and knowledge. A suitably narrowed topic will enable you to move back and forth between general statements and specific details.

2d Gathering ideas for writing

Techniques for gathering ideas, sometimes called **invention techniques**, can help you while you are narrowing your topic. For example, they help you to discover how much you know about a topic before you decide whether or not to write on it. Experienced writers use many techniques for gathering ideas; we will discuss the most common ones in this chapter.

Many writers carry an **idea book**—a small notebook—with them at all times so that they can jot down ideas that spring to mind.

A **journal**, like an idea book, is a record of your ideas, but it is built from daily writing sessions. In your journal you can write about your opinions, beliefs, family, friends, or anything else you wish. The content and tone can be as personal and informal as you wish. Nevertheless, a journal is not a diary for merely listing things done during the day. It is a book for you to fill with what you want to think about.

Keeping a journal can help you in three ways. First, writing every day makes it easier for you to write. Second, a journal encourages close observation and thinking. Third, a journal is an excellent source of ideas when you need to write in response to an assignment.

Freewriting is writing down whatever comes into your mind without stopping to worry about whether the idea is good or the spelling is correct. You do nothing to interrupt the flow. Do not go back to review. Do not cross out. Some days your freewriting might seem mindless, but other days it can reveal interesting ideas. Freewriting works best if you set a goal, such as writing for ten minutes or until one page is filled. Sometimes you may decide to do focused freewriting—writing on a set topic—in preparation for an essay.

In **brainstorming**, you make a list of all the ideas you can think of associated with a topic. The ideas can be listed as words, phrases, or complete sentences. List making, like freewriting, produces its best results when you let your mind work freely, producing many ideas before analyzing them.

Brainstorming is done in two steps. First make your list. Then go back and try to find patterns in the list and ways to group the ideas into categories. Set aside any items that do not fit into groups. The groups with the most items are likely to reflect the ideas that you can write about most successfully.

Another commonly used method for generating ideas is the **journalist's questions**: *who? what? where? why? when?* and *how?* Asking such questions forces you to approach a topic from several different points of view.

Mapping is much like brainstorming, but it is more visual. When you map, begin by writing your subject in a circle in the middle of a sheet of unlined paper. Next draw a line out from the center and name a major division of your subject. Circle it, and from that circle move out to further subdivisions. Keep associating to further ideas and to details related to them. When you finish with one major division of your subject, go back to the center and start again with another major division. As you go along, add anything that occurs to you for any section of the map. Continue the process until you run out of ideas.

All these idea-gathering techniques can help you get onto paper what is already stored in your mind. Reading after you receive an assignment is a good way to get *new* information and to confirm what you already know. Reading, however, is not always part of an assignment. Unless an assignment calls for the use of outside sources, ask your instructor before you do such reading. When you do read to write, be sure to *read critically* (see Chapter 5).

2e | Shaping ideas for writing

To shape the ideas that you have gathered (2d), you need to group them, decide on your tone, draft a thesis statement, and outline.

An essay has three basic parts: an introduction, a body, and a conclusion. The body consists of a number of paragraphs. The introduction and conclusion are usually one paragraph each. Chapter 4 discusses and illustrates various types of paragraphs.

1 Knowing how to group ideas

Effective writing includes both general statements and specific details. In both informative and persuasive writing, general statements must be developed with facts, reasons, examples, and illustrations.

To group ideas, review the material you accumulated while gathering ideas. Look for general ideas. Next group under them related, but less general ideas. If you find that your notes contain only general ideas, or only very specific details, return to gathering techniques to supply what you need.

2 Ordering ideas

Shaping ideas for writing also means placing them into a logical structure. You need to decide what should come first, second, and so on. Within the essay, and within individual body paragraphs, you can order ideas in various ways. The most common organizational strategies are generalization to specifics, climactic order (from least to most important), chronological order (from beginning to end), and spatial order (following a pattern in space, such as top to bottom).

3 Determining your tone

As an adult writing to an adult audience, you are expected to sound sensible and even-tempered. This stance is reflected in your **tone**—*what you say* and *how you say it*. Tone can be broadly described as **informal** or **formal**. Tone is informal in journals and freewriting. As you move from writing for the private you to writing for an audience, you are expected to move toward a more formal tone. This does not mean that you should use overblown language or put on airs that make you sound artificial (see 21d). Most audiences expect a tone midway between informal and highly formal. Your tone should take into account the topic, purpose, and audience of your piece.

4 Drafting a thesis statement

A **thesis statement** is the main idea of an essay. Because it prepares your reader for what you will discuss, the thesis statement must accurately reflect the content of the essay. Following is a list of the basic requirements for a thesis statement.

BASIC REQUIREMENTS FOR A THESIS STATEMENT

1. It states the essay's main idea—the central point you are making to your readers.
2. It is in the form of a complete sentence, not a fragment or a question.
3. It is a generalization.
4. It reflects the essay's purpose—either to give your readers information or to persuade your readers to agree with you.
5. It includes a focus—your assertion that conveys your point of view.
6. It *may* briefly state the major subdivisions of the essay's topic.

Many instructors also require that the thesis statement appear as a single sentence at the end of the introductory paragraph.

In most writing situations you cannot be certain that a thesis statement accurately reflects what you say in the essay until you have written one or more drafts. To start shaping your essay, however, you can use a preliminary thesis statement. Even if it is too broad, it can guide you as you write. When the essay is completed, be sure to revise so that your final thesis statement accurately reflects the content of your essay.

Here are some thesis statements written for 500- to 700-word essays. The first two are for essays with an informative purpose, and the last two are for essays with a persuasive purpose.

TOPIC	rain
No	Rain is important. [too broad]
YES	Rain is part of the earth's water cycle.
TOPIC	radio
No	Everyone listens to the radio. [too broad]
YES	The variety of radio programming ensures there is a program for every taste.
TOPIC	drunk driving
No	Drunk driving is dangerous. [too broad]
YES	Unless drunk drivers are taken off our roads, they will continue to kill and injure thousands of people each year.
TOPIC	adoption
No	Sometimes, adopted children have problems. [too broad]
YES	Adopted children should be able to find out about their birth-parents for psychological, medical, and moral reasons.

5 | Knowing how to outline

Many writers find outlining to be a useful planning strategy. An **outline** helps pull together the results of gathering and ordering ideas and preparing a thesis statement. It also provides a visual guide and checklist. Some instructors require outlines because they want you to practice the discipline of thinking through the arrangement and organization of your writing.

An **informal outline** does not have to follow all the formal conventions of outlining. It simply *lists* the main ideas of an essay—the major subdivisions of the thesis statement—and the subordinate ideas and details.

A **formal outline** follows strict conventions concerning content and format. The material must be displayed so that relationships among ideas are clear and so that the content is orderly. A formal outline can be a **topic outline** or a **sentence outline**: each item in a topic outline is a word or phrase, whereas each item in a sentence outline is a complete sentence.

Here are the conventions to follow in a formal outline.

1. **Numbers, letters, and indentations**: All parts of a formal outline are systematically indented and numbered or lettered. Capitalized Roman numerals (I, II, III) signal major divisions of the topic. Indented capital letters (A, B) signal the next, more specific level of information. Further indented Arabic numbers (1, 2, 3) show the third, even more specific level of information, and so on.

2. **Grouping in pairs**: At all points on an outline there is no I without a II, no A without a B, and so on. If a heading has only one subdivision, you need either to eliminate that subdivision or expand the material so that you have at least two subdivisions.

3. **Levels of generality**: All items in a subdivision are at the same level of generality. A main idea cannot be paired with a supporting detail.

4. **Overlap**: Headings do not overlap. What is covered in A, for example, must be quite different from what is covered in B.

5. **Parallelism**: All entries are grammatically parallel. For example, all items might start with *-ing* forms of verbs or all might be adjectives and nouns (see 18e).

6. **Capitalization and punctuation**: Capitalize only the first word of each heading. In a sentence outline, end each sentence with a period. Do not put periods at the end of items in a topic outline.

7. **Introductory and concluding paragraphs**: The introductory and concluding paragraphs are not part of an outline. Place the thesis statement above the outline.

2e

Here is a formal topic outline of an essay on living alone.

THESIS STATEMENT

Chances are high that adult men and women will have to know how to live alone, briefly or longer, at some time in their lives.

I. Living alone because of circumstances

    A. Grown children moving to other cities
        1. Going away to school
        2. Taking jobs

    B. Married people not being married forever
        1. One out of two marriages ending in divorce
        2. Eight out of ten married women becoming widowed, usually late in life

II. Taking care of practical matters

    A. Opening a checking account
        1. Comparing bank services
        2. Comparing advantages of different kinds of checking accounts

    B. Making major purchases
        1. Replacing a refrigerator
        2. Buying a car

III. Establishing new friendships

    A. Students getting used to going to classes without old friends
        1. Being able to concentrate better
        2. Being able to meet new friends

    B. Single adults going to the beach or parties

IV. Dealing with feelings of loneliness

    A. Understanding the feeling

    B. Avoiding depression
        1. Not overeating
        2. Not overspending
        3. Not getting into unwanted situations
            a. Taking the wrong job
            b. Going into the wrong relationship

    C. Keeping busy

3: DRAFTING AND REVISING

Drafting is getting ideas onto paper in rough sentences and paragraphs. **Revising** is taking a draft from its first to its final version by evaluating, adding, cutting, moving material, editing, and proofreading.

3a Knowing how to get started

If you have trouble getting started when the time arrives for drafting, you are not alone. Even professional writers sometimes have trouble getting started. Here are some time-proven methods experienced writers use to get started when they are blocked.

1. Don't stare at a blank page. Fill up the paper. Write words, scribble, or draw while you think about your topic. The movement of filling the paper while thinking can stimulate your mind to turn to actual drafting.

2. Use "focused freewriting" (2d).

3. Picture yourself writing. Imagine yourself in the place where you usually write, with the materials you need, busy at work.

4. Write your material in a letter to a friend. Doing this gives you a chance to relax. The letter can serve as a rough draft.

5. Write your material as if you were someone else: You can be a friend writing to you, an instructor writing to a class, a person in history writing to you or to someone else. Once you take on a role, you may feel less inhibited about writing.

6. Switch your method of writing. If you usually typewrite or use a word processor, try writing by hand. If you usually use a pen, switch to a pencil.

7. Start in the middle. If you do not know what to write in your introduction, start with a body paragraph.

3b Knowing how to write a draft

First drafts are not meant to be perfect; they are meant to give you something to revise. The direction of drafting is forward: **keep pressing ahead**. Do not stop to check spelling or grammar. If you are not sure a word or sentence is correct, circle it or put an *X* in the margin so that you can return to that spot later.

No single method of drafting an essay works for everyone. Following are a pair of methods you might try—or you might prefer to use another method that you have developed for yourself.

1. Put aside all your notes from planning and shaping. Write a "discovery draft." As you write, be open to discovering ideas and making connections that spring to mind during the physical act of writing. When you finish a discovery draft, you can decide to use it either as a first draft or as part of your notes when you make a structured first draft.

2. Keep your notes from planning and shaping in front of you and use them as you write. Write a structured first draft, working through all your material. If you are working on a long essay, you may want to draft in chunks, a few paragraphs at each sitting.

3c Knowing how to revise

To revise your essay, you must first evaluate it. Then you make improvements and in turn evaluate them in the context of the surrounding material. This process continues until you are satisfied that the essay is in final draft.

STEPS FOR REVISING

1. Shift mentally from suspending judgment (during idea gathering and drafting) to making judgments.
2. Read your draft critically to evaluate it. Be guided by the questions on the Revision Checklist below.
3. Decide whether to write an entirely new draft or to revise the one you have.
4. Be systematic. You need to pay attention to many different elements of a draft, from overall organization to choice of words. Most writers work better when they concentrate on specific elements during separate rounds of revision.

MAJOR ACTIVITIES DURING REVISION

Add. Insert needed words, sentences, and paragraphs. If your additions require new content, return to idea-gathering techniques (see 2d).

Cut. Get rid of whatever goes off the topic or repeats what has already been said.

Replace. As needed, substitute new words, sentences, and paragraphs for what you have cut.

Move material around. Change the sequence of paragraphs if the material is not presented in logical order (see 2e). Move sentences within paragraphs, or to other paragraphs, if arrangements seem illogical (see 4c).

When you revise, you need to pay special attention to your essay's title and thesis statement. Both of these features can help you stay on track, and they tell your reader what to expect.

The **title** of an essay plays an important organizing role. A good title can set you on your course and tell your readers what to expect. A title always stands alone. The opening of an essay should never refer to the essay's title as if it were part of a preceding sentence. For example, after the title "Knowing How to Live Alone," a writer should not begin the essay with the words, "This is very important." The title sets the stage, but it is not the first sentence of the essay.

The **thesis statement** expresses the central idea that controls and limits what the essay will cover. A thesis statement contains the **topic**, narrowed appropriately; the **focus**, which presents what you are saying about the topic; and the **purpose**. If your **thesis statement** does not match what you say in your essay, you need to revise either the thesis statement or the essay—sometimes both (see 2e).

A revision checklist can help you focus your attention as you evaluate your writing. Use a checklist provided by your instructor or compile your own based on the Revision Checklist below.

Revision checklist

The answer to each question on this checklist should be yes. If it is not, you need to revise.

THE WHOLE ESSAY

1. Is the topic of the essay suitable for college writing and is it sufficiently narrow? (2c)
2. Does your thesis statement clearly communicate the topic and focus of the essay? (2e)
3. Does your thesis clearly reflect the purpose of the essay? (1b)
4. Does the essay reflect an awareness of its audience? (1c)
5. Does the essay take into account special requirements—the assignment's time limit, word limit, and other factors?
6. Does your essay have a logical organization pattern? (2e)
7. Is the tone of the essay suitable for its audience? Is the tone consistent? (2e)
8. Is your thesis well supported by the main ideas of the paragraphs? (5e)
9. Do the paragraphs cover separate but related main ideas? (2e-4)
10. Have you covered all the material promised by your thesis statement? (2e-4)
11. Are the connections among the paragraphs clear? (4b and 4e)
12. Does your introduction lead into the thesis statement and the rest of the essay? (4e)
13. Does your conclusion provide a sense of completion? (4e)
14. Have you cut any material that goes off the topic?
15. Does your essay have a title? Does it reflect the content of the essay? (3c)

PARAGRAPHS

1. Does the introduction help your audience make the transition to the body of your essay? (4e)
2. Does each body paragraph express its main idea in a topic sentence as needed? (4a)
3. Are the main ideas—and topic sentences—clearly related to the thesis statement of the essay? (4)
4. Are your body paragraphs developed? Is the development sufficient? (4a and 4d)
5. Does each body paragraph contain specific and concrete support for its main idea? Do the details provide examples, reasons, facts? (4a)
6. Are your facts, figures, and dates accurate?
7. Is each body paragraph arranged logically? (4c)
8. Have you cut any material that goes off the topic?
9. Have you used necessary transitions? (4b and 4e)
10. Do the paragraphs maintain coherence with pronouns (4b), selective repetition (4b), and parallel structures (4b and 18)?

SENTENCES

1. Have you eliminated sentence fragments? (Chapter 13)
2. Have you eliminated comma splices and fused sentences? (14)
3. Have you eliminated confusing shifts? (15a)
4. Have you eliminated misplaced modifiers? (15b)
5. Have you eliminated dangling modifiers? (15c)
6. Have you eliminated mixed sentences? (15d)
7. Have you eliminated incomplete sentences? (15e)
8. Are your sentences concise? (16)
9. Have you used coordination correctly? (17a–17c)
10. Have you used subordination correctly? (17d–17g)
11. Have you used parallelism as needed to help your sentences deliver their meaning? (18)

WORDS

1. Does your word choice reflect your intentions in denotation and connotation? (20b)
2. Have you used specific and concrete language to bring life to general and abstract language? (20b)
3. Does your word choice reflect a level of formality appropriate for your purpose and audience? (21a)
4. Have you avoided sexist language? (21a)
5. Have you avoided slang and colloquial or regional language not appropriate to your audience and purpose? (21a)
6. Have you avoided slanted language? (21a)
7. Have you avoided clichés and artificial language? (21c—d)

3d Knowing how to edit

When you **edit**, you check the correctness of your writing. You pay attention to grammar, spelling, and punctuation, and to correct use of capitals, numbers, italics, and abbreviations. You are ready to edit once you have a final draft that contains suitable content, organization, development, and sentence structure. Once you have edited your work, you are ready to transcribe it into a final copy.

As you edit, be systematic. Use a checklist supplied by your instructor or one you compile from the following Editing Checklist.

Editing checklist

The answer to each question on this checklist should be yes. If it is not, you need to edit.

1. Is the grammar correct? That is, have you used correct verb forms (Chapter 8); have you used the correct case of nouns and pronouns (9); do pronouns refer to clear antecedents (10); do subjects and verbs agree (11); do pronouns agree with their antecedents (11); have you distinguished between adjectives and adverbs (12)?
2. Is the spelling correct? (22)
3. Have you correctly used hyphens? (22)
4. Have you correctly used commas? (24)
5. Have you correctly used semicolons (25), colons (26), apostrophes (27), and quotation marks (28)?
6. Have you correctly used other marks of punctuation? (29)
7. Have you correctly used capital letters, italics, numbers, and abbreviations? (30)

3e Knowing how to proofread

When you **proofread**, you check a final version carefully before handing it in. You need to make sure your work is an accurate and clean transcription of your final draft. Proofreading involves a careful, line-by-line reading of an essay. You should proofread with a ruler so that you can focus on one line at a time. Remember that no matter how hard you have worked on other parts of the writing process, if your final copy is inaccurate or messy, you will not be taken seriously.

Adapting to Your Audience and Purpose

Look at this picture of a flood. Describe the scene for these four different audiences:

Black Star

1. You have just walked home through this flood, and there is a message on your answering machine from your parents (in another state). They want to know if you are all right because they heard about the flood on the radio.
2. You are a businessperson whose basement has been flooded. Write a letter to your insurance company requesting particular action and explaining how you are not to blame for the damage.
3. You are a college senior whose finals have been postponed because of the flood. Write a letter home explaining what has happened on campus and asking your parents to handle the situation at their end (contacting your new employer, notifying your girlfriend/boyfriend, etc.).
4. You are the city official in charge of emergency preparations. Write a bulletin to be read on the radio announcing the extent of the emergency and the availability of shelters. Explain who may use the shelters and what people may bring with them. Use language the general public can understand.

Using Idea-Gathering Techniques

Select four topics from this list, and prepare to write by narrowing each one. Use a different idea-gathering technique for each: freewriting, brainstorming, the journalist's questions, and mapping. Use your own paper, but record your narrowed topic on the line next to each subject you use.

1. success _____

2. being a good friend _____

3. summer in the city (or country) _____

4. laughter _____

5. marriage _____

6. restaurants _____

7. concerts _____

8. children _____

9. sacrifice _____

10. shopping _____

Grouping and Ordering Ideas

Select two of the topics you explored in Exercise 2-2. For each, group ideas in clusters of related material and then order the clusters. Remember that not every item in an idea-generating exercise has to appear in the final essay. Feel free to omit items that do not fit your pattern. If there are gaps, return to idea-gathering techniques to get more material. Your end products will be informal outlines. Use your own paper.

Writing Thesis Statements

A: Most of the following thesis statements are unacceptable because they are too broad or too narrow. Label each thesis *acceptable* or *unacceptable*. Then revise each unacceptable thesis to make it suitable for an essay of about 500 words.

EXAMPLE　　Canada is a nice place to visit.
Its nearness to the United States, its cultural variety, and the lack of a language barrier make Canada an attractive choice for a family vacation.

1. Some people favor the death penalty.

2. People's accents are often clues to their place of birth.

3. Interfaith marriages can have problems.

4. Having more than one husband or wife at the same time is a crime.

5. Although public speaking is hard for some people, learning a few simple techniques can make it less difficult.

6. Cars are getting smaller.

7. Some families cannot afford to take care of their children.

8. ~~Many~~ news broadcasts could be made more interesting.

9. Campers and hikers cannot go onto some private property.

10. Some people think airplanes are safe, and some people do not.

11. Beginning to date again after being divorced or widowed can be difficult.

   _____

12. Supermarkets carry everything these days.

   _____

B: Write thesis statements for the four topics you narrowed in Exercise 2-2 and for six original topics. Be sure that each topic is suitably narrow for an essay of about 500 words and that the thesis statement shows a purpose and a point of view.

EXAMPLE   Topic: *how shopping has been changed by the development of closed malls*

Thesis Statement: *The development of closed malls has led to a revolution in the way Americans shop: we can shop easily at night and in rough weather, we see a greater variety of goods than in any single store, and we are encouraged to think of shopping as fun rather than as a chore.*

1. Topic _____

   Thesis Statement _____

2. Topic _____

   Thesis Statement _____

3. Topic _____

   Thesis Statement _____

4. Topic _____

   Thesis Statement _____

5. Topic _____

   Thesis Statement _____

6. Topic _____

   Thesis Statement _____

7. Topic _____

   Thesis Statement _____

8. Topic _____

   Thesis Statement _____

9. Topic _____

   Thesis Statement _____

10. Topic _____

   Thesis Statement _____

Due Wed.

Planning a Formal Outline

The following topic outline contains twelve errors in form and logic. Revise the outline, using the guidelines listed in 2e. Draw a single line through each error and write your revision just above it.

Thesis Statement: People who live in apartments should be allowed to keep dogs.

I. How dogs contribute to good health
   A. Physical health
      1. Effect on general health
         ~~a. Walking dog—good exercise~~
      2. Effect on heart and blood vessels
         a. Lower blood pressure
         (b.) People who have had a heart attack are less likely to have a second one if they get a dog.
   B. Mental and emotional health
      1. companionship
      2. Responsibility
         a. Feeding
         b. Walking
         c. Health care
      3. Social skills
         a. Talking about dog
         b. Sharing dog with other members of household
         ~~c. Children~~
II. Providing Security
   A. Barking
      ~~1. Protection against burglars~~
   B. Biting—protection against attacks
III. How to Turn Dogs into Good Tenants
   A. Dog owner's responsibilities
      1. Housebreaking
         a. Walk regularly
         b. Clean up accidents thoroughly
      2. ~~Preventing~~ *Prevent* chewing
         a. Provide chew toys
         b. ~~You should repair any damage to walls or rugs.~~
      3. ~~To~~ control barking
      4. Keeping dog on leash when outside

B. Consult trainer if necessary
C. Landlord's responsibilities
    1. Providing a place to walk dogs safely
        a. A dogwalk, if practical
        b. A curb free of broken glass and other sharp objects
    2. Recognize the difference between well-behaved and destructive dogs

---

Making a Formal Outline

EXERCISE 2-6

(2e)

Convert one of the informal outlines you developed in Exercise 2.3 into a formal outline. Write a sentence outline or a topic outline, but be sure not to mix the two types. Begin by placing the thesis statement you developed in Exercise 2-4B at the top of your page. Use the list of conventions in 2e for guidance and as a checklist when you are done. Use your own paper.

Revising, Editing, and Proofreading Essays

A: Here is a middle draft of a short essay. It has already been revised, but it has not yet been edited. Edit the essay, using the Editing Checklist in 3d. If you like, you may also make additional revisions. When you are done, submit a carefully proofread copy of the completed essay to your instructor.

Forks, knives, and spoons seam so natural to most of us that its hard to imagine eaten diner with out them. Yet many people, such as the chinese, use chopsticks instead, and other's use their hands to eat.

Knives are the oldest western utensils. The first ones were made of stone 1.5 million years ago. It was originally use to cut up dead animals after a hunt. The same knife were used to: butcher game slice cooked food, and kill enemies. Even later in History, nobles was the only ones who could afford separate knives for different uses. People use all-purpose knives, pointed like todays steak knives. The round-tipped dinner knife is a modern invention. It became popular in 17th cen. France because hosteses want to stop guests from picking they're teeth with the points of there dinner knives.

The spoon is also an anceint tool. Wooden spoons twenty thousand years old have been found in Asia; spoons of stone, wood, ivory, and even gold have been found in Egyptian tombs. Spoons were originally use to scoop up foods that were to thick to sip from a bowl.

The fork is a newcomer. Forks did not become widely accepted until the eighteenth century; when the French nobility adopted the fork as a status symbol, and eating with ones hands became un-fashionable. At about the same time, individual place settings became the rule to. Previous, even rich people had shared plates and glasses at meals, but know the rich demanded individual plates, glasses, forks, spoons, and knives. Today in America, a full set of utensils is considered a necesity. We forget that as recently as the american revolution some people still considered anyone who use a fork to be a fussy showoff.

B: Here is the first draft of an essay. It needs a great deal of work, as most first drafts do. Revise the essay, using the Revision Checklist in 3c. Then edit your work, using the Editing Checklist in 3d. Finally, submit a carefully proofread copy of the completed essay.

The Suburbs

This morning at registration the clerk who was reviewing my program insulted me when she said, "Why do you live all the way out there?" She said it as if I was a fool to live in the suburbs. It was really crowded, so I didn't tell her what was on my mind. In this essay I will tell you why I like living in the suburbs.

City slickers always have pity on me. "Your so far away from everything" they say. This remark only shows how stupid they are. First, I am not as isolated as they think. To get to school, I drive about 40 minutes on a smooth highway. The highway is uncrowded too. My city friends take an overcrowded bus for forty minutes. Or longer, if there is a traffic jam. When I graduate and begin to work, I probably will not have even the forty-minute drive because local businesses are growing by leaps and bounds. There are factories, shopping malls, and large insurance, law, and advertising firms. All within twenty miles of my home.

I think that if my classmates knew how pleasent suburban life can be, they would join me in a flash. People here are friendlier. First moving onto my block, people I didn't recognize waved to me as I walked my dog. I thought they had me confused with someone else. I later found out that they were just been friendly. I use to live in the city. The only people who notice me when I was walking my dog were the ones who sternly reminded me to "keep the dog off their lawns." Neighbors here keep an eye on one another. Once when I did not move my car for three days a nieghbor knocked on my door to see if I was feeling alright. When I lived in the city, no one cared what I did or how I was, as long as I kept the volume down on the stereo.

Maybe I do not live in the most sophisticated area in the world, but I am not deprived. My stores carry the same fashions as stores in the city, my television recieves the same programs, and my radio carries the same stations. So everything is equal except the suburbs have some advantages I have described to you in this essay. The city is a nice place to visit, but I wouldn't want to live there.

4 Writing Paragraphs

A **paragraph** is a group of sentences that work together to develop a unit of thought. Paragraphing permits you to subdivide material into manageable parts and, at the same time, to arrange those parts into a unified whole that effectively communicates its message.

To signal a new paragraph, you indent the first line five spaces in a typewritten paper and one inch in a handwritten paper.

A paragraph's purpose determines its structure. In college, the most common purposes for writing are *to inform* and *to persuade* (as discussed in 1b). Some paragraphs in informative and in persuasive essays serve special roles: they introduce, conclude, or provide transitions (see 4e). Most paragraphs, however, are **body paragraphs**, also called **developmental paragraphs** or **topical paragraphs**. They consist of a statement of a main idea and specific, logical support for that main idea.

4a Writing unified paragraphs

A paragraph is **unified** when all its sentences relate to the main idea. Unity is lost if a paragraph contains sentences unrelated to the main idea.

The sentence that contains the main idea of a paragraph is called the **topic sentence.** The topic sentence focuses and controls what can be written in the paragraph. Some paragraphs use two sentences to present a main idea. In such cases, the first is the topic sentence and the second is the **limiting** or **clarifying sentence** which narrows the focus of the paragraph.

Topic sentence at the beginning of a paragraph: Most informative and persuasive paragraphs have the topic sentence placed first so that a reader knows immediately what to expect. Placing the topic sentence first also helps to ensure that the entire paragraph will be unified.

> **Many first-jobbers suffer from the "semester syndrome."** Students can usually count on being "promoted" at least twice a year—into the next semester. "Promotions" came regularly and at fixed intervals in school. At work, it's a different story. Promotions don't necessarily occur with any regularity, and sometimes they don't occur at all. This point may seem like a very obvious one, but the fact that

students are used to rapid advancement can make their transitions to work harder. Since as students they become so conditioned to advancement at a fixed rate, many first-jobbers become impatient when they are required to remain in one job or at one task without a promotion for longer than a "semester." They begin to feel they're not moving anywhere, and as a result many leave their first jobs much too soon.

—The staff of *Catalyst, Making the Most of Your First Job*

Topic sentence at the end of a paragraph: Some informative and per-suasive paragraphs present the supporting details before the main idea. The topic sentence, therefore, comes at the end of the paragraph. This technique is particularly effective for building suspense, but it should be used sparingly. In the following paragraph, notice how concrete details build up to the main idea.

I read Dreiser's *Jennie Gerhardt* and *Sister Carrie* and they revived in me a vivid sense of my mother's suffering: I was overwhelmed. I grew silent, wondering about the life around me. It would have been impossible for me to have told anyone what I derived from these novels, for it was nothing less than a sense of life itself. **All my life had shaped me for the realism, the naturalism of the modern novel, and I could not read enough of them.**

—Richard Wright, "The Library Card," from *Black Boy*

Topic sentence implied: Some paragraphs make a unified statement with-out the use of a topic sentence. Writers must construct such paragraphs carefully, so that a reader can easily see the main idea. Paragraphs with implied topic sentences are rare in academic writing.

A topic sentence is usually a generalization. A topical paragraph is **developed** by the sentences that support the topic sentence, offering specific, concrete details. Without development, a paragraph fails to make its point or capture a reader's interest.

The key to successful development of topical paragraphs is detail. Details bring generalizations to life by providing concrete, specific illustrations. A paragraph developed with good detail often has RENNS—an acronym that stands for *r*easons, *e*xamples, *n*umbers, *n*ames, and appeals to the five *s*enses. Use RENNS as a memory device to help you check the development of your paragraphs, but do not feel that every paragraph must have a complete menu of RENNS to be well-developed. Here is a paragraph with two of the five types of RENNS.

However, the first ride I got took me on the way to New York rather than Washington. It was a big Standard Oil truck, heading for Wellsville. We drove out into the wild, bright country, the late November country, full of the light of Indian summer. The red barns glared in the harvested fields, and the woods were bare, but all the world was full of color and the blue sky swam with fleets of white clouds. The truck devoured the road with high-singing tires, and I rode throned in the lofty, rocking cab, listening to the driver telling me stories about all the people who lived in places we passed, and what went on in the houses we saw.

—Thomas Merton, *The Seven Storey Mountain*

This paragraph offers concrete, specific illustrations which describe Merton's first ride on the way to New York. It has *n*ames such as Standard Oil truck (not the general term *truck*), Wellsville, November country, and red barns (not the general term *buildings*). It appeals to the *s*enses by including many references to light and specific colors, as well as to the rocking motion of the cab and the sound of the tires.

4b Writing coherent paragraphs

A paragraph is coherent when its sentences are related to each other, not only in content but also in grammatical structures and choice of words. The techniques of coherence are transitional expressions, pronouns, repetition of key words, and parallel structures. Though they are discussed separately in this section for the sake of clear example, techniques of coherence usually work in unison.

Transitional expressions—words and phrases that signal connections among ideas—can help you achieve coherence in your writing. Here are the most commonly used transitional expressions.

TRANSITIONAL EXPRESSIONS	
SIGNAL	**WORDS**
Addition	also, in addition, too, moreover, and, besides, further, furthermore, equally, important, next, then, finally,
Example	for example, for instance, thus, as an illustration, namely, specifically,
Contrast	but, yet, however, on the other hand, nevertheless, nonetheless, conversely, in contrast, on the contrary, still, at the same time, although,
Comparison	similarly, likewise, in like manner, in the same way, in comparison,
Concession	of course, to be sure, certainly, naturally, granted,
Result	therefore, thus, consequently, so, accordingly, due to this,
Summary	as a result, hence, in short, in brief, in summary, in conclusion, finally, on the whole,
Time sequence	first, firstly, second, secondly, third, fourth, next, then, finally, afterwards, before, soon, later, during, meanwhile, subsequently, immediately, at length, eventually, in the future, currently,
Place	in the front, in foreground, in the back, in the background, at the side, adjacent, nearby, in the distance, here, there,

Notice how transitional expressions (shown in boldface) help to make the following paragraph coherent.

> Doctors have many different ways to help people with asthma. **Sometimes** they give asthmatics a nose or mouth spray, or a pill, or an injection. These medicines help stop the swelling in the bronchial tubes. Doctors **also** tell asthmatics to drink lots of water. This helps the body to thin out the mucus so that it can be coughed up.
>
> —SHEILA L. BURNS, *Allergies and You*

When you use **pronouns** that clearly refer to nouns and other pronouns, you help your reader move from one sentence to the next. Notice how the pronouns (shown in boldface) help make the following paragraph coherent.

> The men and women who perform the daring and often dangerous action that is part of almost every television and motion-picture story today are special people. **They** are professional stunt men and women. **They** know precisely what **they** are doing and how to do it. **Most** are extraordinary athletes with the grace and timing of dancers. **They** plan ahead what **they** must do. And **they** have no intention of getting hurt, although sometimes **they** do.
>
> —GLORIA D. MIKLOWITZ, *Movie Stunts and the People Who Do Them*

You can achieve coherence by repeating **key words** in a paragraph. Notice how the careful repetition of the words *demand, difficulty, game(s), fun*, and *rules* (shown in boldface) help make this paragraph coherent.

> We **demand difficulty** even in our **games**. We **demand** it because without **difficulty** there can be no **game**. A **game** is a way of making something hard for the **fun** of it. The **rules** of the **game** are an arbitrary imposition of **difficulty**. When the spoilsport ruins the **fun**, he always does so by refusing to play by the **rules**. It is easier to win at chess if you are free, at your pleasure, to change the wholly arbitrary **rules**, but the **fun** is in winning within the **rules**. No **difficulty**, no **fun**.
>
> —JOHN CIARDI, "Is Everybody Happy?"

Parallel structures (see Chapter 18) can help you achieve coherence. Using the same form of phrase or clause several times sets up a rhythm which gives unity to the paragraph. Notice how the parallel structures (shown in boldface) make this paragraph coherent.

> **This is** our hope. **This is** the faith with which I return to the South. **With this faith we will be able to** hew out of the mountain of despair a stone of hope. **With this faith we will be able to** transform the jangling discords of our nation into a beautiful symphony of brotherhood. **With this faith we will be able to work together, to pray together, to struggle together, to go to jail together, to stand up for freedom together**, knowing that we will be free one day.
>
> —MARTIN LUTHER KING, "I Have a Dream"

4c Knowing how to arrange a paragraph

Here are some of the most common ways to organize paragraphs.

From general to specific: An arrangement of sentences from the general to the specific is the most common organization for a paragraph. Such paragraphs often begin with a topic sentence and end with specific details.

> **Gifts from parents to children always carry the most meaningful messages.** The way parents think about presents goes one step beyond the objects themselves—the ties, dolls, sleds, record players, kerchiefs, bicycles and model airplanes that wait by the Christmas tree. The gifts are, in effect, one way of telling boys and girls, "We love you even though you have been a bad boy all month" or, "We love having a daughter" or, "We treat all our children alike" or, "It is all right for girls to have some toys made for boys" or, "This alarm clock will help you get started in the morning all by yourself." Throughout all the centuries since the invention of a Santa Claus figure who represented a special recognition of children's behavior, good and bad, presents have given parents a way of telling children about their love and hopes and expectations for them.
>
> —MARGARET MEAD and RHODA METRAUX, *A Way of Seeing*

From specific to general: A less common arrangement moves from the specific to the general. The paragraph ends with a topic sentence and begins with the details that support the topic sentence.

> They live up alongside the hills, in hollow after hollow. They live in eastern Kentucky and eastern Tennessee and in the western part of North Carolina and the western part of Virginia and in just about the whole state of West Virginia. They live close to the land; they farm it and some of them go down into it to extract its coal. Their ancestors, a century or two ago, fought their way westward from the Atlantic seaboard, came up on the mountains, penetrated the valleys, and moved stubbornly up the creeks for room, for privacy, for a view, for a domain of sorts. **They are Appalachian people, mountain people, hill people. They are white yeomen, or miners, or hollow folk, or subsistence farmers**.
>
> —ROBERT COLES, "A Domain (of Sorts)"

From least to most important: A sentence arrangement that moves from the least to the most important is known as a **climactic sequence**. This arrangement holds the reader's interest because the best part comes at the end.

> Joseph Glidden's invention, barbed wire, soon caught on—though not with everyone. Indians called it "devil's rope." Ranchers often cut it down so their cattle could graze freely. Most farmers, however, liked barbed wire. It kept cattle away from their crops. Cattle could break through most wire fences. With barbed wire, they quickly got the point. Eventually, ranchers started using barbed wire. With it, they separated the best cattle from the others to produce better breeds. Barbed wire helped railroads keep cattle off the tracks. As a result, the railroads expanded

into new territory. **Glidden probably didn't realize it at the time, but the few hours he spent twisting wires would help speed the taming of the West.**

—*Small Inventions that Make a Big Difference,*
National Geographic Society

According to location: A paragraph that describes the relative position of objects to one another, often from a central point of reference, uses **spatial sequence**. The topic sentence usually gives the reader the location that serves as the orientation for all other places mentioned.

> The bay in front of the dock was framed by the shores of the mainland, which curved together from both sides to meet in a point. At that vertex another island, rocky and tall, rose from the water. It looked uninhabited; and although a few cabins were scattered along the mainland, between and behind them was unbroken forest. It was my first sight of a natural wilderness. Behind our tent too, and several other tents here and a house in their midst, was the forest. Over everything, as pervasive as sunshine, was the fragrance of balsam firs. It was aromatic and sweet and I closed my eyes and breathed deeply to draw in more of it.
>
> —SALLY CARRIGHAR, *Home to the Wilderness*

According to time: A paragraph arranged according to time uses a **chronological sequence**.

> About 30 years ago, a prince in India found a rare white tiger cub whose mother had been killed. The prince decided to raise the cub, which he named Mohan. When Mohan grew up, he fathered some cubs that were white. One of his cubs, Mohini, was sent to the National Zoo in Washington, D.C. Mohini was used to breed more white tigers for other zoos in the United States.
>
> —"Who-o-o Knows?" *Ranger Rick*, May 1989

4d Knowing patterns for developing a paragraph

If you know a variety of patterns for paragraph development, you have more choices when you are seeking ways to help your paragraphs deliver their meanings most effectively. Although, for the purpose of illustration, the patterns shown here are discussed in isolation, in essay writing paragraph patterns often overlap. Be sure to use the paragraph pattern that communicates your meaning most effectively.

Narration: Narrative writing tells about what is happening or what happened. Narration is usually written in chronological sequence.

> During the 1870s, the business world was not yet ready for the typewriter. Inventor C. Latham Sholes and his daughter Lillian faced two major objections as they demonstrated Sholes's writing machine. "Too expensive and too slow," the businessmen protested. The response discouraged the inventor, but he didn't give up. At his home in Milwaukee, Wisconsin, he designed improvements for his machine. He also invented touch-typing, a system that enables a person to type fast

without looking at the keys. Touch-typing was faster than handwriting. It could save both time and money. That caused businessmen's interest to perk up. By 1900, in offices all over the United States, the *clickety-clack* of typewriters was replacing the scratching of pens.

—*Small Inventions that Make a Big Difference,*
National Geographic Society

Description: Descriptive writing appeals to a reader's senses—sight, sound, smell, taste, and touch—creating a sensual impression of a person, place, or object.

The forest was quiet except for the shrill cries of faraway toucans. Then many leaves began to rustle nearby. Seconds later crickets and cockroaches were hopping and crawling frantically in my direction. *What could be causing these creatures to run for their lives?* I wondered. Then I saw them: Tens of thousands of *army ants* were marching toward their fleeing prey—and me! The swarm of ants looked like a huge moving triangle, with the ants at the head of the swarm forming the widest part. And this part was as long as a school bus.

—Doug Wechsler, "I Met the Rambo Ants"

Process: A process describes a sequence of actions by which something is done or made. It is usually developed in chronological order. If it is to be effective, a process must include all steps. The amount of detail included depends on whether you want to teach the reader how to do something or you merely want to offer a general overview of the process.

To keep the big teams as nearly even as possible in the level of performance, a system called the draft has been devised. This is the way it works. Names of top college players who are graduating and want to turn pro are listed. Team representatives meet for a few days, usually in New York, to select the players they wish from this list. The team that placed last in the standings that year, gets first choice. The team next lowest in the standings gets the next choice, and so on. Naturally the representative will select the player the team needs the most. If one team gets a player that another team wants, that other team may trade an established team member or members for the draft choice. Naturally, a lot of wheeling and dealing goes on at this time.

—Bob and Marguita McGonagle, *Careers in Sports*

Example: A paragraph developed by example uses one or more illustrations to provide evidence in support of the main idea.

Getting right down to the gory details, ever since the earliest days of movie making, stars have been gushing, oozing, trickling, or dripping blood, as the case may be, on screen. Victims in silent movies "bled" chocolate syrup, which looked just like the real McCoy on the kind of black-and-white film used then. If a cowboy in a Western was to get shot, just before the scene was filmed a little chocolate syrup would be poured into the palm of his hand. Then, when the cameras started rolling and the cowboy got "blasted," he merely slapped his hand to his chest and what audiences saw was the bloody aftermath.

—Jane O'Connor and Katy Hall, *Magic in the Movies*

Definition: A paragraph of definition explains the meaning of a word or concept. Because it is more thorough than the definition offered by a dictionary, such a paragraph is called an **extended definition**.

An extended definition may contain any of several elements, but it rarely includes all of them: (1) a dictionary definition, (2) a negative definition—what the term is *not*, (3) a comparison and contrast of definitions used by other people, (4) an explanation of how this term differs from terms with which it is often confused, and (5) an explanation of how the term originated. If the subject is a human quality, the definition may include (6) a discussion of how a person develops the quality and how the quality shows up in the individual's personality.

> Now, consider for a moment just exactly what it is that you are about to be handed. It is a huge, irregular mass of ice cream, faintly domed at the top from the metal scoop, which has first produced it and then insecurely balanced it on the uneven top edge of a hollow inverted cone made out of the most brittle and fragile of materials. Clumps of ice cream hang over the side, very loosely attached to the main body. There is always much more ice cream than the cone could hold, even if the ice cream were tamped down into the cone, which of course it isn't. And the essence of ice cream is that it melts. It doesn't just stay there teetering in this irregular, top-heavy mass; it also melts. And it melts *fast*. And it doesn't just melt—it melts into a sticky fluid that *cannot* be wiped off. The only thing one person could hand to another that might possibly be more dangerous is a live hand grenade from which the pin had been pulled five seconds earlier. And of course if anybody offered you that, you could say, "Oh. Uh, well—no thanks."
>
> —L. Rust Hills, *How to Do Things Right*

Division and classification: **Division** divides things up, and **classification** puts things together. A paragraph developed by division, also known as **analysis**, divides one subject into its component parts. Paragraphs written in this pattern usually start by identifying the one subject and then explain that subject's distinct parts. For example, a football team can be divided into its offensive and defensive teams, which can be divided further into the various positions on each.

A paragraph developed by classification discusses the ways that separate groups relate to one another. The separate groups must be *from the same class*; that is, they must have some underlying characteristic in common. For example, different types of sports—football, Rugby, and soccer—can be classified *together* according to their handling of the ball, their playing fields, the placement of their goals, and the like.

> **There are three kinds of book owners.** The **first** has all the standard sets and best sellers—unread, untouched. (This deluded individual owns wood-pulp and ink, not books.) The **second** has a great many books—a few of them read through, most of them dipped into, but all of them as clean and shiny as the day they were bought. (This person would probably like to make books his own, but is restrained by a false respect for their physical appearance.) The **third** has a few books or many—every one of them dog-eared and dilapidated, shaken and loosened by continual use, marked and scribbled in from front to back. (This man owns books.)
>
> —Mortimer J. Adler, "How to Mark a Book"

Comparison and contrast: **Comparison** deals with similarities, and **contrast** deals with differences between two objects or ideas. Paragraphs using comparison and contrast can be structured in two ways. A **point-by-point structure** allows you to move back and forth between the two items being compared. A **block structure** allows you to discuss one item completely before discussing the other.

POINT-BY-POINT STRUCTURE

Student body: college A, college B
Curriculum: college A, college B
Location: college A, college B

BLOCK STRUCTURE

College A: student body, curriculum, location
College B: student body, curriculum, location

Here is a paragraph structured point-by-point for comparison and contrast.

> Some people say the business about the jolly fat person is a myth, that all of us chubbies are neurotic, sick, sad people. I disagree. Fat people may not be chortling all day long, but they're a hell of a lot *nicer* than the wizened and shriveled. Thin people turn surly, mean, and hard at a young age because they never learn the value of a hot-fudge sundae for easing tension. Thin people don't like gooey soft things because they themselves are neither gooey nor soft. They are crunchy and dull, like carrots. They go straight to the heart of the matter while fat people let things stay all blurry and hazy and vague, the way things actually are. Thin people want to face the truth. Fat people know there is no truth. One of my thin friends is always staring at complex, unsolvable problems and saying, "The key thing is. . . ." Fat people never say that. They know there isn't any such thing as the key thing about anything.
>
> —SUZANNE BRITT JORDAN, "That Lean and Hungry Look"

Here is a paragraph structured block style for comparison and contrast.

> Many people think that gorillas are fierce and dangerous beasts. Stories have been told about gorillas attacking people. Movies have been made about gorillas kidnapping women. These stories and movies are exciting, but they are not true. In real life, gorillas are gentle and rather shy. They rarely fight among themselves. They almost never fight with other animals. They like to lead a quiet life—eating, sleeping, and raising their young.
>
> —SUSAN MEYERS, *The Truth about Gorillas*

Analogy: Analogy is a type of comparison. By comparing objects or ideas from different classes, an analogy explains the unfamiliar in terms of the familiar. For example, the fight to find a cure for a disease might be compared to a war. Often a paragraph developed with analogy starts with a simile or metaphor (see 21b).

> If clothing is a language, it must have a vocabulary and a grammar like other languages. Of course, as with human speech, there is not a single language of dress, but many: some (like Dutch and German) closely related and others (like Basque) almost unique. And within every language of clothes there are many different

dialects and accents, some almost unintelligible to members of the mainstream culture. Moreover, as with speech, each individual has his own stock of words and employs personal variations of tone and meaning.

—ALISON LURIE, *The Language of Clothes*

Cause-and-effect analysis: Cause-and-effect analysis involves examining the origin or outcome of something that happened or might happen. Causes are what lead up to an event; effects are what result.

When a person is weightless, the slightest exertion causes motion. For example, if you pushed yourself away from a chair, you would continue to move away from it. There would be nothing to stop the motion. You would float in space. Should you let go of your book, it would hang in space. Push it ever so slightly, and the book would move in a straight line. Splash water, and it would form into round drops moving in all directions.

—FRANKLYN M. BRANLEY, *Mysteries of Outer Space*

4e Knowing how to write special paragraphs

Introductory paragraphs, concluding paragraphs, and transitional paragraphs have special roles in an essay. **Introductions** prepare a reader for the topical paragraphs that follow, **conclusions** bring the topical paragraphs to a close for a reader, and **transitional paragraphs** help the reader move through complex material. Generally, special paragraphs are shorter than topical paragraphs.

Introductory paragraphs: In informative and persuasive writing, an introductory paragraph prepares readers for what lies ahead. For this reason, your introduction must relate clearly to the rest of your essay. If it points in one direction and your essay goes off in another, your reader will be confused—and may even stop reading.

In college writing, many instructors want an introductory paragraph to include a statement of the essay's **thesis**—its central idea. Although professional writers do not always use thesis statements in their introductory paragraphs, they can help student writers who need to practice clear essay organization. Here is an example of an introductory paragraph ending with a thesis statement.

Basketball is a team game. Individual stars are helpful, but in the end, the team that plays together is the team that wins. No one player can hog the ball; no one player should do all the shooting. Every player, every coach and every fan knows that. But once in a while, a team needs a super effort by an individual. **In a National Basketball Association playoff game between Boston and Syracuse, Boston's Bob Cousy made one of the most spectacular one-man shows ever seen.**

—HOWARD LISS, *True Sports Stories*

An introductory paragraph often includes an **introductory device** to lead into the thesis and to stimulate reader interest. To be effective, an introductory

4e

device must relate clearly to the essay's thesis and to the material in the topical paragraphs. Some of the most common introductory devices are listed below.

SELECTED DEVICES FOR INTRODUCTORY PARAGRAPHS

Provide relevant background information.

Tell an interesting brief story or anecdote.

Give a pertinent statistic or statistics.

Make a stimulating statement.

Ask a stimulating question or questions.

Use an appropriate quotation.

Make a useful analogy.

Define a term used throughout the essay.

Here is a guide to what to avoid in introductory paragraphs.

WHAT TO AVOID IN INTRODUCTORY PARAGRAPHS

1. Don't be too obvious. Avoid bald statements such as "In this paper I will discuss the causes of falling oil prices."
2. Don't apologize. Avoid self-critical statements such as "I do not have much background in this subject" or "I am not sure if I am right, but here is my opinion."
3. Don't use overworn expressions. Avoid empty statements such as "Love is what makes the world go round" or "Haste makes waste."

Concluding paragraphs: In informative and persuasive writing, a conclusion brings discussion to a logical and graceful end. Too abrupt an ending leaves your reader suddenly cut off, and a conclusion that is merely tacked onto an essay does not give the reader a sense of completion. In contrast, an ending that flows gracefully and sensibly from what has come before it reinforces your ideas and increases the impact of your essay. The most common ways of concluding an essay are listed below.

SELECTED WAYS TO CONCLUDE AN ESSAY

Use the devices suggested in this chapter for introductory paragraphs—but avoid using the same device in the introduction and conclusion of an essay.

Summarize the main points of an essay.

Call for awareness and action.

Point toward the future.

The concluding paragraph below summarizes Cousy's "show."

> In that game Bob Cousy scored a total of 50 points. He made 25 of them in regulation time, and 25 more in the four overtime periods. And he made 30 out of 32 foul shots. Even more important, he had scored his points at the right time. Four times he scored in the final seconds to keep the game going. Then he helped his team pull away. Basketball may be a team game, but most teams would not be sorry to have an individual performer like Bob Cousy.
>
> —HOWARD LISS, *True Sports Stories*

Here is a list of what to avoid when writing concluding paragraphs.

WHAT TO AVOID IN WRITING CONCLUDING REMARKS

1. Don't go off the track. Avoid introducing an entirely new idea or adding a fact that belongs in the body of the essay.

2. Do not merely reword your introduction. Also do not simply list the main idea in each topic sentence or restate the thesis. While a summary can refer to those points, it must tie them into what was covered in the essay. If the introduction and conclusion are interchangeable, you need to revise.

3. Don't announce what you have done. Avoid statements such as "In this paper I have tried to show the main causes for the drop in oil prices."

4. Don't use absolute claims. Avoid statements such as "This proves that. . . ." or "If we take this action, the problem will be solved." Always qualify your message with expressions such as "This seems to prove. . . ." or "If we take this action, we will begin working toward a solution of the problem."

5. Don't apologize. Avoid casting doubt on your material by making statements such as "I may not have thought of all the arguments, but. . . ."

Transitional paragraphs: A transitional paragraph usually consists of one or two sentences that help the reader move from one major point to another in long essays. Here is a transitional paragraph that moves the reader between a series of details and an explanation of their possible source.

> Now that we've sampled some of the false "facts" that clutter our storehouse of knowledge, perhaps you'd like to consider some of the possible reasons why we seem so susceptible to misinformation.
>
> —WILLIAM P. GOTTLIEB, *Science Facts You Won't Believe*

Identifying Sentences that Do Not Fit the Topic Sentence

Identify the topic sentence in each paragraph, and write its number in the first column. Then identify any irrelevant sentences (those that do not fit the topic sentence), and write their numbers in the second column.

	Topic Sentence	Irrelevant Sentences
EXAMPLE ¹The first attempts to popularize the use of toilet paper were failures. ²An American tried to sell packaged toilet paper in 1857. ³James Buchanan was president at the time. ⁴People were not interested, though, because they were used to using old newspapers and sales pamphlets for this purpose. ⁵It seemed foolish to spend money on new paper for the bathroom. ⁶Twenty years later an Englishman introduced rolls of toilet paper. ⁷However, it was now the middle of the Victorian age, and advertising toilet paper was difficult because of people's modesty about bodily functions. ⁸The Victorian Age gets its name from the British Queen Victoria, who ruled from 1837 to 1901.	*1*	*3, 8*

1. ¹Throwaway tissues have had a short but active history. ²Originally, tissues were called Cellucotton. ³Cellucotton had been developed as a cotton substitute late in World

War I. [4]Because it was highly absorbent, Cellucotton was used as bandages and even as gas mask filters. [5]I've seen pictures of gas masks, and they look uncomfortable. [6]I'm not sure where the filters were in them, but they must have been inside because I cannot see any white in the photos. [7]After the war, the manufacturer had a huge surplus and began looking for different ways to use Cellucotton.

2. [1]The major use of Cellucotton after the war was as a coldcream remover. [2]Movie stars appeared in magazine advertisements urging people to buy these towels. [3]A package of one hundred cost sixty-five cents. [4]Although I'm not sure how much money the average person earned, I think that was a lot of money in 1916. [5]In spite of the high price, sales were strong, but something odd happened. [6]People wrote letters saying how good the little towels were as disposable handkerchiefs. [7]Eventually, the company questioned its customers and found that most people were buying the product to blow their noses. [8]The company adjusted its advertising, and sales continued to grow.

_____   _____

3. [1]Other paper goods have equally interesting histories. [2]For example, the paper cup actually began as part of one man's plan to sell drinking water in public places. [3]An early water cooler was invented in 1908. [4]At that time, water was available for free in many public places, but drinkers shared an unwashed tin cup. [5]The risk of disease was great. [6]In order to encourage people to spend money for water, the inventor

_____   _____

provided free cups and advertised the safety of drinking from his coolers. [7]There should be free cups at water fountains today too because of all the diseases going around. [8]Luckily for the inventor, many states were passing laws prohibiting the use of shared water cups in public places. [9]More and more places began using paper cups, and the company grew quickly, eventually changing its name to the Dixie Cup Company.

4. [1]Many people associate the clarinet with jazz or the Big Bands of the forties. [2]However, the clarinet has been around since ancient times. [3]The clarinet can be hard to play. [4]The first clarinet appeared in Egypt before 2700 B.C. [5]The double clarinet appeared about eight hundred years later. [6]The first modern Westerner to compose for the clarinet was a sixteenth century German, Johann Christoph Denner. [7]He improved the clarinet by making it of wood, using a single rather than a double reed, and increasing its length from one foot to two feet.

_____   _____

5. [1]The trumpet is another instrument with a long history. [2]The first trumpets were made of bamboo cane or eucalyptus branches. [3]The eucalyptus tree is found in Australia and is the chief food source for koalas. [4]The first metal trumpets, made of silver, were found in the tomb of King Tutankhamen of Egypt, who died about 1350 B.C. [5]The Greek trumpets of the fifth century B.C. were made of carved ivory. [6]Like us, the Romans had both straight and J-shaped trumpets. [7]The Romans are often depicted in paintings as enjoying music.

_____   _____

Identifying Transitions

Underline all the transitional words and expressions in these paragraphs. Then list the transitions on the lines provided.

1. The lion is called the King of Beasts, but the tiger really deserves the title. Male lions are six to eight feet long, not counting their tails. They are about three feet high at the shoulder, and they weigh four to five hundred pounds. In contrast, the tiger can grow up to a foot longer, several inches taller, and a hundred pounds heavier.

   _____

2. Most people think the boomerang is found only in Australia; however, this is not so. People use curved hunting sticks in four other parts of the world: Indonesia, eastern Africa, the Indian subcontinent, and the southwestern United States. In the United States, the Hopi, Acoma, and Zuni Indians use such sticks to hunt small animals. Few boomerangs are designed to return to their owners, but the Australian aborigines have perfected a kind that does return. In fact, the word ''boomerang'' comes from the aborigines' name for such a hunting stick.

   _____

3. Despite its name, The *Encyclopaedia Britannica* is not a British enterprise, nor has it ever been. The *Britannica* was founded in 1771 by a group of ''Gentlemen in Scotland'' who ran it until 1815, when a second group of Scotsmen took over. The British finally became involved in 1910, but as partners to Americans. Since the 1920s, the *Britannica* has been a completely American project. From 1928 to 1943, it was owned by Sears, Roebuck. Since 1943, the *Britannica* has been owned by the University of Chicago.

   _____

4. Everyone knows the story of Cinderella. She was treated as a servant by her stepmother and stepsisters, helped by a fairy godmother, and finally rescued by a prince who identified her because her small foot fit the glass slipper that his ''mystery woman'' had left behind at the ball. Were glass slippers fashionable centuries ago, or did someone make a mistake? Someone certainly made a mistake. In 1697, Charles Perrault translated Cinderella from Old French into English. Unfortunately, he mistranslated *vair* as ''glass.'' Actually, *vair* means ''white squirrel fur.'' So, Cinderella's shoes were much more comfortable than we had been told.

   _____

Identifying Devices that Provide Coherence

Read this paragraph carefully, and then answer the questions that follow.

[1]Have you ever wondered how the painted lines in the road are made straight? [2]No one painting freehand could consistently keep lines straight, so machines are used. [3]Before a small road or street is painted, a highway crew marks it at twenty-foot intervals, following an engineer's plan. [4]Then a gasoline-powered machine, about the size of a large lawnmower, is pushed along by one person. [5]The operator follows the marks on the road, while air pressure forces out a stream of paint or hot plastic. [6]Hot plastic lasts from eighteen months to three years; paint lasts from three to six months. [7]Of course, this machine is too slow for use on highways. [8]Instead, four-person crews use a large truck equipped with a pointer that can be used to follow the median strip, so there is no need to mark the road before painting. [9]The truck is faster than the one-person machine for other reasons as well: it has *two* adjustable sprayguns that paint lines at the required distances apart, and it moves at five miles an hour. [10]Crew members must have great skill. [11]In fact, they receive up to a year of training.

1. Which words and phrases serve as transitional devices? _____

   _____

2. What key words are repeated (include all forms of the words)? _____

   _____

3. How does parallelism function in sentences 6 and 9? _____

   _____

4. What key words are later replaced by pronouns? List the nouns and the pronouns that substitute for them. _____

   _____

Organizing Sentences to Create a Coherent Paragraph

Rearrange the sentences in each set to create a coherent paragraph. Write the letters of the sentences in their new order on the lines given. Then write out the paragraph, using your own paper.

1. a. Second, compare fees for special services, such as stopping checks.
   b. Always compare several banks before you open a checking account.
   c. Finally, make sure the bank's hours are convenient for you.
   d. First, find out the monthly fee each bank charges.
   e. Next, see if you will be earning interest on your account.

   _____

2. a. Early humans imitated these "natural bridges" by chopping down tall trees and placing them across water.
   b. It was built of many logs tied together with rope.
   c. The first bridges were simply trees that had, by chance, fallen across streams.
   d. The bridge over the Euphrates River lasted for decades.
   e. The first genuine bridge was laid across the Euphrates River at Babylon about 700 B.C

   _____

3. a. Ruth Handler noticed that her daughter Barbie ignored these baby dolls, preferring to play with teenage paper dolls that had fancy clothes.
   b. In 1958 Mrs. Handler brought out the Barbie doll, an adult doll with many beautiful outfits.
   c. In the 1940s and early 1950s, most dolls were round-faced babies.
   d. The Barbie doll was so popular that in 1961 the Handlers created a boyfriend doll, Ken, named after their son.
   e. Toy manufacturers Ruth and Elliot Handler, founders of the Mattel toy company in 1945, created some of the most popular American dolls.

   _____

4. a. The 206 bones of the human skeleton are not lifeless.
   b. They are made of millions soft living cells encased in a hard framework.
   c. In adults, blood-forming marrow is usually found only in the bones of the trunk, but in young children all bones have active blood-forming marrow.
   d. At the center of some bones is a soft tissue called the marrow that manufactures blood cells.
   e. This framework is made of minerals, and that is why milk, a rich source of minerals, is very important for strong bones.

   _____

Supporting the Topic Sentence

For each topic sentence below, supply three to five relevant details. Then, using your own paper, write a unified and coherent paragraph using the topic sentence and your supporting details.

1. Topic Sentence: Women should (should not) serve in combat units in the U.S. armed forces.

    Details:

2. Topic Sentence: Raising a child today is very expensive.
    Details:

3. Topic Sentence: The _____ have contributed many
(members of an ethnic group)
things to American culture.

    Details:

4. Topic Sentence: Leaving home is difficult.
    Details:

5. Topic Sentence: _____ is a challenging course.
    Details:

6. Topic Sentence: _____ can be an exciting (relaxing) hobby.
    Details:

Organizing Details within Paragraphs

Details in a paragraph are often organized in one of four patterns: chronological order (time), spatial order (location), general to specific, or climactic order (least important to most important). For each pattern, select a subject from the ones given, construct a topic sentence, and list three to five supporting details. Then, on your own paper, use the topic sentence and details to write a unified and coherent paragraph of at least four sentences. It may be possible to combine two closely related details in one sentence.

1. CHRONOLOGICAL ORDER: the steps in getting a driver's license; preparing for a big date; how to arrange a surprise party
   Topic Sentence:
        Details:

2. SPATIAL ORDER: the view from my bedroom window; people waiting to enter a popular club or theater; the positions of the players around a baseball diamond
   Topic Sentence:
        Details:

3. GENERAL TO SPECIFIC: the advantages (disadvantages) of living with one's parents; the expense of going to college; the reasons _____ is my favorite holiday
   Topic Sentence:
        Details:

4. CLIMACTIC ORDER: why I am attending college; how I know when I am in love; the steps to be taken to make my city a better place to raise children
   Topic Sentence:
        Details:

Using Examples in Paragraphs

Write two paragraphs in which examples are used to support your topic sentence. In the first paragraph, use three to five short examples; in the second, use one extended example. First compose a topic sentence. Next, list the supporting example(s) you will use. After that, write your paragraph, using your own paper.

Select your topics from this list: the risks of walking alone at night; my favorite actor/actress; the advantages (disadvantages) of playing on a school team; how peer pressure can be hard to resist; professional athletes are overpaid (underpaid); the difficulty of adjusting to a new neighborhood, school, or job

1. MULTIPLE EXAMPLES

   Topic Sentence: _____

   Examples: a. _____

              b. _____

              c. _____

              d. _____

              e. _____

2. EXTENDED EXAMPLE

   Topic Sentence: _____

   Example: _____

Using Paragraph Development Strategies

Most paragraphs are developed through a combination of several of the strategies discussed in this chapter. Usually one strategy predominates, however. For each development strategy listed below, select a topic from the list; compose a topic sentence; list three to five details, examples, or other pieces of support; and then, using your own paper, write the paragraph.

1. NARRATIVE
   Topics: a time I proved I was right; an embarrassing situation; a time I learned the truth about someone; a narrow escape

   Topic Sentence: _____

   Events: a. _____

            b. _____

            c. _____

            d. _____

            e. _____

2. DESCRIPTION
   Topics: describe your room at its messiest; describe the crowd at a concert or sports event; describe your most interesting professor; describe Michael Jackson or Duke Ellington (see photographs on pages 46 and 47)

   Topic Sentence: _____

   Details: a. _____

            b. _____

            c. _____

            d. _____

            e. _____

3. PROCESS
   Topics: how to act at a job interview; how to organize your time; how to buy a used car; how to select a college

   Topic Sentence: _____

   Steps: a. _____

            b. _____

            c. _____

       d. _____

       e. _____

4. DEFINITION
   Topics: my perfect vacation; my ideal boyfriend or girlfriend; panic; rock and roll

   Topic Sentence: _____

   Qualities: a. _____

          b. _____

          c. _____

          d. _____

          e. _____

5. DIVISION AND CLASSIFICATION (pick one)
   Topics for Division: types of students; types of friendships; types of worry; types of success

   Topic Sentence: _____

   Subgroups: a. _____

          b. _____

          c. _____

          d. _____

          e. _____

   Topics for Classification: summer jobs; pets; parents; restaurants

   Topic Sentence: _____

   Individual
   Components: a. _____

          b. _____

          c. _____

          d. _____

          e. _____

UPI/Bettmann Newsphotos

UPI/Bettmann Newsphotos

6. COMPARISON AND CONTRAST
   Topics: I and my same-sex parent; being a student and being an employee; watching a sports event on television and attending one in person; Michael Jackson's stage personality and that of another performer

   Topic: _____

   Points of Comparison
   and Contrast: a. _____

                 b. _____

                 c. _____

                 d. _____

                 e. _____

7. ANALOGY
   Topics: a possessive person and a spider in its web; starting a new job (attending a new school) and jumping into a cold pool; a lie and a forest fire; daydreaming and going for a walk

   Topic Sentence: _____

   Similarities: a. _____

                 b. _____

                 c. _____

                 d. _____

                 e. _____

8. CAUSE AND EFFECT
   Topics: why I chose the college I am now attending; what happened when I changed my appearance (lost or gained weight, cut hair, dressed differently); how divorce or remarriage affected the children in one family; the effects Michael Jackson or Duke Ellington have had on popular music

   Topic Sentence: _____

   Causes
   or Effects: a. _____

               b. _____

               c. _____

               d. _____

               e. _____

Revising Introductions and Conclusions

Each of these introductions and conclusions is inadequate as part of a 500-word essay. Determine what is wrong with each. Then, using your own paper, revise each paragraph. Some may need to be completely rewritten.

1.   THE EXPLORATION OF THE ANTARCTIC

   Introduction: I think the Antarctic is very interesting, so even though I didn't have time to do a lot of research I'm going to tell you what I know about its exploration.

   Conclusion: In this paper I have tried to show how brave all these explorers were to face the terrible cold and loneliness of Antarctica. By the way, Antarctica is the *South* Pole.

2.   THE CAUSES OF VOLCANIC ERUPTIONS

   Introduction: There are 850 active volcanoes in the world. More than 75 percent of them are located in the "Ring of Fire," an area that goes from the west coasts of North and South America to the east coast of Asia, all the way down to New Zealand. Twenty percent of these volcanoes are in Indonesia. Many are also in Japan, the Aleutian Islands (off Alaska), and Central America. Other big groups of volcanoes are in the Mediterranean Sea and Iceland. In contrast, there are only six volcanoes in Africa and three in Antarctica.

   Conclusion: So this is why volcanoes erupt.

3.   SHOULD CAPITAL PUNISHMENT BE RESTORED IN OUR STATE?

   Introduction: Yes, I agree with the question. Every year the rate of serious crime in our state rises. Now is the time to get the murderers and rapists off the streets.

   Conclusion: In this essay, I have proven beyond any doubt that the death penalty will discourage people from committing violent crimes, that it will save the taxpayers a lot of money, and that hardly anybody will be executed by accident.

4.   LET'S NOT LIMIT PRESIDENTS TO TWO TERMS

   Introduction: The twenty-second amendment to the Constitution, limiting presidents to two elected terms, should be repealed.

   Conclusion: Fourth, the twenty-second amendment was ratified in 1951 as a Republican reaction to the earlier four-term election of Democrat Franklin Roosevelt. Now the strategy has backfired; although the American people may be very happy with a president, they cannot keep him in office long enough to successfully put all his policies to work.

5.

Introduction: In this essay I will discuss why it is important for Americans to speak and read more than one language. Knowing a second language helps people to explore another culture, keeps them in touch with their roots, and can make traveling abroad much easier and more interesting. Therefore, all Americans should learn a second language.

Conclusion: There are, then, three good reasons to learn a second language. First, knowing a language such as French or German enables a person to read some of the world's most important literature, philosophy, and science. Second, learning the language of our ancestors may help us to learn about our families and ourselves and may help us to preserve vanishing ways. Third, travel in Europe, Asia, or South America is easier when the traveler is able to speak to the inhabitants in their own language. Finally, once we have struggled to learn a new language we can understand how newcomers struggle to learn English. This can make us more patient and understanding, leading to better relations with our neighbors and co-workers.

Writing Introductions and Conclusions

EXERCISE **4-10**
(4e)

Write introductory and concluding paragraphs for three of the topics listed here. Refer to the chapter for suggested strategies. Before writing, list your thesis statement and strategies on the lines below. Use a different strategy for each paragraph. Use your own paper.

TOPICS: selecting a sensible diet for life; violence in the stands at sports events; applying for a student loan; dealing with difficult neighbors; noise pollution; motorcycles; old movies; talking to your doctor; teenage marriage; computers in the classroom; science fiction monsters

ESSAY 1

Thesis Statement: _____

Strategy for Introduction: _____

Strategy for Conclusion: _____

ESSAY 2

Thesis Statement: _____

Strategy for Introduction: _____

Strategy for Conclusion: _____

ESSAY 3

Thesis Statement: _____

Strategy for Introduction: _____

Strategy for Conclusion: _____

5 and 6 | Reading and Thinking Critically; Writing Argument

5: READING AND THINKING CRITICALLY

5a | Understanding the reading process

Purposes for reading vary. In college, most reading involves reading to learn new information, to appreciate literary works, or to review notes on classes or assignments. These types of reading involve rereading.

Your purpose in reading determines the speed at which you can expect to read. When you are hunting for a particular fact, you can skim the material until you come to what you want. When you read material about a subject you know well, you can move somewhat rapidly through most of it, slowing down when you come to new material. When you are unfamiliar with the subject, your brain needs time to absorb the new material, so you have to read slowly.

In reading for the purpose of learning, three steps are common to all materials. These are similar to the steps in the writing process.

UNIVERSALS IN READING TO LEARN	
Skim	Like *planning* in the writing process, skimming means getting ready to read.
Read	Like *drafting* in the writing process, reading means moving through the material, according to your purpose for reading.
Reinforce	Like *revising* and *editing* in the writing process, reinforcing means re-reading, making clear, fine tuning, and getting into final form.

Here is a structured system, known as SQ3R, that will help you apply these universals to studying and thinking critically.

S = Survey: Surveying is part of *skimming*. You survey to get an overview of the material before you start reading closely. Look at the title, the subtitles or other headings, the first and last paragraphs, and any illustrations. Make predictions about what you expect to find in the piece of writing. Decide how quickly or slowly the piece should be read.

Q = Question: Questioning is also a part of *skimming*. Turn the title and any subtitles into questions. Doing this makes reading an active rather than a passive activity and results in better comprehension and recall. The goal is to get your thinking started so that you will be alert to focus on key matters as you read.

R = Read: *Reading* is the central activity. Read carefully; you cannot read a textbook as quickly as you might read a novel. See how what you read fits your predictions, and modify those predictions as you need to. Concentrate on key sections and paragraphs; read less important sections more quickly. Read in suitable surroundings: if you must have quiet, find a quiet place; if you study best in the early morning, set aside a few mornings a week for work. Above all, leave yourself enough time to read all your assignments at a comfortable pace.

R = Recite: Reciting is part of *reinforcing*. Look away from the page and repeat the main points, aloud or to yourself. Recite in chunks—subsections of textbook chapters, for example. Knowing ahead of time that when you finish a section you will have to recite stimulates concentration. If you cannot recite the material, reread it and try again. If you still have trouble, go back to surveying, questioning, and rereading.

R = Review: Reviewing is the second part of *reinforcing*. When you finish reading, survey again to refresh your memory of the material. Doing this gives you a framework into which to fit the new material you have just learned. If you cannot recall a point clearly, reread that section.

5b Reading to think critically

The full meaning of a passage develops on three levels: the literal, the inferential, and the evaluative. Most people stop reading at the literal level, but unless you move on to the next two steps you will not fully understand what you read.

1. Reading for **literal** meaning means understanding what is said. The literal level involves (a) the key facts, the central points in an argument, or the major details of plot and character, and (b) the minor details that fill out the picture.

2. Reading to make **inferences** means understanding what is implied (that is indicated indirectly) but not stated. Often you have to infer information, or background, or the author's purpose.

3. **Evaluative** reading, necessary for critical thinking, occurs after you know an author's literal meaning and you have drawn as many inferences as possible from the material.

5c

A major evaluative reading skill is **differentiating fact from opinion.** The difference between fact and opinion is sometimes quite obvious, but at other times telling fact from opinion can be tricky. Keep in mind that facts (numbers, statistics, dates, quotations) can be proven. Opinions, in contrast, reflect individual biases. Consider these examples:

OPINIONS	FACTS
California is too crowded.	California has the largest population of any U.S. state—over 25 million people.
Living in Alaska must be lonely.	Alaska has a population density of only .88 persons per square mile.
New Jersey has the best scenery on the East Coast.	New Jersey's official nickname is the Garden State.

5c Using evidence to think critically

The most important part of reasoning is **evidence**—facts, statistics, examples, and expert opinion.

GUIDELINES FOR USING EVIDENCE EFFECTIVELY

1. **Evidence should be plentiful.** In general, the more evidence, the better. A survey that draws upon 100 people is more likely to be reliable than a survey involving only ten.
2. **Evidence should be representative.** Do not trust a statement if it is based on only some members of the group being discussed; it must be based on a truly *representative*, or typical, sample of the group.
3. **Evidence should be relevant.** Be sure the evidence you present truly supports your point and is not simply an interesting but irrelevant fact. For example, declining enrollment at a college *might* indicate poor teaching—but it also might indicate a general decline in the student population of the area, a reduction in available financial aid, higher admissions standards, or any number of other factors.
4. **Evidence should be qualified.** Avoid words such as *all, certainly, always,* or *never.* Conclusions are more reasonable if they are qualified with words such as *some, many, a few, probably, possibly, may, usually,* and *often.*
5. **Evidence should be accurate.** Evidence must come from reliable sources.

5d Evaluating cause and effect to think critically

Cause and effect is a type of thinking that seeks the relationship between two or more pieces of evidence. You may seek either to understand the effects of a known cause or to determine the cause or causes of a known effect.

5e

GUIDELINES FOR EVALUATING CAUSE AND EFFECT

1. **Clear relationship.** Causes and effects normally occur in chronological order: *First* a door slams; *then* a pie that is cooling on a shelf falls. However, a cause-and-effect relationship must be linked by more than chronological sequence. The fact that B happened after A does not prove that it was caused by A.

2. **A pattern of repetition.** To establish the relationship of A to B, there must be proof that every time A was present, B occurred.

3. **No oversimplification.** The basic pattern of cause and effect—single cause, single effect—rarely gives the full picture. Most complex social or political problems have *multiple causes*, not a single cause and a single effect.

cause 1
cause 2   ⟶   produce   ⟶   effect B
cause 3

Similarly, one cause can produce *multiple effects:*

cause A   ⟶   produces   ⟶   effect 1
                                                      effect 2
                                                      effect 3

5e   Understanding reasoning processes to think critically

Induction and **deduction** are reasoning processes. They are natural thought patterns that people use every day to think through ideas and to make decisions.

Induction is the process of arriving at general principles from particular facts or instances. Suppose you go to the supermarket and when you get home you notice that the eggs are smashed because the packer put a melon on top of them. The next week you come home from the market after the same person has bagged your groceries to find that a package of spaghetti has split open. The week after that the same packer puts a container of yogurt in upside down. It opens and you have to wash your groceries before you can put them away. You decide never to go on that person's line again because you want your groceries packed properly. You have arrived at this conclusion by means of induction.

Once you have become convinced that a certain grocery packer at your supermarket does a sloppy job, you will probably stay off that person's line—even if it is the shortest one. Your reasoning might go like this:

A. That grocery packer smashes groceries.
B. I can choose to get on that person's line or not.
C. If I choose to get on that person's line, my groceries will get smashed.

You reached this decision by means of deduction. Deduction moves from two or more general principles (A and B above) to a conclusion (C) about a specific instance.

A COMPARISON OF INDUCTIVE AND DEDUCTIVE REASONING

	INDUCTION	DEDUCTION
Where the argument begins	with specific evidence	with a general claim
Type of conclusion	a general claim	a specific statement
Main use	to discover something new	to apply what is known

6: WRITING ARGUMENT

When **writing argument** for your college courses, you seek to convince a reader to agree with you concerning a topic open to debate. A written argument states and supports one position about the debatable topic. Support for that position depends on evidence, reasons, and examples chosen for their direct relation to the point being argued.

Written argument differs from everyday, informal arguing. Informal arguing often originates in anger and might involve bursts of temper or unpleasant emotional confrontations. An effective written argument, in contrast, sets forth its position calmly, respectfully, and logically.

6a   Choosing a topic for written argument

When you choose a topic for written argument, be sure that it is **open to debate**. Be careful not to confuse facts with matters of debate. A fact is the name of a college course or how many credits are required in a college curriculum. An essay becomes an argument when it takes a position concerning the fact or other pieces of information. For example, some people might think that college students should be free to choose whatever courses they want, while other people might think that certain courses should be required of all students.

A written argument could take one of these opposing positions and defend it. If you cannot decide what position to agree with because all sides of an issue have merit, do not get blocked. Instead, concentrate on the merits of one position, and present that position as effectively as you can.

6b Developing an assertion and a thesis statement for written argument

An **assertion** is a statement that reflects a position about a debatable topic that can be supported by evidence, reasons, and examples (see 4a). The assertion acts as a preliminary form of your thesis statement. Although the wording of the assertion often does not find its way into the essay itself, the assertion serves as a focus for your thinking and your writing.

TOPIC	Buying on credit
ASSERTION	Buying on credit can be helpful.
ASSERTION	Buying on credit can be dangerous.

Next, based on your assertion, you compose a **thesis statement** (see 2e) to use in the essay. It states the *exact* position that you present and support in the essay.

THESIS STATEMENT	Buying on credit enables people to make necessary purchases without straining their budgets.
THESIS STATEMENT	Buying on credit causes people to go dangerously into debt.

To stimulate your thinking about the topic and your assertion about the topic, use the techniques for gathering ideas explained in 2d. Jot down your ideas as they develop. Many writers of arguments make a list of the points that come to mind. Use two columns to visually represent two contrasting points of view. Head the columns with labels that emphasize contrast: for example, *agree* and *disagree* or *for* and *against*.

6c Structuring written argument

No one structure fits all written argument. However, for college courses, most written arguments include certain elements.

ELEMENTS IN A WRITTEN ARGUMENT

1. **Introductory paragraph**: Sets the context for the position that is argued in the essay. (See 4e.)

2. **Thesis statement**: States the position being argued. In a short essay, it often appears at the end of the introductory paragraph. (See 2e.)

3. **Background information**: Gives the reader basic information needed for understanding the position being argued. This information can be part of the introductory paragraph or can appear in its own paragraph.

4. **Reasons or evidence**: Supports the position being argued. This material is the heart of the essay. The discussion of each reason or type of evidence usually

---

> **ELEMENTS IN A WRITTEN ARGUMENT** *(continued)*
>
> consists of a general statement backed up with specific details or specific examples. Depending on the length of the essay, one or two paragraphs are devoted to each reason or type of evidence. The best order for presenting support depends on the impact you want to achieve. (See 4c.)
>
> 5. **Anticipation of opposing positions**: Mentions positions in opposition to the one being argued and responds to them briefly. This counter-argument can appear in its own paragraph, just before the conclusion or immediately after the introduction.
>
> 6. **Concluding paragraph**: Brings the essay to a logical end. It does not cut off the reader abruptly. (See 4e.)

6d Considering the audience for written argument

When a topic is emotionally charged, chances are high that any position being argued will elicit either strong agreement or strong disagreement in the reader. For example, topics such as abortion, capital punishment, and gun control arouse very strong emotions in many people.

The degree to which a reader might be friendly or hostile can influence what strategies you use to try to convince that reader. For example, when you anticipate that many readers will not agree with you, consider discussing common ground before presenting your position. Common ground in a debate over capital punishment might be that both sides agree that crime is a growing problem. Once both sides agree about the problem, there might be more tolerance for differences of opinion concerning whether capital punishment is a deterrent to crime.

6e Defining terms in written argument

When you **define terms**, you clarify the meaning of key words. Key words are terms that are central to your message. Key words that are **open to interpretation** should be replaced with other, more specific words.

No   Buying on credit is **bad.**

Yes   Buying on credit **encourages people to buy things they do not need.**

Yes   Buying on credit **makes it hard to see how much one is actually spending.**

Some key words might **vary with the context** of a discussion and should be explained. Abstract words such as *love, freedom,* and *democracy* have to be explained because they have different meanings in different situations.

Many students wonder whether they should use actual dictionary definitions in an essay. Looking up words in the dictionary to understand precise meanings is a very important activity for writers. Quoting a dictionary definition, however, is rarely wise. Using an **extended definition** is usually more effective. See the extended definition of an ice cream cone in 4d.

6f Reasoning effectively in written argument

The basis for a debatable position is often personal opinion or belief, and in such cases it is unrealistic to expect to change someone's mind with one written argument. Nevertheless, you still have an important goal: to convince your reader that your point of view has value. You can achieve this by combining three strategies:

1. **Be logical**: use solid evidence; analyze cause and effect carefully; and distinguish between fact and opinion.
2. **Enlist the emotions of the reader**: appeal to the values and beliefs of the reader, usually by arousing the "better self" of the reader.
3. **Establish credibility**: show that you can be relied upon as a knowledgeable person with good sense by being accurate and not distorting facts.

6g Establishing a reasonable tone in written argument

To achieve a reasonable tone, **choose your words carefully**. Avoid exaggerations and artificial language (see 21d). No matter how strongly you disagree with opposing arguments, never insult the other side. Name calling is impolite, shows poor self control, and demonstrates poor judgment.

Distinguishing Fact from Opinion

Identify each passage as *fact* or *opinion*. Be prepared to explain your answers.

EXAMPLES   The first shoes were sandals.   _____*fact*_____

Wearing sandals to work is rude.   _____*opinion*_____

A.   1. The oldest shoe ever found is an Egyptian sandal   _____
from 2000 B.C.

2. Ancient sandals were made of various materials,   _____
including leather, rope, and strong grasses.

3. Roman soldiers who wore sandals while marching   _____
were probably uncomfortable.

4. The first non-sandal shoe was a leather moccasin.   _____

5. The Romans were the first to have professional   _____
shoemakers.

6. Not having electric tools, the Roman shoemakers   _____
must have worked very hard.

7. Shoemakers today probably like their jobs.   _____

8. Their prices are very low.   _____

9. The style and color of a Roman's shoes were signs   _____
of social rank.

10. Upper-class Roman women wore red or white closed   _____
shoes, but lower-class women wore natural-colored
sandals.

11. An outfit does not look right without matching   _____
shoes.

12. I would hate it if I had to wear sandals all year round.   _____

13. The Romans were the first to make shoes shaped to   _____
fit right and left feet.

14. Roman shoes did not have brand names, but some   _____
shoemakers were in greater demand and could
charge more because they made better shoes.

B. 1. Before the fourteenth century, shoe sizes were not standardized. _____

2. Even expensive, custom-made shoes could vary in size from one shoemaker to another. _____

3. There is no point in being rich if a person cannot get comfortable shoes. _____

4. In 1305 King Edward I of Britain standardized basic measurements used in trade. _____

5. One new standard was the inch; it was declared to be the length of three grains of barley. _____

6. Children's shoe sizes were also measured in barley grains; for example, a size ten was ten barley grains long. _____

7. People must have been happy about the new standards. _____

8. Barley was a strange thing to select as a basis for measurement. _____

9. The fourteenth century had some of the oddest fashions ever created. _____

10. Long spiked toes became popular for a while. _____

11. Luckily for us today, spiked toes did not stay popular. _____

12. High heels did not develop until sixteenth-century France—where they were worn mostly by men. _____

13. King Louis XIV popularized high heels. _____

14. He added inches to his boots to hide his shortness. _____

15. He was imitated by his nobles. _____

7 Parts of Speech and Structures of the Sentence

PARTS OF SPEECH

Knowing grammar helps you understand how language works. Grammar describes the forms and structures of words. In this way, it offers an explanation of how language operates and how words make meaning to deliver their messages. Grammar also sets down the standards accepted by people who write and speak for educated audiences.

If you know the parts of speech, you have a basic vocabulary for identifying words, their various forms, and the sentence structures they build. The first part of this chapter explains each part of speech to help you identify words and their functions. Being able to do this is important because sometimes the same word can function as more than one part of speech. To identify a word's part of speech, you have to see how the word functions in a sentence.

We drew a **circle** on the ground. [*Circle* is a noun.]
Sometimes planes **circle** the airport before landing. [*Circle* is a verb.]

Running is good exercise. [*Running* is a noun.]
Running shoes can be very expensive. [*Running* is an adjective.]

7a Recognizing nouns

A **noun** names a person, place, thing, or idea.

Most nouns change form to show number: *week, ox* (singular); *weeks, oxen* (plural) (see 22d-4). Nouns also change form for the possessive case: *the **mayor's** decision* (see 27a). Nouns function as subjects (7j-1), objects (7k), and complements (7l): ***Marie saw a fly in the soup*** (subject, direct object, object of preposition); ***Marie is a vegetarian*** (subject, subject complement).

	NOUNS	
TYPE	**FUNCTION**	**EXAMPLE**
Proper	Names specific people, places, or things (first letter is always capitalized)	**John Lennon** **Paris** **Buick**
Common	Names general groups, places, people, things, or activities	**singer** **city** **car** **talking**
Concrete	Names things that can be seen, touched, heard, smelled, tasted	**landscape** **pizza** **thunder**
Abstract	Names things *not* knowable through the five senses	**freedom** **shyness**
Collective	Names groups	**family** **team** **committee**
Mass	Names "uncountable" things	**water** **time**

Articles often appear with nouns. The articles are *a, an*, and *the*, and they signal whether a noun is meant generally or specifically in a particular context.

Give me **a** pen. [General: any pen will do.]
Give me **the** pen on the desk. [Specific: only one pen will do.]

7b Recognizing pronouns

A **pronoun** takes the place of a noun.

Peter is an engineer. [noun]
He is an engineer. [pronoun]

The word (or words) a pronoun replaces is called its **antecedent**.
Some pronouns change form to show **number**: *I, she, yourself* (singular); *we, they, themselves* (plural). Many pronouns change form to show **case**: *I, who* (subjective); *me, whom* (objective); *my, mine, whose* (possessive) (see Chapter 9).

PRONOUNS

Type	Function	Example
Personal *I, you, they, we, her, its, our,* and others	Refers to people or things	**I** saw **her** take **your** books to **them**
Relative *who, which, that, what, whomever,* and others	Introduces certain noun clauses and adjective clauses	**Whoever** took the book **that** I left must return it.
Interrogative *who, whose, what, which,* and others	Introduces a question	**Who** called?
Demonstrative *this, these, that, those*	Points out the antecedent	Is **this** a mistake?
Reflexive; Intensive *myself, yourself, herself, themselves,* and all *-self* or *-selves* words	Reflects back to the antecedent; intensifies the antecedent	They claim to support **themselves**. **I** **myself** doubt it.
Reciprocal *each other, one another*	Refers to individual parts of a plural antecedent	We respect **each other.**
Indefinite *all, anyone, each*	Refers to nonspecific persons or things	**Everyone** is welcome here.

7c   Recognizing verbs

A **verb** expresses an action, an occurrence, or a state of being.

I **leap**. [action]
Claws **grab**. [action]
The sky **becomes** cloudy. [occurrence]
He **seems** sad. [state of being]

A **linking verb** connects a subject with one or more words—called a **subject complement**—that rename it or describe it.

Eleanor Roosevelt **was** First Lady. [*Eleanor Roosevelt* = subject, *was* = linking verb, *First Lady* = subject complement]
Eleanor Roosevelt **was** popular. [*Eleanor Roosevelt* = subject, *was* = linking verb, *popular* = subject complement]

	VERBS	
TYPE	**FUNCTION**	**EXAMPLE**
Main *ask, begin, choose, dangle, eat, follow, go, hear, investigate,* and thousands more	Delivers verb meaning	I **drove** yesterday.
Linking *be, appear, become, look, seem,* and others	Acts as main verb but delivers meaning by linking a subject (7j) to a complement (7l)	You **seem** angry.
Auxiliary *can, could, may, might, must, should, would,* and others	Combines with main verb to make a verb phrase (7m) that delivers information about tense (8f, g), mood (8i), and voice (8j)	If I **had** driven last week, you **would be** driving now.

The most common linking verb is *be* (8c). Verbs describing the workings of the senses sometimes function as linking verbs: *feel, smell, taste, sound, look,* and so on. Other linking verbs include *appear, seem, become, remain,* and *grow.*

Auxiliary verbs, also known as **helping verbs,** are forms of *be, do, have,* and several other verbs that combine with main verbs to make verb phrases.

> This season many new television series **have imitated** last year's hit shows. [*have* = auxiliary, *imitated* = main verb, *have imitated* = verb phrase]

> Programs **are becoming** more and more alike. [*are* = auxiliary, *becoming* = main verb, *are becoming* = verb phrase]

> Soon we **may** not **be able to tell** the programs apart. [*may be able* = auxiliary verb, *to tell* = main verb, *may be able to tell* = verb phrase]

7d Recognizing verbals

Verbals are made from verb parts but they can not function as verbs, because they do not change form to show time (tense) changes. They function as nouns, adjectives, or adverbs.

VERBALS		
TYPE	**FUNCTION**	**EXAMPLE**
Infinitive *to* + simple form of verb	1. Noun: names an action, state, or condition 2. Adjective or adverb: describes or modifies	**To eat** now is inconvenient. Still, we have far **to go**.
Past participle *-ed* form of regular verb	Adjective: describes or modifies	**Boiled, filtered** water is usually safe to drink.
Present participle *-ing* form of verb	1. Adjective: describes or modifies 2. Noun; see *gerund,* below	**Running** water may not be safe.
Gerund *-ing* form of verb	Noun: names an action, state, or condition	**Eating** in turnpike restaurants can be an adventure.

7e Recognizing adjectives

An **adjective** modifies—that is, describes—a noun or a pronoun. Adjectives also modify word groups—clauses and phrases—that function as nouns.

He received a **low** grade on the first quiz. [*Low* modifies noun *grade.*]

His second grade was **higher**. [*Higher* modifies noun phrase *his second grade.*]

That he achieved a B average was **important**. [*Important* modifies noun clause *that he achieved a B average.*]

Descriptive adjectives such as *low* and *higher* show levels of "intensity," usually by changing form (*low, lower, lowest*). For more information about these changes, see Chapter 12.

Some words that are quite different from descriptive adjectives still function to limit nouns, so they are classified as adjectives. Articles, one type of these limiting adjectives, are discussed in 7a. The chart on the next page lists other types.

Sometimes words that usually function as nouns function as adjectives.

The **fire** destroyed the hotel. [*Fire* is a noun.]

The **fire** extinguisher is in the hall. [*Fire* is an adjective describing *extinguisher.*]

LIMITING ADJECTIVES

Demonstrative
this, these, that, those | **Those** students rent **that** house.

Indefinite
any, each, other, some, few, and others | **Few** films today have complex plots.

Interrogative
what, which, whose | **What** answer did you give?

Numerical
one, first, two, second, and others | The **fifth** question was tricky.

Possessive
my, your, their, and others | **My** violin is older than **your** cello.

Relative
what, which, whose, whatever, whichever, whoever | We don't know **which** road to take.

7f Recognizing adverbs

An **adverb** modifies—that is, describes—a verb, an adjective, another adverb, or a clause.

In winter the ice on ponds may freeze **suddenly**. [*Suddenly* modifies verb *may freeze.*]

It is **very** tempting to go skating. [*Very* modifies adjective *tempting.*]

People die **quite** needlessly when they fall through the ice. [*Quite* modifies adverb *needlessly.*]

Always wait until the ice has thickened enough to hold your weight. [*Always* modifies entire clause.]

Most adverbs are easily recognized because they are formed by adding *-ly* to adjectives (*wisely, quickly, devotedly*). Yet some adjectives also end in *-ly* (*motherly, chilly*). Also, many adverbs do not end in *-ly* (*very, always, not, yesterday, well*). See Chapter 12 for an explanation of how confusion between adverbs and adjectives can be avoided.

Conjunctive adverbs are a group of adverbs that function (1) to modify the sentences to which they are attached, and (2) to help create logical connections in meaning between independent clauses.

CONJUNCTIVE ADVERBS (WORDS OF TRANSITION)	
FUNCTION	**EXAMPLES**
Indicate addition	**also, furthermore, moreover**
Indicate contrast	**however, still, nonetheless, nevertheless, conversely**
Indicate comparison	**similarly**
Indicate summary or result	**therefore, thus, consequently**
Indicate time	**next, then, meanwhile, finally**
Indicate emphasis	**indeed, certainly**

Construction has slowed traffic on the interstate; **therefore**, people are looking for other routes to work.

People have been complaining for weeks. **Finally**, one more lane has been opened during rush hour.

7g Recognizing prepositions

A **preposition** signals the beginning of a prepositional phrase. It is followed by a noun or pronoun (called the **object of the preposition**), and it indicates the relationship of that noun or pronoun to another word. Here is a complete list of prepositions.

about	despite	over
above	down	past
across	during	regarding
after	except	round
against	excepting	since
along	for	through
among	from	throughout
around	in	till
as	inside	to
at	into	toward
before	like	under
behind	near	underneath
below	next	unlike
beneath	of	until
beside	off	up
between	on	upon
beyond	onto	with
but	out	within
by	outside	without
concerning		

Prepositional expressions are formed by combinations of single-word prepositions.

according to	due to	instead of
along with	except for	in the midst of
apart from	in addition to	on account of
as for	in back of	on top of
as regards	in case of	out of
as to	in front of	up to
because of	in lieu of	with reference to
by means of	in place of	with regard to
by reason of	in regard to	with respect to
by way of	in spite of	with the exception of

A **prepositional phrase** consists of a preposition (or prepositional expression), its object, and any modifying words. A prepositional phrase always starts with a preposition: *above their heads, in the pool, in front of the store.*

7h Recognizing conjunctions

A **conjunction** connects words, phrases, or clauses. **Coordinating conjunctions** join two or more grammatically equivalent structures.

COORDINATING CONJUNCTIONS

and	or	for
but	nor	so
		yet

And, but, yet, or, and *nor* can join structures of any kind: two or more nouns, verbs, adjectives, adverbs, phrases, and all types of clauses.

Joe is majoring in Computer Technology **and** Engineering. [nouns]

He finds his course interesting **but** demanding. [adjectives]

In his spare time, he works on his car, **and** he helps care for his grandfather. [independent clauses]

For and *so* can connect only independent clauses.

Joe helps his grandfather, **for** he does not want the man to move to a nursing home.

Correlative conjunctions function in pairs, joining equivalent grammatical constructions.

CORRRELATIVE CONUNCTIONS

both . . . and	neither . . . nor
either . . . or	not only . . . but (also)
whether . . . or	

Both the United States *and* the Soviet Union are worried about nuclear proliferation.

Subordinating conjunctions begin certain dependent clauses that function as modifiers.

SUBORDINATING CONJUNCTIONS

after	even though	though	where
although	if	unless	wherever
as	once	until	whether
because	since	when	while
before	so that	whenever	

Because of the unpredictability of hurricanes, many lives are lost each year.

People sometimes refuse to evacuate *although* they are warned in plenty of time.

7i Recognizing interjections

An **interjection** is a word or expression used to convey surprise or other strong emotions. An interjection can stand alone, usually punctuated with an exclamation point, or can be part of a sentence, usually set off with commas. Interjections occur only rarely in academic writing.

Oh no!

Darn! I lost my keys.

Well, how much will it cost to fix my car?

STRUCTURES OF THE SENTENCE

The *sentence* can be defined in several ways. On its most basic level, a sentence starts with a capital letter and finishes with a period, question mark, or exclamation point. Sentences can be classified according to purpose. Most sentences are **declarative**; they make a statement:

Pizza is fattening.

Some sentences are **interrogative**; they ask a question:

How fattening is pizza?

Some sentences are **imperative**; they give a command:

Give me a pizza!

Some sentences are **exclamatory**; they exclaim:

What a large pizza!

Grammatically, a sentence contains at least one **independent clause**, that is, a group of words that can stand alone as an independent unit, in contrast to a

dependent clause, which cannot stand alone. Sometimes a sentence is described as a "complete thought," but the concept of "complete" is too vague to be useful.

To begin your study of the sentence, consider its basic structure. A sentence consists of two parts: a subject and a predicate.

7j Recognizing subjects and predicates

1 Recognizing subjects

The **simple subject** is the word or group of words that acts, is acted upon, or is described. In the sentence *The saxophonist played*, the simple subject is the one word *saxophonist*. The **complete subject** is the simple subject and all the words related to it.

THE SENTENCE		
Complete Subject	**+**	**Complete Predicate**
The talented saxophonist ↑ SIMPLE SUBJECT		played.

The **pianist** sang. [simple subject]
The new pianist sang. [complete subject]

A subject can be **compound**, that is, can consist of two or more nouns or pronouns and their modifiers.

THE SENTENCE		
Complete Subject	**+**	**Complete Predicate**
The talented saxophonist and the trumpeter ↖ ↗ COMPOUND SUBJECT		played.

The audience and **the club manager** applauded. [compound subject]

2 Recognizing predicates

The **predicate** is the part of the sentence that says what the subject is doing or experiencing, or what is being done to the subject. The predicate usually comes after its subject, and it always contains a verb. The **simple predicate** contains only the verb. The **complete predicate** is the simple predicate and all the words related to it.

THE SENTENCE

Complete Subject	+	Complete Predicate
The talented saxophonist		played passionately.
		↑
		SIMPLE PREDICATE

The pianist **sang**. [simple predicate]

The pianist **sang beautifully**. [complete predicate]

A predicate can be **compound**, that is, consisting of two or more verbs.

THE SENTENCE

Complete Subject	+	Complete Predicate
The talented saxophonist		strutted and played.
		↖ ↗
		COMPOUND PREDICATE

The pianist **sang** and **swayed**. [compound predicate]

7k Recognizing direct and indirect objects

1 Recognizing direct objects

A **direct object** occurs in the predicate of a sentence. It receives the action of a transitive verb (8d), completing its meaning.

THE SENTENCE		
Complete Subject	**+**	**Complete Predicate**
Their agent		negotiated a contract.
		↑ ↑
		VERB DIRECT OBJECT

Their agent called **the music critics** [direct object]

To find the direct object, make up a *whom?* or *what?* question about the verb. (The agent negotiated what? *A contract.* The agent called whom? *The music critics.*) A direct object may be compound:

They played **their hit** and **a new song**.

2 Recognizing indirect objects

An **indirect object** occurs in the predicate of a sentence. It answers a *to whom?, for whom?, to what?*, or *for what?* question about a verb.

THE SENTENCE		
Complete Subject	**+**	**Complete Predicate**
Their agent	got	the group a contract.
	↑	↑ ↑
	VERB	INDIRECT OBJECT DIRECT OBJECT

He tried to get **them** an album deal. [indirect object]

71 Recognizing complements, modifiers, and appositives

1 Recognizing complements

A **complement** occurs in the predicate of a sentence. It renames or describes the subject or object. A **subject complement** is a noun or adjective that follows a linking verb, such as *was* or *seems*, and renames or describes the subject.

THE SENTENCE		
Complete Subject	+	**Complete Predicate**
The club manager		was the owner.
		↑ ↑
		LINKING SUBJECT
		VERB COMPLEMENT

The owner was **a jazz lover**. [noun as subject complement]
The owner was **generous**. [adjective as subject complement]

An **object complement** is a noun or adjective that immediately follows the direct object and either renames or describes it.

THE SENTENCE		
Complete Subject	+	**Complete Predicate**
The owner		called himself Artie.
		↑ ↑ ↑
		VERB DIRECT OBJECT
		OBJECT COMPLEMENT

The group considered itself **lucky**. [adjective as object complement]
Artie called them **exceptional**. [adjective as object complement]
He began to consider himself **a patron of the arts**. [noun phrase as object complement]

2 Recognizing modifiers

Modifiers are words or groups of words that describe other words. There are two basic kinds of modifiers: adjectives and adverbs.

Adjectives modify only nouns or words acting as nouns, such as pronouns, noun phrases, or noun clauses. They may appear in the subject or the predicate of a sentence.

THE SENTENCE

Complete Subject	+	Complete Predicate
The talented saxophonist ↑ ADJECTIVE		played a mellow tune. ↑ ADJECTIVE

Adverbs modify verbs, adjectives, other adverbs, or independent clauses. They may appear in the subject or the predicate of a sentence.

THE SENTENCE

Complete Subject	+	Complete Predicate
The saxophonist		played very passionately. ↖ ↗ ADVERBS

The audience responded **warmly**. [Adverb *warmly* modifies verb *responded*.]

They swayed **quite** excitedly in their seats. [Adverb *quite* modifies adverb *excitedly*.]

Enthusiastically, they demanded more. [Adverb *enthusiastically* modifies independent clause.]

3 Recognizing appositives

An **appositive** is a word or group of words that renames the word or group of words preceding it. Generally, appositives are nouns used to rename other nouns, although adjectives and verbs are also sometimes renamed by appositives.

THE SENTENCE

Complete Subject	+	Complete Predicate
The group, Diamond in the Rough,		looked like a hit.

↑
APPOSITIVE

Their manager, **Jon Franklin**, was ready to take the next step. [*Jon Franklin* renames the noun *manager.*]

He picked his targets: **the record companies and the television shows**. [*The record companies and the television shows* renames the noun *targets.*]

7m Recognizing phrases

A **phrase** is a group of words that lacks a subject (7j-1) or a predicate (7j-2). Phrases function as parts of speech. They cannot stand alone as sentences.

A **noun phrase** functions as a noun in a sentence.

Some political terms have unusual histories.

The seating plan in the French congress during their Revolution gives us our names for political radicals, conservatives, and moderates.

A **verb phrase** functions as a verb in a sentence.

The members **were seated** in a semicircular room. The most radical members **were located** to the left of the chairperson's platform, the more conservative to the right.

A **prepositional phrase** functions as an adjective or adverb. It is formed by a preposition (7g) followed by a noun or pronoun.

This arrangement enabled members **with similar views** to talk **during meetings**. [*with similar views* modifies *members; during meetings* modifies *to talk.*]

An **absolute phrase**, which consists of a participle (7d, 8b) preceded by a subject, modifies the entire sentence to which it is attached. An absolute phrase cannot stand alone as a sentence because it lacks a true verb.

> **The moderates being in the center**, physical fights were avoided. [*Being* is the present participle of *to be; the moderates* acts as a subject.]

Verbal phrases use forms of verbs that do not express time (7d), so they cannot function as verbs in sentences. Instead, they function as nouns or modifiers. Verbal phrases are formed with infinitives, past participles, or present participles.

Infinitive phrases contain a verb's simple form preceded usually, but not always, by the word *to*. Infinitive phrases function as nouns, adjectives, or adverbs.

> Politicians love **to debate every issue**. [infinitive phrase = noun as object of verb *love*]
>
> Physically separating politicians works **to prevent debates from becoming fist fights**. [infinitive phrase = adverb modifying verb *works*]

Gerund phrases use the present participle—a verb's *-ing* form—as nouns.

> **Understanding the origin of certain terms** helps us recognize the repetition of historical patterns. [gerund phrase = noun functioning as sentence subject]

(In the example above, notice *recognize the repetition of historical patterns* too. It is an infinitive phrase, but one that does not use *to*.)

Participial phrases function as adjectives. They are formed from a verb's present participle—its *-ing* form—or from its past participle—the *-ed* form of a regular verb.

> **Imitating the French plan**, we now call radicals leftists, conservatives right-wingers, and moderates centrists. [present participle phrase = adjective modifying *we*]
>
> These labels, **copied by many governments**, continue long after the revolution that gave them birth. [past participle phrase = adjective modifying *labels*]

Telling the difference between a gerund phrase and a present participle phrase can be tricky because both contain a verb form that ends in *-ing*. Remember that a gerund phrase functions *only* as a noun, and a participial phrase functions *only* as an adjective.

> **Seeing liver on the dinner menu**, I decided to fast. [participial phrase as adjective describing *I*]
>
> **Seeing liver on the dinner menu** made me want to fast. [gerund phrase as subject of sentence]

7n Recognizing clauses

A **clause** is a group of words that contains a subject and a predicate (7j). Clauses are divided into two categories: **independent clauses** (also known as **main clauses**) and **dependent clauses** (including **subordinate clauses** and **relative clauses**).

1 Recognizing independent clauses

An **independent clause** contains a subject and a predicate. It can stand alone as a sentence. However, it cannot begin with a subordinating conjunction (7h) or a relative pronoun (7b) because those words make a clause dependent (7n-2).

THE SENTENCE		
Complete Subject	+	**Complete Predicate**
The saxophonist		played.

2 Recognizing dependent clauses

A **dependent clause** contains a subject and a predicate and usually starts with a word that makes the clause unable to stand alone as a sentence. A dependent clause must be joined to an independent clause.

Some dependent clauses start with **subordinating conjunctions**. These are called **subordinate clauses**. Each subordinating conjunction indicates a relationship between the meaning in the dependent clause and the meaning in the independent clause. For a chart listing these relationships, see 17e.

THE SENTENCE		
Dependent (Adverb) Clause	+	**Independent Clause**
When **the applause** stopped,		**the saxophonist** played.
SUBORDINATING COMPLETE COMPLETE CONJUNCTION SUBJECT PREDICATE		COMPLETE COMPLETE SUBJECT PREDICATE

Subordinate clauses function as adverbs. Because of this, they are also known as **adverb clauses**. They modify verbs, adjectives, other adverbs, and entire independent clauses. Adverb clauses may appear in different parts of sentences, but they always begin with a subordinating conjunction. They usually answer some question about the independent clause: *how? why? when?* or *under what conditions?*

> Many Americans wait to travel to Europe **until they can get low air fares**.
>
> **If a family has relatives in another country**, an international vacation can be relatively inexpensive.
>
> The number of Americans visiting China has grown rapidly **since full diplomatic relations were established in 1979**.

♣ PUNCTUATION ALERT: When an adverb clause comes before an independent clause, separate the clauses with a comma. ♣

> **Since full diplomatic relations were established in 1979**, the number of Americans visiting China has grown rapidly.

Other dependent clauses act as adjectives. These **adjective clauses** start with relative pronouns or *when, where*, or *why*. **Relative pronouns** include *who, that, which, whom, whose, whoever, whomever, whichever, what*, and *whatever*. Another name for these clauses is **relative clauses**. Adjective clauses modify nouns, pronouns, and groups of words functioning as nouns.

THE SENTENCE		
First Part of Independent Clause	**Dependent (Adjective) Clause**	**Second Part of Independent Clause**
The talented saxophonist ↑ COMPLETE SUBJECT	who led the band ↑ RELATIVE PRONOUN	signed autographs. ↑ COMPLETE PREDICATE

The word starting an adjective clause refers to something specific—an antecedent—in the independent clause.

> The concert hall, **which held 12,000 people**, was sold out in one day.
>
> The tickets **that I bought** were the last ones in the balcony.

See 10f for a discussion of when to use *who, which*, or *that*. See 24e for a discussion of when to use commas with relative clauses.

Noun clauses function as subjects, objects, or complements. Noun clauses begin with many of the same words as adjective clauses: *that, who, which*, (in all their forms), as well as *when, where, whether, why*, or *how*. Noun clauses do not modify. They replace a noun or pronoun with a clause.

> **It** depends on your generosity. [pronoun as subject]
>
> **Whether I can buy the camera** depends on your generosity. [noun clause as subject]
>
> **Whoever wins the contest** will appear in publicity photos. [noun clause as subject]

Because they start with similar words, it is easy to confuse noun clauses and adjective clauses. A noun clause *is* a subject, object, or complement; an adjective clause *modifies* a subject, object, or complement. The word at the start of an adjective clause has a specific antecedent elsewhere in the sentence; the word that starts a noun clause does not.

Elliptical clauses are grammatically incomplete in order to be brief and to the point. Usually the omission is limited to *that, which*, or *whom* in adjective clauses, the subject and verb in adverb clauses, or the second half of a comparison.

Lima is one of the places **[that] I want to visit this summer**. [relative pronoun omitted from adjective clause]

After [I visited] São Paolo, I decided to return to South America. [subject and verb omitted from adverb clause]

An apartment has less storage space **than a house [has]**. [second half of comparison omitted]

70 | Recognizing sentence types

Sentences have four basic structures: simple, compound, complex, and compound-complex.

A **simple sentence** is composed of a single independent clause with no dependent clauses. It has one subject and one predicate. However, a simple sentence is not always short. The subject or predicate may be compound, and the sentence may contain modifying words or phrases.

The beagle is one of the world's most popular dogs.

It is a member of the hound family.

The basset and the harrier are also hounds.

A **compound sentence** is composed of two or more independent clauses joined by a coordinating conjunction or a semicolon. There are seven coordinating conjunctions: *and, but, or, nor, for, so*, and *yet*. Compound sentences operate according to principles of coordination. ✤ PUNCTUATION ALERT: Always use a comma before a coordinating conjunction that joins two independent clauses. ✤

The beagle is known for its large, velvety ears, **but** its hazel eyes are even more attractive.

The beagle is believed to be one of the oldest breeds of hounds, **and** it is still used to hunt.

A **complex sentence** is composed of one independent clause and one or more dependent clauses. ♣ PUNCTUATION ALERT: Always use a comma after a dependent clause when it occurs before an independent clause. ♣

Because it has an erect, white-tipped tail, the beagle can be seen and followed even in high grass and bushes.

Although the beagle lost some of its popularity at the beginning of this century, it has become recognized as the ideal pet for anyone **who wants a medium-sized hound**.

A **compound-complex sentence** contains two or more independent clauses and one or more dependent clauses.

The beagle gets along well with other dogs **since it is a pack animal, and** it is patient with boisterous children **who might be too rough to allow near less sturdy pets**.

Although the beagle can be a delight, it is not an easy animal to keep **because it loves to wander off hunting and investigating, so** an owner needs to be alert.

Writing Different Types
of Sentences

A: Combine these groups of simple sentences according to the directions in parentheses. It will be necessary to add coordinating conjunctions, subordinating conjunctions, or relative pronouns. Sometimes it will be necessary to drop or change a few words. Since most passages can be combined in several ways, take the time to draft a few alternatives and then select the version you like best. Try to use at least one elliptical clause in this exercise.

EXAMPLE   Sometimes people repress their memories. They cannot recall anything about an event.   (compound)

Sometimes people repress memories, so they cannot recall anything about an event.

1. Psychoanalysis helps people deal with these forgotten memories. Psychoanalysis works at exploring them consciously.   (compound)

   _____

   _____

2. Repression can make life difficult. Repression is the burying in the unconscious of fearful experiences.   (complex)

   _____

   _____

3. People repress frightening thoughts and experiences. Then they try to go on living normally.   (compound)

   _____

   _____

4. People repress experiences. They avoid having to relive them. They feel better for a time.   (compound-complex)

   _____

   _____

5. Experiments show something. People forget bad experiences quickly. People forget good experiences less quickly.   (complex)

   _____

   _____

6. Repression occurs in the mentally ill.
   It occurs also in mentally healthy people.   (compound)

   _____

   _____

7. A certain kind of learning atmosphere leads to better memory.
   This kind of learning atmosphere is the kind where people can
   relax.   (complex)

   _____

   _____

8. Any student knows this.
   So does any teacher.   (compound)

   _____

   _____

9. People are often distracted in stressful situations.
   They simply do not see everything.
   Therefore, they cannot remember everything.   (compound-complex)

   _____

   _____

10. This may explain something.
    Accident victims often do not recall details of their experiences.   (complex)

    _____

    _____

11. Many people do not remember much from their childhoods.
    This does not mean that they are repressing bad memories.   (compound)

    _____

    _____

12. They may have been too interested in some events to notice any others.
    These other events were happening at the same time.
    Maybe their childhoods were simply too boring to remember.   (compound-complex)

    _____

    _____

Name _____   Date _____

B: Using independent and dependent clauses, expand each of these simple sentences, making
   a compound, then a complex, and finally a compound-complex sentence.

EXAMPLE   He is always late.
          (compound) *He is always late, and his brother is always early.*
          (complex) *He is always late because he oversleeps.*
          (compound-complex) *He is always late when there is a test, so the*
          teacher is moving him to a later class.

1. Fast food is not cheap.

   (compound) _____

   (complex) _____

   (compound-complex) _____

   _____

2. The movie theater was crowded.

   (compound) _____

   (complex) _____

   (compound-complex) _____

   _____

3. Read contracts before you sign them.

   (compound) _____

   (complex) _____

   (compound-complex) _____

   _____

4. Ice cream is a popular dessert.

   (compound) _____

   (complex) _____

   (compound-complex) _____

   _____

5. Grocery stores should be open twenty-four hours a day.

   (compound) _____

   (complex) _____

   (compound-complex) _____

C: Write complete sentences by adding one or more independent clauses to each of these subordinate clauses.

EXAMPLE   if I have a chance
            If I have a chance, I'll learn to draw.

1. because she has a pet snake

2. whoever has the flu

3. before the union votes on the contract

4. even though they paid the electric bill

5. where the keys are

6. that cost a dollar

7. who has the prize-winning ticket

8. since she learned to drive

9. whether the bus stops on that corner

10. if the milk is sour

8 Verbs

Verbs provide information about what is happening, what has happened, and what will happen. In English, a verb tells of an action (*move, juggle, race*), an occurrence (*become, change, happen*), or a state of being (*be, seem, feel, exist*).

> Americans **enjoy** sports. [action]
> Football **becomes** more popular every year. [occurrence]
> Soccer **is** a new favorite of many people. [state of being]

VERB FORMS

8a Recognizing the forms of main verbs

Changes in form help verbs deliver information about tense, person, and number. For a discussion of person and number, see Chapter 11.

Every main verb has three principal parts: a **simple form**, a **past tense**, and a **past participle**. The simple form is also known as the **dictionary form** or the **base form**. The simple form shows action (or occurrence or state of being) taking place in the present for *I, you, we,* and *they: I travel, they explore.*

The **past-tense** form is the second principal part. It indicates an action or occurrence or state of being completed in the past. The past tense of all regular verbs adds final *-ed* or *-d* to the simple form. Many verbs, however, are irregular. That is, their past-tense forms, and often their past participles as well, either change in spelling or use different words instead of adding *-ed* or *-d: ring, rang, rung; fly, flew, flown.* The principal parts of common irregular verbs are listed in 8b-2. Except for the past tense of *be* (8c), the past tense form of each verb is the same for all persons and numbers.

The **past participle** is the third principal part. In regular verbs, the past participle has the same form as the past tense. However, for many irregular verbs these forms differ and must be memorized (see 8b-2).

To function as a verb, a past participle must combine with an auxiliary verb (8c) in a **verb phrase**. Verb phrases formed with past participles make the **perfect** tenses (8f) and **passive** constructions (8j): *I have succeeded; they are shocked.* For a discussion of other uses of the past participle, see 7d.

8b Using the -*s* form correctly

Except for *be* and *have* (8c), all verbs in the present tense add an -*s* or -*es* ending to the simple form when the subject is third person singular: *Everybody likes candy.*

Be and *have*—irregular verbs—do not use their simple forms in the third person singular of the present tense. Instead, *be* uses *is* and *have* uses *has*:

Candy **is** fattening; it **has** a lot of calories.

Some dialects of English use forms such as *candy be* and *it have* for third person singular in the present tense. Academic writing requires *is* and *has*.

Also, if you drop the -*s* or -*es* ending when you speak, you may forget to use it when you write. Be sure to proofread your writing to make sure you have used the -*s* form correctly.

8c Recognizing regular and irregular verbs

1 Forming the past tense and past participle of a regular verb by adding -*ed* or -*d*

A **regular verb** is one that forms its simple past and past participle by adding -*ed* or -*d* to the simple form. Most verbs in English are regular: *walk, walked, walked; bake, baked, baked.* Some regular verbs, however, require spelling changes at the end of the simple form: *deny, denied.* (See Chapter 22.)

Some speakers omit the -*ed* sound in the past tense. If you are unused to hearing or pronouncing this sound, you may forget to add it when you write the past tense or past participle. Nevertheless, written English requires the -*ed* ending, so be sure to proofread your writing for -*ed* endings.

2 Memorizing the principal parts of irregular verbs

About two hundred of the most common verbs in English are **irregular**: They do not add the -*ed* or -*d* to form the past tense or past participle. They form the past and past participle in different ways. Some irregular verbs change an internal vowel in the simple form to make the past tense and past participle: *ring, rang, rung.* Some change an internal vowel and add an ending other than -*ed* or -*d: rise, rose, risen.* Some use the simple form throughout: *cost, cost, cost.*

Unfortunately, a verb's simple form does not indicate whether the verb is irregular or regular. If you do not know the principal parts of a verb you are using, you need to find them in a college dictionary.

Common irregular verbs

SIMPLE FORM	PAST TENSE	PAST PARTICIPLE
arise	arose	arisen
awake	awoke *or* awaked	awaked *or* awoken
be (is, am, are)	was, were	been
beat	beat	beaten
become	became	become
begin	began	begun
bend	bent	bent
bite	bit	bitten *or* bit
blow	blew	blown
break	broke	broken
bring	brought	brought
build	built	built
buy	bought	bought
catch	caught	caught
choose	chose	chosen
come	came	come
cost	cost	cost
creep	crept	crept
cut	cut	cut
deal	dealt	dealt
dig	dug	dug
dive	dived *or* dove	dived
do	did	done
draw	drew	drawn
drink	drank	drunk
drive	drove	driven
eat	ate	eaten
fall	fell	fallen
feel	felt	felt
fight	fought	fought
find	found	found
flee	fled	fled
fly	flew	flown
forbid	forbade *or* forbad	forbidden
forget	forgot	forgotten *or* forgot
freeze	froze	frozen
get	got	got *or* gotten
give	gave	given
go	went	gone
have	had	had
hear	heard	heard
hide	hid	hidden
hit	hit	hit
hold	held	held

Common irregular verbs *(continued)*

SIMPLE FORM	PAST TENSE	PAST PARTICIPLE
hurt	hurt	hurt
keep	kept	kept
know	knew	known
lay	laid	laid
lead	led	led
leave	left	left
lend	lent	lent
let	let	let
lie	lay	lain
lose	lost	lost
make	made	made
mean	meant	meant
meet	met	met
pay	paid	paid
quit	quit	quit
read	read	read
ride	rode	ridden
ring	rang	rung
rise	rose	risen
run	ran	run
say	said	said
see	saw	seen
seek	sought	sought
send	sent	sent
set	set	set
shake	shook	shaken
shoot	shot	shot
sing	sang	sung
sit	sat	sat
sleep	slept	slept
speak	spoke	spoken
spend	spent	spent
spring	sprang *or* sprung	sprung
stand	stood	stood
strike	struck	struck
swim	swam	swum
swing	swang	swung
take	took	taken
teach	taught	taught
tear	tore	torn
tell	told	told
think	thought	thought
throw	threw	thrown
wear	wore	worn
write	wrote	written

8d Recognizing *be*, *do*, *have*, and other auxiliary verbs

The verbs *be, do,* and *have* function both as main verbs and as auxilliary (or helping) verbs. *Be,* the most common verb in English, is the most irregular as well.

THE FORMS OF *BE*

Simple Form	be
Past Tense	was, were
Past Participle	been
***-s* Form**	is
Present Participle	being

PERSON	PRESENT TENSE	PAST TENSE
I	am	was
you (singular)	are	were
he, she, it	is	was
we	are	were
you (plural)	are	were
they	are	were

Do and *have* are not as irregular as *be.*

THE FORMS OF *DO* AND *HAVE*

Simple Form	do		**Simple Form**	have
Past Tense	did		**Past Tense**	had
Past Participle	done		**Past Participle**	had
***-s* Form**	does		***-s* Form**	has
Present Participle	doing		**Present Participle**	having

When used as main verbs, forms of *be* are **linking verbs**. They join a subject to a **subject complement** (7I), a word or group of words that renames or describes the subject.

Water pollution **is** a danger to many communities. [*is* = linking verb, *water pollution* = subject, *a danger to many communities* = subject complement]

113

Underground streams **are** sources of well water. [*are* = linking verb, *underground streams* = subject, *sources of well water* = subject complement]

When used alone as main verbs, *have* is transitive and *do* can be transitive. Transitive verbs must be followed by a direct object (see 8d).

Combined with participles of main verbs, forms of *be* and *have* are **auxiliary verbs**, or **helping verbs**, that help the participles to show tense (8f, g) and mood (8i).

I **am waiting.** [auxiliary verb *am* + present participle *waiting* = present progressive tense]

The news **has been expected** for days. [auxiliary verb *has* + auxiliary verb *been* + past participle *expected* = present perfect tense in the passive voice]

The auxiliary verbs *will* and *shall* help to create two tenses: the future (*I shall try, you will pass*) and, with *have* and past participles of main verbs, the future perfect (*I shall have tried, you will have passed*). *Will* and *shall* never change form. Formal writing reserves *shall* for the first person (*I, we*) and *will* for all other persons (*you, he, she, it, they*).

The verbs *can, could, may, might, should, would, must,* and *ought to* are called **modal auxiliary verbs**. Modal auxiliary verbs have only one form; they do not change, no matter what constructions they appear in.

Modal auxiliaries add to the main verb a sense of needing, wanting, or having to do something, or a sense of possibility, permission, or ability.

The ant **can carry** many times its own weight. [ability]

Ants **may be observed** gathering around crumbs on the sidewalk. [possibility]

We **must sweep** up dropped food or we **might attract** ants in our homes. [necessity, possibility]

8e Using intransitive and transitive verbs correctly, especially *sit* and *set, lie* and *lay, rise* and *raise*

The difference between *I see clearly* and *I see a fire* is that the first sentence tells *how* the subject does something while the second points to *what* the subject does. In the first sentence, the verb is **intransitive**—it stops with the action. In the second sentence, the verb is **transitive**—the action of the verb carries over to whatever is named in the **direct object**. Many verbs in English can be both intransitive and transitive depending upon how they are used in particular sentences.

INTRANSITIVE (NO OBJECT)	TRANSITIVE (WITH AN OBJECT)
The trees **shook** in the wind.	The boys **shook** the apple tree.
The train **leaves** tonight.	The train **leaves** the station.

Three important pairs of verbs are not this flexible. In these pairs—*sit* and *set, lie* and *lay, rise* and *raise*—one verb is intransitive, the other transitive.

SUMMARY OF FORMS FOR *SIT, LIE, RISE,* AND *SET, LAY, RAISE*

INTRANSITIVE (NO OBJECT)

Simple Form	Past Tense	Past Participle	-s Form	Present Participle
sit	sat	sat	sits	sitting
lie	lay	lain	lies	lying
rise	rose	risen	rises	rising

TRANSITIVE (WITH AN OBJECT)

Simple Form	Past Tense	Past Participle	-s Form	Present Participle
set	set	set	sets	setting
lay	laid	laid	lays	laying
raise	raised	raised	raises	raising

To *sit* means to seat oneself; to *set* means to place something else down.

INTRANSITIVE	I **sit** down. I **sat** down. [*down* = modifier]
TRANSITIVE	I **set** the stapler on the desk. [*stapler* = direct object]

To *lie* means to place oneself down or to recline; to *lay* means to place something else down.

INTRANSITIVE	Oscar **lies** on the couch. Oscar **lay** on the coach. [*on the couch* = modifier]
TRANSITIVE	Oscar **lays** bricks for a living. Oscar **laid** bricks for a living. [*bricks* = direct object]

To *rise* means to stand up, to get up out of bed, or to elevate oneself in some other way; to *raise* is to lift up or elevate someone or something else.

INTRANSITIVE	Wendy **rises** every morning at 6:30. Wendy **rose** every morning at 6:30. [*every morning at 6:30* = modifier]
TRANSITIVE	Wendy **raises** the rent. Wendy **raised** the rent. [*the rent* = direct object]

8f

VERB TENSE

8f | Understanding verb tense

The **tense** of a verb indicates *when* the action, occurrence, or state of being it expresses takes place. Verbs are the only words that change form to express time.

English verb tenses are divided into two general groups: simple and perfect.

The three **simple tenses** divide time into present, past, and future. The **present** tense describes what is happening, what is true at the moment, and what is always true. It uses the simple form (8a-1) and the *-s* form (8a-2).

> I **study** Italian at the university.
> Joe **studies** hard all the time.

The **past tense** tells of a completed action or a condition that has ended. It uses the past tense form (8a-1, 8b).

> We **joined** the Italian conversation group.
> We **hoped** to practice speaking.

The **future tense** indicates action not yet taken. This tense uses the auxiliary verbs *will* or *shall* and the simple form (8c).

> We **shall see** an Italian movie at the next meeting.

The second group of tenses are the **perfect tenses**. They also divide time into present, past, and future (8f).

All six tenses also have **progressive forms**, made from the *-ing* form and the verb *to be* (8g).

8g | Using the simple present tense correctly

The **simple present tense** describes what is happening or what is true at the moment. It also has special functions, summarized below.

SUMMARY OF USES FOR THE SIMPLE PRESENT TENSE

DESCRIBING WHAT IS HAPPENING NOW, IN THE PRESENT

You **work** efficiently.
The gale **rattles** the windows.

DESCRIBING A HABITUAL OR REGULARLY OCCURRING ACTION

My accounting class **meets** at 10:00 on Tuesdays.
Horror movies **give** him nightmares.

> **SUMMARY OF USES FOR THE SIMPLE PRESENT TENSE** *(continued)*
>
> **EXPRESSING A GENERAL TRUTH OR WIDELY HELD OPINION**
>
> A kilogram **is** roughly 2.2 pounds.
> Good fences **make** good neighbors.
>
> **DESCRIBING A FIXED-TIME FUTURE EVENT**
>
> The semester **ends** on May 30.
> The ship **leaves** port at midnight.
> His birthday **falls** on a Sunday this year.
>
> **DISCUSSING "TIMELESS" EVENTS AND ACTIVITIES AND INTENTIONS OF THOSE WHO CREATE THEM**
>
> Jay Gatsby **wants** it all.
> Luke Skywalker and Hans Solo repeatedly **save** Princess Leia.
> Einstein **speaks** of matter as something that is interchangeable with energy.

8h Using the perfect tenses correctly

The perfect tenses usually describe actions or occurrences that have already been completed or that will be completed before another point in time.

The **present perfect tense** shows that an action begun in the past continues into the present, or that an action completed in the past affects the present.

Betty **has applied** for a summer job.
We **have** always **tried** to do our best.

The **past perfect tense** indicates that an action was completed before another one took place.

The blizzard **had trapped** the climbers before they could get down the mountain.

The **future perfect tense** indicates that an action will be complete before some specified or predictable time.

The space craft **will have sent** back pictures of the outer planets before it flies out of the solar system.

8i Using the progressive form of each tense correctly

The progressive form uses the present participle along with the various forms of *be* and other auxiliary verbs. It shows that an action or condition is ongoing.

The **present progressive** indicates something taking place at the time it is written or spoken about.

Rents **are rising**.

The **past progressive** shows the continuing nature of a past action.

The fire **was spreading** rapidly when the firefighters arrived.

The **future progressive** shows that a future action will continue for some time.

After vacation, **we shall be returning** to our study of verb tenses.

The **present perfect progressive** describes something that began in the past and is likely to continue in the future.

The kitchen tap **has been dripping** for weeks.

The **past perfect progressive** describes an ongoing condition in the past that has been ended by something stated in the sentence.

The stereo **had been playing** well until the movers dropped it.

The **future perfect progressive** describes an action or condition continuing until some specific future time.

On November 11, **we shall have been going** together for two years.

SUMMARY OF TENSES INCLUDING PROGRESSIVE FORMS

SIMPLE TENSES

	REGULAR VERB	IRREGULAR VERB	PROGRESSIVE FORM
Present	I talk	I eat	I am talking, I am eating
Past	I talked	I ate	I was talking, I was eating
Future	I will talk	I will eat	I will be talking, I will be eating

PERFECT TENSES

	REGULAR VERB	IRREGULAR VERB	PROGRESSIVE FORM
Present Perfect	I have talked	I have eaten	I have been talking, I have been eating
Past Perfect	I had talked	I had eaten	I had been talking, I had been eating
Future Perfect	I will have talked	I will have eaten	I will have been talking, I will have been eating

8j   Using verbs in accurate tense sequence

Sentences often have more than one verb, and these verbs often refer to actions taking place at different times. Showing the right time relationships—that is, using accurate tense sequences—is necessary to avoid confusion. The tense of the verb in an independent clause determines the possibilities for verb tense in that sentence's dependent clauses.

SUMMARY OF SEQUENCE OF TENSES

WHEN INDEPENDENT-CLAUSE VERB IS IN THE SIMPLE PRESENT TENSE, FOR THE DEPENDENT-CLAUSE VERB:

Use the present tense to show same-time action.

> The director **says** that the movie **is** a tribute to factory workers.
> I **avoid** shellfish because I **am** allergic to it.

Use the past tense to show earlier action.

> I **am** sure that I **deposited** the check.

Use the present perfect tense to show a period of time extending from some point in the past to the present.

> They **claim** that they **have visited** the planet Venus.

Use the future tense for action to come.

> The book **is** open because I **will be reading** it later.

WHEN INDEPENDENT-CLAUSE VERB IS IN THE PAST TENSE, FOR THE DEPENDENT-CLAUSE VERB:

Use the past tense to show earlier action.

> I **ate** dinner before you **offered** to take me out for pizza.

Use the past perfect tense to emphasize earlier action.

> The sprinter **knew** she **had broken** the record.

Use the present tense to state a general truth.

> Christopher Columbus **discovered** that the world **is** round.

WHEN INDEPENDENT-CLAUSE VERB IS IN THE PRESENT PERFECT OR PAST PERFECT TENSE, FOR THE DEPENDENT-CLAUSE VERB:

Use the past tense.

> The milk **has become** sour since I **bought** it last week.
> The price of sugar **had** already **declined** when artificial sweeteners first **appeared**.

(continued on next page)

SUMMARY OF SEQUENCE OF TENSES *(continued)*

WHEN INDEPENDENT-CLAUSE VERB IS IN THE FUTURE TENSE, FOR THE DEPENDENT-CLAUSE VERB:

Use the present tense to show action happening at the same time.

   You **will be** rich if you **win** the prize.

Use the past tense to show earlier action.

   You **will** surely **win** the prize if you **remembered** to mail the entry form.

Use the present perfect tense to show future action earlier than the action of the independent-clause verb.

   The river **will flood** again next year unless we **have built** a better dam by then.

WHEN THE INDEPENDENT-CLAUSE VERB IS IN THE FUTURE PERFECT TENSE, FOR THE DEPENDENT-CLAUSE VERB:

Use either the present tense or the present perfect tense.

   Dr. Chang **will have delivered** 5,000 babies by the time she **retires**.
   Dr. Chang **will have delivered** 5,000 babies by the time she **has retired**.

MOOD

8k Understanding mood

The **mood** of a verb conveys a writer's attitude toward a statement. The most common mood in English is the **indicative mood**. It is used for statements about real things, or highly likely ones, and for questions about fact: *The car started; how much does that jacket cost?* Most statements are in the indicative mood.

The **imperative mood**, which always uses the simple form of the verb, expresses commands and direct requests. The subject is often omitted in an imperative sentence. It is assumed to be *you: Sit down! Please do not smoke in here.*

The **subjunctive mood** expresses conditions including wishes, recommendations, indirect requests, and speculations (see 8i). The subjunctive mood in English is rare. Therefore, its forms are less familiar than those of the indicative mood and the imperative mood.

8l Using correct subjunctive forms

The **present subjunctive** of all verbs except *be* uses the simple form of the verb for all persons and numbers. The present subjunctive of *be* is *be* for all persons and numbers.

VERBS

It is important that the vandals **be** [not *are*] found
I am demanding that he **pay** [not *pays*] his bill.

The **past subjunctive** uses the same form as the past indicative. The past subjunctive of *be* for all persons and numbers is the same as the past plural indicative, *were*.

He wishes he **were** [not *was*] richer.

Although the subjunctive is not as common as it once was, it is still used in four situations:

1. Use the subjunctive in *if* clauses and some *unless* clauses for speculations or conditions contrary to fact.

   Unless a meltdown **were** [not *was*] to take place, the risks from a nuclear power plant are small.

2. Use the subjunctive for judgments introduced by *as if* or *as though*.

   The runner looks as though he **were** [not *was*] about to collapse.

3. Use the subjunctive in *that* clauses for wishes, indirect requests, recommendations, and demands.

   I wish that this building **were** [not *was*] air-conditioned.
   Her mechanic recommended that she **look** [not *looked*] for a new car.

4. Use the subjunctive in certain standard expressions.

   Please let me **be**.   **Come** what may. . . .
   Be that as it may. . . .   Far **be** it from me. . . .

VOICE

Understanding voice

The **voice** of a verb indicates whether a subject does or receives the action named by the verb. English has two voices: active and passive.
In the **active voice**, the subject performs the action.

Roaches **infest** most cities.

In the **passive voice**, the subject is acted upon, and the person or thing doing the action often appears as the object of the preposition *by*.

Roaches **are considered** a nuisance by many people.

The passive voice uses verb phrases. A past participle indicates the action, and a form of *be* specifies person, number, and tense: *is seen, were seen, have been seen*.

8n Writing in the active voice, not the passive voice, except to convey special types of emphasis

The active voice emphasizes the doer of the action, so active constructions have a more direct and dramatic effect. Active constructions also use fewer words than passive constructions. Therefore, use the active voice wherever you can. Most sentences in the passive voice can easily be converted to the active voice.

PASSIVE   Bicycling tours of Canada **are often taken by young travelers**.

ACTIVE   **Young travelers often take** bicycling tours of Canada.

However, the passive voice is useful in two special situations.

1. You should use the passive voice when the doer of the action is unknown or unimportant.

   The painting **was stolen** some time after midnight. [Who stole the painting is unknown.]

2. You can also use the passive voice to focus attention on the action rather than the doer of the action. For example, in a passage about important contributions to the history of biology, you might want to emphasize a doer by using the active voice.

   William Harvey **studied** the human circulatory system.

   However, in a passage summarizing what scientists know about circulation, you might want to emphasize what was done.

   The human circulatory system **was studied** by William Harvey.

9 Case of Nouns and Pronouns

The **case** (form) of a noun or pronoun shows how that word relates to other words in a sentence. For example, *we, us* and *our* are three different cases of the first-person-plural pronoun:

> As **we** walked through the park, a crowd gathered around **us** to see **our** pet alligator.

English has three cases: **subjective, objective**, and **possessive**. Nouns use one form for the subjective and objective cases and have a separate possessive form, made with the apostrophe. Many pronouns, however, have three distinct forms for the three cases. **Personal pronouns**, the most common type of pronouns, have a full range of forms (cases) that show changes in **person** (first, second, and third person) and **number** (singular and plural). (For an explanation of *person*, see Chapter 11.)

CASES OF PERSONAL PRONOUNS			
	SUBJECTIVE	**OBJECTIVE**	**POSSESSIVE**
	Singular/Plural	Singular/Plural	Singular/Plural
First person	I we	me us	my/mine our/ours
Second person	you you	you you	your/yours your/yours
Third person	he they she it	him them her it	his her/hers its their/theirs

The plural of *you* is simply *you*. Avoid the nonstandard plural *yous*.

A pronoun in the **subjective case** functions as a subject of a sentence or clause.

> **We** needed an apartment. [*We* is the subject.]

A pronoun in the **objective case** functions as a direct object or an indirect object.

> A friend called **us** one night. [*Us* is the direct object.]
> He told **us** a secret. [*Us* is the indirect object.]
> He had a surprise for **us**. [*Us* is the object of a preposition.]

A pronoun in the **possessive case** indicates possession or ownership.

♣ PUNCTUATION ALERT: Do not use an apostrophe for a personal pronoun in the possessive case. ♣

> He said that **his** neighbor was moving next month.
> We called the neighbor and agreed to sublet **her** apartment.
> **Its** windows look out over a park.

9a Using the same cases for pronouns in compound constructions as in single constructions

A compound construction contains more than one subject or object (see 7j-1, 7k-1). This compounding has no effect on the choice of a pronoun case.

> **He** and **I** saw the eclipse of the sun. [compound subject.]
> The beauty of the eclipse astounded both **him** and **me**. [compound object]

If you are unsure which case to use, try this "drop test." Temporarily *drop all of the compound element except the pronoun in question*, and then you will be able to tell which pronoun case is needed. Here is how the method works for compound subjects.

EXAMPLE	**Janet and (me, I)** read that the moon has one-eightieth the mass of the earth.
STEP 1	Drop *Janet and*.
STEP 2	Which reads correctly: "**Me** read that the moon has one-eightieth the mass of the earth" or "**I** read that the moon has one-eightieth the mass of the earth"?
STEP 3	Answer: Janet and **I** read that the moon has one-eightieth the mass of the earth.

The same test works for compound objects:

EXAMPLE	The instructor told **Janet and (I, me)** that the moon has one-fiftieth the volume of the earth.
STEP 1	Drop *Janet and*.
STEP 2	Which reads correctly: "The instructor told **I** that the moon has one-fiftieth the volume of the earth" or "The instructor told **me** that the moon has one-fiftieth the volume of the earth"?
STEP 3	Answer: The instructor told Janet and **me** that the moon has one-fiftieth the volume of the earth.

When pronouns in a **prepositional phrase** (7m) occur in compound constructions (*The book was about* **him** *and* **me**), the pronouns often appear in the wrong case. You may hear people say "with he and I" or "between you and I," but this usage is incorrect. A prepositional phrase always includes an object, so any pronouns that follow words such as *with, to, from, for, after*, or *between* must be in the objective case. See 7g for a complete list of prepositions.

No	The reward will be divided **between you and I**. [*I* is in the subjective case and cannot follow a preposition.]
YES	The reward will be divided **between you and me**. [*Me* is in the objective case, so it is correct.]

9b Matching noun and pronoun cases

When one or more pronouns occurs in an **appositive** (7l-3)—a word or group of words that renames the noun or noun phrase next to it—the pronoun takes the same case as the noun replaced.

No	**Us** working women lead productive lives. [*Working women* is the subject, so *us*, an objective pronoun, is incorrect.]
YES	**We** working women lead productive lives. [*We* is a subjective pronoun: correct.]
No	Someone ought to give working mothers, **she** and **I**, better job opportunities. [*Working mothers* is the object, so *she* and *I*, subjective pronouns, are incorrect.]
YES	Someone ought to give working mothers, **her** and **me**, better job opportunities. [*Her* and *me* are objective pronouns: correct.]

9c **Using the subjective case after linking verbs**

A **linking verb** connects the subject to a word that renames it. Such a renaming word is called a **complement**. Because a pronoun coming after a linking verb renames the subject, that pronoun must be in the subjective case.

> Is Lee at home? This is **he**. [*He* renames *this*, the subject, so the subjective case is required.]
>
> Who is there? It is **I**. [*I* renames *it*, the subject, so the subjective case is required.]
>
> The winner of the speed skating event was **she**. [*She* renames *the winner*, the subject, so the subjective case is required.]

In speech and informal writing the objective case is often used in these situations, but academic writing is more formal and requires the subjective case.

9d **Using *who* and *whoever* whenever the subjective case is needed; using *whom* and *whomever* whenever the objective case is needed**

Who and *whoever*, which function as both **relative** and **interrogative pronouns** (7b), change forms in the different cases. Within each case, however, they remain the same for all persons and for singular and plural.

CASES OF RELATIVE AND INTERROGATIVE PRONOUNS

SUBJECTIVE	OBJECTIVE	POSSESSIVE
who	whom	whose
whoever	whomever	————

To determine whether *who, whom, whoever,* or *whomever* is correct in a dependent clause (7n-2), temporarily drop everything in the sentence up to the pronoun in question, and then make substitutions—remembering that *he, she, they, who,* and *whoever* are subjects, and *him, her, them, whom,* and *whomever* are objects.

STEP 1   I asked (**who, whom**) attended the World Series.

STEP 2   Omit *I asked*.

STEP 3   Test what other pronoun would make a sensible sentence: "**He** attended the World Series" or "**Him** attended the World Series."

STEP 4   Answer: "**He** attended the World Series."

STEP 5   Therefore, because *he* is subjective, *who*, which is also subjective, is correct: "I asked **who** attended the World Series."

The subjective case is called for even when expressions such as *I think* and *he says* come between the subject and the verb. Ignore these expressions when determining the correct pronoun.

> He is the pitcher **who** [I think] will be elected Most Valuable Player.

This process also works for the objective case (*whom*), as well as for *whoever* and *whomever*.

At the beginning of questions, use *who* if the question is about the subject and *whom* if the question is about the object. If you are unsure, reword the question as a statement.

> **Who** repaired the radio? ["*I* repaired the radio" uses the subjective pronoun *I*, so *who* is correct.]
>
> Jacques admires **whom**? ["Jacques admires *him*" uses the objective pronoun *him*, so *whom* is correct.]
>
> To **whom** does Jacques speak about becoming an electrician? ["Jacques speaks to *me* about becoming an electrician" uses the objective pronoun *me*, so *whom* is correct.]

In speech and informal writing, *who* is often used for both subjects and objects (*Who does Jacques ask?*), but such practice is nonstandard and should be avoided in academic writing.

9e Using the pronoun case that reflects your intended meaning after *than* or *as*

When a pronoun follows *than* or *as*, the pronoun case carries essential information about what is being said. For example, the following two sentences convey two very different messages, simply because of the choice between the words *me* and *I* after *than*.

1. My sister photographs landscapes more **than** *me*.
2. My sister photographs landscapes more **than** *I*.

Sentence I means "My sister photographs landscapes more *than she photographs me*." On the other hand, sentence 2 means "My sister photographs landscapes more *than I photograph landscapes*." To make sure that any sentence of comparison is clear, either include all the words in the second half or mentally fill in the words to check whether you have chosen the correct pronoun case.

9f Using the objective case when a pronoun is the subject or the object of an infinitive

Objective pronouns occur as both subjects and objects of infinitives (7d).

> His nephew wanted **him** to challenge **me** to a raft race. [*Him* is the subject of the infinitive *to challenge; me* is the object of the infinitive; both are in the objective case.]

9g Using the possessive case before gerunds

A **gerund** is the *-ing* form of a verb that functions as a noun: *Singing in the shower is a common pastime.* When a noun or pronoun precedes a gerund, the possessive case is called for.

Igor's singing annoyed the neighbors.
His singing annoyed the neighbors.

In contrast, the **present participle** is the *-ing* form that functions as an adjective. It does not take the possessive case.

Igor, **singing in the shower**, annoyed the neighbors.

9h Reserving *-self* forms of pronouns for reflexive or intensive use

Reflexive pronouns reflect back on the subject or object.

The diver prepared **herself** for the finals.
She had to force **herself** to relax.

Reflexive pronouns should not be used as substitutes for subjects or objects.

The diver and **I** [not *myself*] wished the sportscasters would go away.
They bothered her and **me** [not *myself*] for interviews.

Intensive pronouns provide emphasis.

The diver felt that competing **itself** was stressful enough without giving interviews.
The sportscasters acted as though they **themselves** were the only reason for the event.

Avoid the following nonstandard forms of reflexive and intensive pronouns in academic writing: *hisself*, nonstandard for *himself*; *theirself, theirselves, themself,* and *themselfs*, nonstandard for *themselves*.

10 Pronoun Reference

The meaning of a pronoun comes from its **antecedent**, the noun or pronoun to which the pronoun refers. In order for your writing to communicate its message clearly, each pronoun must relate directly to an antecedent. You can accomplish this by following a few simple rules.

10a Making a pronoun refer clearly to a single antecedent

To be understood, a pronoun must refer to a specific single (or compound) antecedent.

> Daniel Boone was born near Reading, Pennsylvania, in 1734, but as a youngster **he** moved to the North Carolina frontier with **his** family.

Often the same pronoun fits more than one possible antecedent. This situation can be confusing.

> Boone is often confused with Davy Crockett. **He** was born in eastern Tennessee in 1786. **His** family was just as poor as **his**; both had little formal education. **He** became a member of the Tennessee legislature in 1821 and eventually died at the Alamo in 1836. **He** became famous for opening up Kentucky to settlers, and **he** died in 1820—long before the Battle of the Alamo.

A writer can clarify such a passage by replacing some pronouns with nouns so that each remaining pronoun clearly refers to a single antecedent.

> **Boone** is often confused with **Davy Crockett. Crockett** was born in eastern Tennessee in 1786. **His** family was just as poor as **Boone's**; both had little formal education. **Crockett** became a member of the Tennessee legislature in 1821 and eventually died at the Alamo in 1836. **Boone** became famous for opening up Kentucky to settlers, and **he** died in 1820—long before the Battle of the Alamo.

Using *said* and *told* with pronouns that appear to refer to more than one person is especially likely to create confusion. Use quotation marks and slightly reword the sentence to make the meaning clearer.

No	Her aunt told her she was returning to school.
Yes	Her aunt told her, "You are returning to school."
Yes	Her aunt told her, "I am returning to school."

10b Placing pronouns close to their antecedents for clarity

If too much material comes between a pronoun and its antecedent, unclear pronoun reference results. Readers lose track of the meaning of a passage if they have to trace too far back to find the antecedent of a pronoun.

No	**Patrick Henry**, who said "Give me liberty, or give me death," turned down many important political positions: a seat in the Senate, ambassadorships to Spain and France, Secretary of State, and Chief Justice of the Supreme Court. **He** did, however, serve as Governor of Virginia for five terms. **He** was elected to a sixth, but refused to serve. [Although *he* can refer only to *Patrick Henry*, too much material comes between the first pronoun and its antecedent.]

Yes	**Patrick Henry**, who said "Give me liberty, or give me death," turned down many important political positions: a seat in the Senate, ambassadorships to Spain and France, Secretary of State, and Chief Justice of the Supreme Court. **Henry** did, however, serve as Governor of Virginia for five terms. **He** was elected to a sixth, but refused to serve.

10c Making a pronoun refer to a definite antecedent

A noun in its possessive form (*the car's exhaust*) cannot also serve as the subject (*The car stalled*) or object (*I sold the car*) of its sentence. Thus a pronoun cannot refer back to a noun in its possessive form.

No	**Galen's** formula for cold cream has not changed much since **he** invented it 1,700 years ago. [*He* cannot refer to the possessive *Galen's*.]
Yes	**Galen's** formula for cold cream has not changed much since **the Roman physician** invented it 1,700 years ago.

An adjective serves as a modifier, not as a subject or object. Thus a pronoun cannot refer back to an adjective.

No	Janet works at the **cosmetics** counter. **They** are inexpensive. [*They* cannot refer to the adjective *cosmetics*.]
Yes	Janet works at the cosmetics counter. **The products** are inexpensive.

Pronouns such as *it, that, this,* and *which* are particularly prone to unclear reference. As you write and revise, check carefully to see that each of these pronouns refers to only one antecedent that can be determined easily by your readers. When necessary, replace the confusing pronoun with a noun.

No   Annie Taylor, a 43-year-old widow, was the first person to go over Niagara Falls in a barrel. **This** was fantastic. [What does *this* refer to? Her age? Her being a widow? A female being the first person to go over the Falls?]

Yes   Annie Taylor, a 43-year-old widow, was the first person to go over Niagara Falls in a barrel. **That anyone would want to do this** was fantastic.

No   After going over the Falls, Taylor admitted she could not swim. **It** was very dangerous. [What does *it* refer to?]

Yes   After going over the Falls, Taylor admitted she could not swim. **Her stunt** was very dangerous.

In speech, such statements as *it said in the papers* and *at the United Nations they say* are common. Such expressions are inexact, however, and should be avoided.

The newspapers report [not *It said in the newspapers*] that many United Nations officials receive high salaries.

A United Nations spokesperson says [not *At the United Nations they say*] that the high salaries are rewards for doing difficult jobs well.

A piece of writing has to stand on its own, so when you are referring to a title, be sure to repeat or reword whatever part of the title you want to use. Do not use a pronoun in the first sentence of an essay to refer to the essay's title.

Title   *Airport Security Must Be Strict*
No   Yes, I agree with this.
Yes   Because of the dangerous state of world affairs, airport security must be strict.

10d Avoiding overuse of *it*

It has three different uses in English.

1. *It* is a personal pronoun: *Rachel decided which VCR she wants, but she doesn't have enough money to buy **it** yet.*
2. *It* is an expletive, a word that postpones the subject: ***It is lucky that the price of VCR's is falling.***
3. *It* is part of idiomatic expressions of weather, time, or distance: ***It is raining.***

All of these uses are acceptable, but combining them in the same sentence can create confusion.

No   It was fortunate that I tried the new restaurant on the day that **it** opened an outdoor cafe section, because **it** was a sunny day.

Yes   I was fortunate to try the new restaurant on the day that the outdoor cafe section opened, because **it** was a sunny day.

10e Using *you* only for direct address

You is used frequently in speech and informal writing to refer to general groups of people (*You can never tell what fashions will be popular*). In academic writing, however, *you* is acceptable only if the writer is directly addressing the reader. For example, *you* is used in this workbook because we, the authors, are directly addressing you, our reader. Similarly, your instructor might write on one of your essays: "Your introduction makes me want to read on."

You should not be used in academic writing to refer to people in general, however.

No   At many libraries, *you* can check books out for two weeks. [Does this mean that libraries have a special circulation period just for the reader?]

Yes   At many libraries, *borrowers* can check books out for two weeks.

10f Using *who*, *which*, and *that* correctly

Who refers to people or to animals with names or special talents.

The Pied Piper was a real man, **who** led all the plague-carrying rats out of Hamlin, Germany, on July 22, 1376.

The movie *Willard* featured a rat named Ben, **who** was the hero's friend.

Which and *that* refer to animals, things, and sometimes anonymous or collective groups of people. The choice between *which* and *that* depends on whether the clause introduced by the pronoun is restrictive (essential) or nonrestrictive (nonessential). Use *that* with restrictive clauses and *which* with nonrestrictive clauses. Use *who* for people in both kinds of clauses. ❖ COMMA CAUTION: Set off nonrestrictive clauses with commas. For a fuller explanation, see 24e. ❖

Rats, **which** often carry disease-bearing fleas, are health problems.

Garbage, **which** rats love, must be cleaned up before the rats can be driven out.

Rats **that** have been inbred for generations are the ideal lab animals.

All traits **that** might interfere with experiments have been eliminated.

Lab workers **that** handle rats every day probably are not repelled by them.

11 Agreement

SUBJECT–VERB AGREEMENT

Subject–verb agreement occurs at least once per sentence. To function correctly, subjects and verbs must match in number (singular or plural) and in person (first, second, or third).

The human **brain weighs** about three pounds. [*brain* = singular subject in the third person; *weighs* = singular verb in the third person]

Human **brains weigh** about three pounds. [*brains* = plural subject in the third person; *weigh* = plural verb in the third person]

A QUICK REVIEW OF PERSON FOR AGREEMENT

The **first person** is the speaker or writer. *I* (singular) and *we* (plural) are the only subjects that occur in the first person.

Singular   *I* see a field of fireflies.

Plural   *We* see a field of fireflies.

The **second person** is the person spoken or written to. *You* (both singular and plural) is the only subject that occurs in the second person.

Singular   *You* see a shower of sparks.

Plural   *You* see a shower of sparks.

The **third person** is the person or thing being spoken or written of. Most rules for subject–verb agreement involve the third person. A subject in the third person can vary widely—for example, *student* and *students* (singular and plural people), *table* and *tables* (singular and plural things), and *it* and *they* (singular and plural pronouns).

Singular   The **scientist sees** a cloud of cosmic dust.

She (he, it) sees a cloud of cosmic dust.

Plural   The **scientists see** a cloud of cosmic dust.

They see a cloud of cosmic dust.

11a

11a Using the final -s or -es fo plural subjects or for singular verbs

Subject–verb agreement often involves e letter: *s*. The key is the difference between the -*s* added to subjects and the -*s* ded to verbs.

Plural subjects are usually formed adding -*s* or -*es* to singular nouns. **Singular verbs** in the present tense of th iird person are formed by adding -*s* or -*es* to the simple form—with the excep s of *be (is)* and *have (has)*.

Visualizing how the *s* works in a ment can help you remember when it is needed. The -*s* (or -*es* when the wor eady ends in *s*) can take only one path at a time, either the top or the bottom in this diagram.

SINGULAR		**PLURAL**	
tudent		students	
-s		-s	
works		work	
mother		mothers	
-s		-s	
kisses		kiss	

Even tho the final -*s* does not appear in some subjects, the principle of the memory ice holds. This final -*s* does not appear in the following situations: in subjects are plural without an -*s* (such as *people, children*); in plural personal pronou *we, you, they*); in the plural demonstrative pronouns (*these, those*); and in cert indefinite pronouns when they are used as plurals (*few, some, more, many, st, all*).

rson on a diet often **misses** sweets.

ple enjoy** candy or cake after meals.

ey learn** to substitute fruit for pastry.

♣ U 3E ALERT: Do not add -*s* to the third-person singular main verb after a modal au y verb (a helping verb such as *can, might, must, would*—see 8c). ♣

11b For the purposes of agreement, ignoring words that come between a subject and verb

Words that separate the subject from the verb can cause confusion about what the verb should agree with. To locate the subject of the sentence, ignore prepositional phrases or phrases that start with *including, together with, along with, accompanied by, in addition to, except,* or *as well as.*

The best **workers** in the bookkeeping department **have** received raises.

The top selling sales **representative**, along with her husband, **is going** to visit San Diego as a bonus.

11c Using a plural verb for subjects connected by *and*

When two or more subjects are joined by *and*, they function as a group; therefore, they need a plural verb.

Soda and iced tea are popular summer drinks.

My friend and I prefer cold milk.

However, if the word *each* or *every* precedes subjects joined by *and*, use a singular verb.

Each cat and dog in the animal shelter **deserves** a home.

When *each* or *every* follows subjects joined by *and*, however, it does not affect the basic rule: use a plural verb for subjects joined by and:

The ASPCA and the Humane Society each **need** our support.

The one exception to the *and* rule occurs when the parts combine to form a single thing or person.

Beans and rice is a popular vegetarian dish.

My husband and business partner keeps our tax records.

11d Making the verb agree with the subject closest to it

When you join subjects with *or* or *nor* or correlative conjunctions, *either . . . or, neither . . . nor, not only . . . but (also),* make the verb agree with the subject closest to it. Unlike *and*, these conjunctions do not create plurals. For the purpose of agreement, ignore everything before the final subject.

~~Neither Benny Goodman nor~~ **Louis Armstrong is** heard on the radio often.

~~Either the Andrews Sisters or~~ **Frank Sinatra was** my mother's favorite singer.

11e Making sure the verb agrees with its subject in cases of inverted word order

In questions, the verb comes before the subject. Be sure to look ahead to check that the subject and verb agree.

Is jazz popular?

Expletive constructions postpone the subject by using *there* or *here* plus a form of the verb *be*. Check ahead in such sentences to identify the subject, and make the form of *be* agree with the subject.

There were many **bands** that played swing in the forties.
There is still a dedicated **audience** for this music.

Introductory *it* plus a form of the verb *be* can be an expletive construction as well, but one that always takes a singular verb.

It is young musicians who strive to capture the sound of the Big Bands.

11f Using singular verbs for most indefinite pronouns

Indefinite pronouns do not refer to any particular person, thing, or idea. They take their meanings from context. Indefinite pronouns are usually singular, and therefore they take singular verbs. Here is a list of indefinite pronouns:

each	everyone	no one
every	everybody	nobody
one	everything	nothing
either	anyone	someone
neither	anybody	somebody
another	anything	something

Everybody talks about the weather but **no one does** a thing about it.
No matter what **someone forecasts, something** different **seems** to happen.

A few indefinite pronouns—*none, some, more, most, any,* and *all*—may be either singular or plural, depending on the meaning of the sentence.

All of the weather forecasts we hear **are** based on probabilities.
We hate bad weather, but **some is** inevitable.

11g Using singular or plural verbs according to context with collective nouns

A **collective noun** names a group of people or things: *family, group, audience, class, number, committee, team*. When the group acts as one unit, use a singular verb. When the members of the group act individually, use a plural verb.

> The **jury is** hearing evidence. [*Jury* refers to a single unit, so the verb is singular.]
>
> The **jury disagree** on a verdict [The jury members take separate action, so the verb is plural.]

11h Making sure a linking verb agrees with the subject—not the subject complement

Even when the **subject complement** (7-1) that follows a linking verb (7c) differs in number (singular and plural) from the subject, the verb must agree with the subject.

> The best **part** of the week **is** Saturday and Sunday.

but

> **Saturday and Sunday are** the best part of the week.

11i Using verbs that agree with the antecedents of *who*, *which*, and *that* when these pronouns appear as subjects

Who, which, and *that* have the same form in singular and plural, so you must find their antecedents (10a) before you can decide whether the verb is singular or plural.

> The **tenants who move** into this apartment will need to paint it. [*Who* refers to *tenants*, so the verb *move* is plural.]
>
> The **tenant who moves** into this apartment will need to paint it. [*Who* refers to *tenants*, so the verb *moves* is singular.]

Be especially careful to identify the antecedent of *who, which*, or *that* when you see *one of the* or *the only one of the* in a sentence.

> George Boyd is one of the **tenants who want** to hire a new janitor. [*Who* refers to *tenants*, so *want* is plural.]
>
> George Boyd is the only **one** of the tenants **who wants** to hire a new janitor. [*Who* refers to *one*, so *wants* is singular.]

11j Using singular verbs with subjects that specify amounts and with singular subjects that are plural in form

Subjects that refer to sums of money, distance, or measurement are considered singular and take singular verbs.

Seventy-five cents is the toll over the bridge.
One and six-tenths kilometers makes a mile.

Many words that end in *-s* or *-ics* are singular in meaning despite their plural appearance. These include *news, ethics, economics, mathematics, physics, politics, sports, statistics* (as a course of study).

Mathematics is necessary for many daily tasks.
Athletics demands total commitment.

In contrast, other words are plural even though they refer to one thing. These include *jeans, pants, scissors, clippers, tweezers, eyeglasses, thanks, riches.*

The **scissors are** on the desk.

11k Using singular verbs for titles of written works, companies, and words as terms

Arm and Hammer is a popular brand of baking soda.
Cats, the musical, **is** based on a book of poems by T. S. Eliot.

PRONOUN–ANTECEDENT AGREEMENT

The form of most pronouns depends on what their **antecedents** are (10a), so the connection between a pronoun and its antecedent must be clear. These connections are reflected by agreement in number (singular or plural), person (first, second, or third), and gender (male or female).

Singular pronouns must refer to singular antecedents, and plural pronouns must refer to plural antecedents.

The **ocean** has **its** own plant and animal life.
The **oceans** have **their** own plant and animal life.

First person pronouns must refer to first person antecedents, second person pronouns to second person antecedents, and third person pronouns to third person antecedents.

Beginning **divers** have to watch **their** [third person: not *your*] instructors for directions.

11l Using a plural pronoun when antecedents are joined by *and*

Two or more antecedents joined by *and* require a plural pronoun, even if each antecedent by itself is singular.

Miami and San Francisco are centers of ocean exploration because of **their** coastal locations.

When *each* or *every* precedes singular nouns joined by *and*, use a singular pronoun.

Each scuba diver and sailor hopes to locate a sunken treasure for **herself** or **himself.**

Also when the singular nouns joined by *and* refer to the same person or thing, use a singular pronoun.

Our **captain and diving instructor** warned us to stay near **her.**

11m Making the pronoun agree with the antecedent closest to it

Antecedents joined by the conjunctions *or* or *nor*, or correlative conjunctions (such as *either... or, neither... nor*), often mix masculine and feminine or singular and plural nouns. To find the needed pronoun, ignore everything before the final antecedent.

~~Either the seals or~~ the **porpoise** will do **its** act.
~~Either the porpoise or~~ the **seals** will do **their** act.
~~Neither Bob nor~~ **Jane** likes to share **her** training methods.
~~Neither Jane nor~~ **Bob** likes to share **his** training methods.

11n Using a singular pronoun to refer to most indefinite-pronoun antecedents

Indefinite pronouns (see 11f for a list) are usually singular, so the pronouns that refer back to them should also be singular.

Everyone should know **his or her** Social Security number.
No one can be expected to know **his or her** driver's license number.

Using the masculine pronouns appropriately

Until about twenty-five years ago the masculine pronoun was used to refer to indefinite pronouns as well as to nouns and pronouns that name general categories to which any person might belong: *Everyone should admit his mistakes*. Today people are more conscious that *he, his, him,* and *himself* exclude women. Many writers try to avoid using masculine pronouns to refer to the entire population.

HOW TO AVOID USING ONLY THE MASCULINE PRONOUN TO REFER TO MALES AND FEMALES TOGETHER

Solution 1 Use a pair—but try to avoid a pair more than once in a sentence or in many sentences in a row.

Everyone hopes that **he or she** will win the scholarship.

A successful doctor knows that **he or she** has to work long hours.

Solution 2 Revise into the plural.

Many people hope that **they** will win the scholarship.

Successful doctors know that **they** have to work long hours.

Solution 3 Recast the sentence.

Everyone hopes to win the scholarship.

Successful doctors should expect to work long hours.

Some indefinite pronouns can be either singular or plural, depending on the meaning of the sentence. When the indefinite pronoun is plural, then the pronouns that refer back to it should be plural.

Many students do not realize they have a talent for mathematics. **Some** have learned this attitude from **their** parents.

11o Using singular or plural pronouns according to context to match collective-noun antecedents

A **collective noun** names a group of people or things: *family, group, audience, class, number, committee, team,* and the like. When the group acts as one unit, use a singular pronoun to refer to it. When the members of the group act individually, use a plural pronoun.

The **committee** has elected **its** new chairperson. [The *committee* is acting as one unit, so the pronoun is singular.]

The **committee** expressed **their** opinions about the election campaign. [The *committee* is acting as individuals, so the pronoun is plural.]

Making Subjects and Verbs Agree

A: Fill in the blanks on the right with the present tense forms of the verbs in parentheses. Be sure the verb agrees in person and number with the subject of the sentence. (11a)

EXAMPLE Some people (to believe) that cutting hair makes it grow faster.   *believe*

1. This (to be) not true.   *is*
2. Many things (to influence) how quickly hair (to grow).   _____

3. However, a haircut (to have) no effect.   _____
4. Dead cells (to form) chains that we (to call) hairs.   _____

5. The scalp (to produce) new hair cells constantly.   _____
6. Haircuts (to take) off only old, dead cells.   _____
7. The new cells (to remain) unaffected by even close haircuts.   _____
8. Hair (to increase) in length an average of five inches per year.   _____
9. Growth (to seem) to be quicker for women than men.   _____
10. The longest hair (to belong) to a man in India: 26 feet long.   _____

B: Fill in the blanks on the right with the appropriate present-tense forms of the verbs in parentheses. (11b-d)

EXAMPLE The average doctor, not only sports medicine specialists, (to treat) more sports-related injuries than ever.   *treats*

1. The rate of injuries among weekend athletes (to appear) headed toward a new high.   _____
2. Recreational basketball, running, and tennis (to lead) to the kind of injuries previously found only among professional and college athletes.   _____
3. Nine activities, including football, (to account) for three-quarters of all recreational sports injuries.   _____
4. Overuse, repeated shocks to muscles and bones, (to cause) more than two-thirds of all injuries.   _____

5. Not only tennis and running, but also aerobic dancing (to be) a frequent cause of overuse injuries. _____

6. Acute injuries, sudden damage such as a broken bone, (to make) up the remaining injuries. _____

7. Skiing, football, basketball, or soccer (to be) usually involved in an acute injury. _____

8. Skiing and aerobic dancing (to turn) out to be more dangerous than realized. _____

9. Skiing, not football and soccer, (to produce) the most injuries. _____

10. Aerobic dancing, although it seems gentler than other sports, (to give) rise to more fractures than any other recreational activity. _____

2 correct

C: Circle the subjects and underline the verbs. If the verb does not agree with the subject, cross it out and write the correct form on the line to the right. If the verb does agree, write *correct* on the line. (11e,h)

EXAMPLE (Stage fright) ~~are~~ really several problems. _____*is*_____

1. It are amazing (to realize) that stage fright affects 80 percent of us. _____*is*_____

2. There are a difference between stage fright and shyness, although they are connected. _____

3. The same person are usually a shy conversationalist and a fearful public speaker. _____

4. However, the two problems is not one. _____

5. From feelings of awkwardness in childhood come shyness. _____

6. There is usually nothing but inexperience causing stage fright. _____

7. There are a successful cure based on speech writing and self-confidence lessons. _____

8. Relaxation exercises is another method. _____

9. On building self-confidence, others concentrate. _____

10. It are the goal of such courses to make people feel comfortable speaking in front of others. _____

D: Fill in the blanks on the right with the present tense forms of the verbs in parentheses. (11f-g)

EXAMPLE Everybody in Britain (to be) covered by the National Health Service. _____*is*_____

1. Everyone (to get) basic medical care for free. _____*gets*_____

2. Most medical services are included, although some, such as eyeglasses, (to carry) a small fee.   _____

3. No one (to be) turned away.   _____

4. The population (to have) become healthier.   _____

5. The working class (to be) much better off now than in 1948, when the system started.   _____

6. Not everybody (to like) the system, though.   _____

7. A common doctors' complaint is the lack of hospital space; another (to be) the heavy paperwork.   _____

8. Also, anyone wanting unrequired surgery (to need) to wait for months, or even years.   _____

9. The average medical team (to work) with inadequate equipment because the government cannot afford to supply everything wanted.   _____

10. All the people are served, but none (to become) pampered or spoiled.   _____

E: Circle the antecedent of each italicized *who, which,* or *that.* Then fill in the blanks on the right with the appropriate present-tense forms of the verbs in parentheses. (11i)

EXAMPLE   The British (system) *that* (to keep) politically powerful people in line works by giving out honors and titles, such as knighthoods.   *keeps*

1. The king or queen's ability to grant titles might seem to be a (custom) *that* (to serve) little purpose in our modern world.   *serves*

2. Yet, titles can be valued rewards for people *who* (to deserve) recognition for their contributions to society.   _____

3. Someone *who* (to hope) for a title is also less likely to do things *that* (to displease) the government.   _____

4. Awards, *which* (to be) usually given only for service to the country, may sometimes be given to union and business leaders to encourage cooperation with government policies.   _____

5. Although the monarch grants the awards, he or she gives them only to people *who* (to have) been recommended by the prime minister.   _____

6. A small government staff, *which* (to be) composed of civil service employees, makes the actual recommendations.   _____

7. The awards, *which* (to lead) to great competition and pride, include knighthoods and other royal titles.   _____

8. Some orders of knights go back to the thirteenth and fourteenth centuries, *which* (to increase) their snob appeal.   _____

9. A person *who* (to receive) a title gains social status in a way not possible in the United States.   _____

10. Nevertheless, Americans *who* (to follow) the comings and goings of the British royal family seem to be saying they would like to have royalty and titles here too.   _____

F: Fill in the blanks on the right with the appropriate present-tense forms of the verbs in parentheses. (11j-k)

EXAMPLE   Two and a half centimeters (to equal) approximately one inch.   ___*equals*___

1. Six dollars (to seem) like a lot of money to see just one movie.   _____

2. The news (to be) available 24 hours a day on some radio and television stations.   _____

3. *Bonnie and Clyde* (to show) moviegoers the violent rise and fall of a Depression-era gang.   _____

4. Twenty-five-thousand miles (to be) the circumference of the earth at the equator.   _____

5. When there are children in a home, scissors (to belong) in a safe place.   _____

6. Four hundred and fifty-four grams (to make) one pound.   _____

7. Simon & Schuster (to publish) books through its many divisions, including Prentice Hall.   _____

8. Physics (to deal) with the basic principles governing our universe.   _____

9. Eyeglasses (to get) lost easily because once we take them off we cannot see well enough to look for them.   _____

10. Dun and Bradstreet (to rate) businesses so people can see if a company is a safe investment.   _____

G: Fill in the blanks on the right with the appropriate present-tense forms of the verbs in parentheses. (11a-k)

EXAMPLE   Everyone (to dream) during sleep.   ___*dreams*___

1. No one (to know) why we (to dream).   _____
   _____

2. Dreams (to occur) during a special kind of sleep, known as REM.   _____

3. REM (to stand) for Rapid Eye Movement. _____

4. A total of about two hours a night (to get) spent in this _____
dream state.

5. There (to be) many theories about why people dream _____
and what the rapid movement of our eyeballs (to mean). _____

6. Some (to suggest) that REM sleep occurs when the _____
brain rids itself of unnecessary images.

7. According to this theory, dreams (to represent) random _____
signals.

8. Others (to believe) that dreaming helps the brain _____
establish patterns for thinking.

9. Human newborns, they say, (to spend) about half their _____
sleep time dreaming.

10. The babies, who (to receive) huge amounts of new _____
information every day, may be developing plans for
processing what they see and hear.

11. In contrast, the elderly (to devote) only fifteen percent _____
of their sleep time to dreaming.

12. Why we dream and what dreams mean (to form) a big _____
mystery.

13. Psychologists (to think) dreams help people deal with _____
emotional issues.

14. The population often (to lack) the time necessary to _____
cope with complicated emotional situations.

15. For example, people in the middle of divorce often (to _____
have) long, detailed dreams.

16. In contrast, people with peaceful lives generally (to _____
claim) their dreams are dull.

17. Sigmund Freud said that dreams (to protect) us from _____
painful truths.

18. There (to exist) a radical new theory which (to propose) _____
that dreams do something entirely different. _____

19. While awake, people (to learn) about the environment, _____
but in dreams the flow of new information about the
world is cut off.

20. Each dream (to combine) new information with _____
information already in the brain, and new ways of _____
dealing with the world (to be) rehearsed.

Making Pronouns
and Antecedents Agree

Select a personal pronoun that agrees with the subject of each of these sentences. Write your answers on the lines to the right.

EXAMPLE   The group has _____ meeting here.   _____*its*_____

1. Anyone can get _____ name in the news.   _____his/her_____

2. None of the checks were cashed; _____ finally expired.   _____

3. The chef cut _____ on the thumb while peeling carrots.   _____

4. A person should insure _____ valuables.   _____

5. The family has _____ eye on a new house.   _____

6. The codebreakers shared _____ secrets.   _____

7. Everybody has _____ own dreams and goals.   _____

8. One can be happy only if _____ has respect for _____ .   _____
_____

9. Children never realize how loud _____ can be.   _____

10. The senior class wore _____ rings proudly.   _____

11. My mother and her sister took _____ vacation together.   _____

12. Either Mike or John wears a patch over _____ eye.   _____

13. All are welcome; _____ just need to call for directions to the party.   _____

14. Neither documentaries nor the news is given enough money by _____ network.   _____

15. San Jose and San Diego get _____ names from Spanish.   _____

16. Either Eleanor Roosevelt or Ellen Wilson is believed to have covered for _____ husband during presidential emergencies.   _____

17. Cars cost more than _____ owners expect them to.   _____

18. Venus and Mars have _____ orbits nearer to Earth than to any other planets.   _____

19. The band starts _____ tour tomorrow night.   _____

20. Any of the candidates could win; _____ are very much alike.   _____

Drop

*Revising Sentences
for Agreement*

EXERCISE **11-3**
(11a-o)

Revise each of these passages so that all pronouns agree with their antecedents in person, number, and gender. You may also have to change verbs or other words. Most sentences can be revised in more than one way. Take the time to try several, and select the version you like best.

EXAMPLE   The human population creates most environmental problems because they have minimum requirements for food and space.
The human population creates most environmental problems because it has minimum requirements for food and space.

1. The number of people that needs to be absorbed into the United States each month is 150,000. They are made up of 120,000 births and 30,000 immigrants.

   _____

2. All need to have basic services. He needs food, clothing, and shelter.

   _____

3. A higher birth rate and a greater survival rate are modern trends. Together, it makes the world population double in 35 years.

   _____

4. Either disease or war may be the result, some people say. They will be ways of reducing the population.

   _____

5. There are theories about how many people the earth can support, but it varies from 500,000 (12 percent of the current population) to 15 billion (about four times the current population).

   _____

6. Anyone in a world of 15 billion people would not have many luxuries in their lives.

   _____

7. Life in the poorest tropical countries is horrible. They are often very short and miserable.

   _____

8. The food supply in these countries is already too small, but rapidly growing populations means they will become even less adequate.

_____

9. Nobody can be sure of the outcome if we do not make some changes. They can be sure, however, that more people will go hungry.

_____

10. Neither the dependence on only a few grain crops nor the beef-eating habit is likely to last much into the future. They are too wasteful of food resources.

_____

12 | Using Adjectives and Adverbs

Both **adjectives** and **adverbs** are **modifiers**—words or groups of words that describe other words. Because adjectives and adverbs function similarly in sentences, distinguishing between them is sometimes difficult.

ADJECTIVE	The **quick** messenger delivered the payroll.
ADVERB	The messenger **quickly** delivered the payroll.

The key to distinguishing between adjectives and adverbs is that they modify different types of words or groups of words.

SUMMARY OF DIFFERENCES BETWEEN ADJECTIVES AND ADVERBS

WHAT ADJECTIVES MODIFY	EXAMPLE
nouns	The **busy** *lawyer* rested.
pronouns	*She* felt **triumphant**.

WHAT ADVERBS MODIFY	EXAMPLE
verbs	The lawyer *spoke* **quickly**.
adverbs	The lawyer spoke **very** *quickly*.
adjectives	The lawyer was **extremely** *busy*.
independent clauses	**Therefore**, *the lawyer rested*.

Adjectives and adverbs are sometimes confused because of the *-ly* ending. In many cases, an adverb is formed by adding *-ly* to an adjective: *soft, softly; grand, grandly; beautiful, beautifully*. However, even though many adverbs end in *-ly*, some do not: *well, very, worse*. Also some words that end in *-ly* are adjectives: *lively, friendly*. The *-ly* ending, therefore, is not a foolproof way to identify adverbs.

To determine whether an adjective or an adverb is called for, see how the word functions in its sentence. If a noun or pronoun is being modified, use an adjective. If a verb, adjective, or other adverb is being modified, use an adverb.

12a Using adverbs—not adjectives—to modify verbs, adjectives, and other adverbs

Only adverbs modify verbs. You should avoid the nonstandard use of adjectives in the place of adverbs.

No   It snowed **heavy** last night. [Adjective *heavy* cannot modify verb *snowed*.]

Yes   It snowed **heavily** last night. [Adverb *heavily* modifies the verb *snowed*.]

Good–well: The words *good* and *well* can be confusing. As an adjective, *good* can modify nouns or noun substitutes.

The **good** news spread. [Adjective *good* modifies noun *news*.]

The reopened factory would be **good** for the town. [Adjective *good* modifies noun phrase *the reopened factory*.]

Good cannot modify verbs. Only *well*, an adverb, can modify verbs.

No   The project started off **good**. [Adjective *good* cannot modify verb *started off*.]

Yes   The project started off **well**. [Adverb *well* modifies verb *started off*.]

Yes   The **good** project started off **well**.

One exception exists: *well* is used as an adjective to describe conditions of health.

I don't feel **well**.
The patient is **well**.

Only adverbs modify adjectives and other adverbs.

No   This is a **true fattening** dessert. [Adjective *true* cannot modify adjective *fattening*.]

Yes   This is a **truly fattening** dessert. [Adverb *truly* modifies adjective *fattening*.]

12b Not using double negatives

A **double negative** is a statement that contains two negative modifiers. Negative modifiers include *no, never, not, none, nothing, hardly, scarcely*, and *barely*. They should not occur in the same sentence.

No   Some people do **not** have **no** pity for the needy.

Yes   Some people do **not** have any pity for the needy.

No   They **never** donate **no** food.

Yes   They **never** donate food.

No   She could **not hardly** pay the rent.

Yes   She could **hardly** pay the rent.

12c Using adjectives—not adverbs—as complements after linking verbs

Linking verbs indicate a state of being or a condition. They serve to connect the subject to a word that renames or describes it. If the subject is being described after a linking verb, an adjective is needed. If, however, the verb is being described, an adverb is needed.

> The bee was **angry**. [Adjective *angry* describes the subject *bee* after linking verb *was*.]
>
> The bee attacked **angrily**. [Adverb *angrily* describes the action verb *attacked*.]

Bad–badly: The words *bad* (adjective) and *badly* (adverb) are often misused with linking verbs, especially verbs related to the senses, such as *feel*. Only the adjectives *bad* or *good* are correct when a verb is operating as a linking verb.

FOR DESCRIBING A FEELING	The coach felt **bad**. [not *badly*]
FOR DESCRIBING A SMELL	The locker room smelled **bad**. [not *badly*]
FOR DESCRIBING A SOUND	The half-time band sounded **good**. [not *well*]

12d Using correct comparative and superlative forms of adjectives and adverbs

By using special forms of adjectives and adverbs, you can make comparisons. Most adjectives and adverbs show degrees of comparison by means of *-er* and *-est* endings or by being combined with the words *more* and *most*. (All adjectives and adverbs show diminishing or negative comparison by combining with the words *less* and *least: less jumpy, least jumpy; less surely, least surely.*)

FORMS OF COMPARISON FOR REGULAR ADJECTIVES AND ADVERBS

FORM	FUNCTION
Positive	Used for a statement when nothing is being compared
Comparative	Used when only two things are being compared—with *-er* endings or *more* (or *less*)
Superlative	Used when three or more things are being compared—with *-est* ending or *most* (or *least*)

On the following page is a list that contrasts the three forms. Consider the messages of comparison in the sentences after the list.

POSITIVE	COMPARATIVE	SUPERLATIVE
green	greener	greenest
happy	happier	happiest
selfish	less selfish	least selfish
beautiful	more beautiful	most beautiful

Her tree is **green**.

Her tree is **greener** than his tree.

Her tree is the **greenest** one on the block.

The choice of whether to use *-er/-est* or *more/most* depends largely on the number of syllables in the adjective or adverb. With **one-syllable words**, the *-er/ -est* endings are most common: *large, larger, largest* (adjective); *far, farther, farthest* (adverb). With **words of three or more syllables**, *more/most* are used: *energetic, more energetic, most energetic*. With **adverbs of two or more syllables**, *more/ most* are used: *easily, more easily, most easily*. With **adjectives of two syllables**, practice varies. Often you will form comparatives and superlatives intuitively, based on what you have heard or read for a particular adjective. If neither form sounds natural for a given adjective, consult your dictionary for the recommended form.

Be careful not to use a **double comparative** or **double superlative**. The words *more* or *most* cannot be used if the *-er* or *-est* ending has been used.

Some comparative and superlative forms are irregular. Learn this short list.

IRREGULAR COMPARATIVES AND SUPERLATIVES

POSITIVE (1)	COMPARATIVE (2)	SUPERLATIVE (3+)
good (adjective)	better	best
well (adjective and adverb)	better	best
bad (adjective)	worse	worst
badly (adverb)	worse	worst
many	more	most
much	more	most
some	more	most
little	less	least

12e Avoiding using too many nouns as modifiers

Sometimes nouns can modify other nouns: *bird watching, fishing pole, fire drill*. These terms create no problems, but when nouns pile up in a list of modifiers, it can be difficult to know which nouns are being modified and which nouns are doing the modifying.

No   I misplaced my **electric garage door opener rebate coupon**.

YES   I misplaced **the coupon needed to get a rebate on the electric opener for my garage door**.

Identifying Adjectives and Adverbs

On the lines to the right, identify each of the italicized words as an adjective or an adverb.

EXAMPLE Surveys show that vanilla is the most *popular* ice cream flavor.   *adjective*

1. Sales figures indicate the *same* thing.   _____

2. *Most* ice cream is eaten by people over 55.   _____

3. They eat it more than once *every* week.   _____

4. People between 19 and 34 eat the *least* ice cream.   _____

5. They are *probably* all on diets.   _____

6. *Surprisingly*, the most ice cream per person is eaten by New Englanders.   _____

7. It is not *known* why New Englanders eat more ice cream than people in the hot southern states.   _____

8. The *average* American eats 22 quarts of ice cream per year.   _____

9. *This* figure includes sherbets and ices.   _____

10. The most popular sherbet is *orange* sherbet.   _____

11. It is *quickly* followed in popularity by pineapple and lime.   _____

12. Eskimo Pie was the *entirely* appropriate name of the first chocolate-covered ice cream bar.   _____

13. The Popsicle was invented *accidentally*.   _____

14. A man left a glass of lemonade near an open window one *winter* night.   _____

15. The glass had a spoon in it *too*.   _____

16. In the morning he had the first *frozen* juice bar.   _____

17. There are *many* different stories about the first ice cream cone.   _____

18. The most *likely* story is that the ice cream cone was invented at the 1904 St. Louis World's Fair.   _____

19. An ice cream booth *suddenly* ran out of serving dishes.   _____

20. The *panicky* owner went to a neighboring waffle booth for help.   _____

21. He rolled the waffles into cones to hold his ice cream and *immediately* created a hit.   _____

22. If you keep ice cream *tightly* covered in a cold freezer, it will stay fresh for two months.   _____

23. To be *legally* called ice cream, a product must contain at least 20 percent butterfat. _____

24. This high fat content is why ice cream is more *fattening* than sherbet and ice milk. _____

25. The *ice cream* sundae was invented about 1890. _____

26. The *exact* truth about its invention is not clear. _____

27. The most *commonly* believed version is this one. _____

28. *Old* laws in the Midwest banned the sale of soda on Sunday. _____

29. Store owners served soda-less ice cream sodas on *that* day. _____

30. The combinations of ice cream, syrup, and fruit became so *well* liked that people began to ask for them during the week too. _____

Distinguishing Adjectives from Adverbs

From the choices in parentheses, select the correct modifier for each sentence. Write your answers on the lines to the right.

EXAMPLE   Aspirin can cause a (severe, severely) upset stomach in some people. _____*severely*_____

1. Pain sufferers (annual, annually) spend a quarter of a billion dollars on aspirin. _____

2. Over 200 kinds of headache medicines containing aspirin are (available, availably). _____

3. Many of us feel taking aspirin can make us (good, well). _____

4. However, aspirin has many (serious, seriously) side effects. _____

5. Aspirin (common, commonly) causes bleeding in the stomach. _____

6. This can make us feel (bad, badly). _____

7. Bleeding occurs when an undissolved aspirin tablet lies on the (delicate, delicately) stomach wall. _____

8. For most of us, the amount of blood lost is not (dangerous, dangerously). _____

9. However, some (slow, slowly) dissolving tablets can cause prolonged bleeding, leading to great discomfort. _____

10. (High, Highly) quality aspirin dissolves more quickly and   _____
    is less likely to cause a problem.
11. Aspirin has a (lengthy, lengthily) history.   _____
12. Our (ancient, anciently) ancestors chewed the leaves   _____
    and bark of the willow tree.
13. They contain a substance (chemical, chemically) related   _____
    to aspirin.
14. Aspirin itself was introduced as a painkiller and fever   _____
    reducer more (recent, recently).
15. Coming on the market in 1899, it (quick, quickly)   _____
    became the best-selling nonprescription drug in the
    world.
16. The tablet form so (popular, popularly) today was   _____
    introduced by Bayer in 1915.
17. Taking an aspirin a day has (late, lately) been claimed to   _____
    be good for the heart.
18. Some research shows that men who take aspirin   _____
    (regular, regularly) after a heart attack are less likely to
    have another attack.
19. No one knows why this is so, but some healthy people   _____
    have been (quick, quickly) to start taking aspirin daily.
20. Doctors advise us to think (careful, carefully) before we   _____
    do this because there is no evidence that aspirin
    prevents first heart attacks.

Using Comparatives and Superlatives

EXERCISE 12-3
(12d)

A: Fill in the comparative and superlative forms of the adjectives and adverbs listed
   on the left.

	Comparative	Superlative
EXAMPLE tall	_taller_	_tallest_
1. *bad*	_____	_____
2. *badly*	_____	_____
3. *forgiving*	_____	_____
4. *free*	_____	_____

5. *good* _____ _____
6. *gracefully* _____ _____
7. *handsome* _____ _____
8. *hot* _____ _____
9. *little* _____ _____
10. *loudly* _____ _____
11. *many* _____ _____
12. *much* _____ _____
13. *powerfully* _____ _____
14. *pretty* _____ _____
15. *quickly* _____ _____
16. *some* _____ _____
17. *sweetly* _____ _____
18. *sympathetically* _____ _____
19. *talented* _____ _____
20. *well* _____ _____

B: Use the adjectives and adverbs above in sets of sentences that show how the three forms are related to changes in meaning. Use your own paper.

EXAMPLE I am tall. (positive)

~~Drop~~

I am taller than my sister. (comparative)

I am the tallest person in my family. (superlative)

Writing with Adjectives and Adverbs

> **EXERCISE 12-4**
> **(12)**

~~Drop~~

Write a paragraph describing someone, something, or someplace wonderful. Some suggestions: your favorite restaurant, your favorite movie star, an exciting amusement park, your most treasured possession.

Be sure to have a topic sentence (4a). Develop your idea with four to six sentences, each containing strong and appropriate adjectives and adverbs. Try not to use so many modifiers in any one sentence that the main idea gets lost. Use your own paper.

13 Sentence Fragments

A **sentence fragment** is part of a sentence punctuated as though it were a complete sentence. You can avoid writing sentence fragments if you recognize the difference between a fragment and a complete sentence.

13a Knowing how to test for sentence completeness

If you write sentence fragments frequently, you need a system to check that your sentences are complete. Here is a test to use if you suspect that you have written a sentence fragment.

TEST FOR SENTENCE COMPLETENESS

1. **Is there a verb?** If not, there is a sentence fragment.
2. **Is there a subject?** If not, there is a sentence fragment.
3. **Do the subject and verb start with a subordinating word—and lack an independent clause to complete the thought?** If they do, there is a sentence fragment.

QUESTION 1: Is there a verb?

If there is no verb, you are looking at a sentence fragment.

FRAGMENT	Yesterday the math lab hiring tutors.
REVISED	Yesterday the math lab **was** hiring tutors.
FRAGMENT	Today the math lab hiring tutors.
REVISED	Today the math lab **is** hiring tutors.

Fragment	Selected for their math ability.
Revised	The tutors **are** selected for their math ability.
Revised	Selected for their math ability, the tutors also **work** well with other students.

Fragment	Each tutor to work with eight students.
Revised	Each tutor **works** with eight students.
Revised	Each tutor **is assigned** to work with eight students.

QUESTION 2: Is there a subject?

If there is no subject, you are looking at a sentence fragment. To find a subject, ask a "who?" or "what?" question about the verb.

Fragment	Worked in the library. [Who worked? Unknown]
Revised	**The students** worked in the library.

Every sentence must have its own subject. A sentence fragment without a subject often results when the missing subject is the same as the subject in the previous sentence.

No	In September, the new dormitories were opened. **Were occupied immediately.**
Yes	In September, the new dormitories were opened. **They were occupied immediately.**

Imperative statements—commands and some requests—are an exception. Imperative statements imply the word *you* as the subject.

Sit down! = (You) sit down!

QUESTION 3: Do the subject and verb start with a subordinating word— and lack an independent clause to complete the thought?

If the answer is yes, you are looking at a sentence fragment. Clauses that begin with subordinating words are called **dependent clauses**, as explained in 7n-2. To be part of a complete sentence, a dependent clause must be joined to an independent clause.

One type of subordinating word is a **subordinating conjunction**. Some of the most frequently used are *after, although, because, if, when, where,* and *until.*

Fragment	**If** I see him.
Revised	**If** I see him, I'll give him your message.

Fragment	**Where** the park is.
Revised	The city will build a hospital **where** the park is.

❖ PUNCTUATION ALERT: When a dependent clause starting with a subordinating conjunction comes before an independent clause, a comma always separates the clauses. ❖

Another type of subordinating word is a **relative pronoun**. The most frequently used are *who, which, that, what, whoever*, and *whatever*.

FRAGMENT	The class **that** we wanted.
REVISED	The class **that** we wanted was full.
FRAGMENT	The students **who** registered early.
REVISED	The students **who** registered early got the classes they wanted.

Questions are an exception—they can begin with words such as *when, where, who*, and *which* without being sentence fragments.

When is the meeting?
Who is your favorite author?

13b Revising dependent clauses punctuated as sentences

To correct a dependent clause punctuated as a sentence (see the discussion of Question 3 in 13a), you can do one of two things: (1) You can join the dependent clause to an independent clause that comes directly before or after—sometimes you will need to add words so that the combined sentence makes sense. (2) You can drop the subordinating conjunction or relative pronoun and, if necessary, add words to create an independent clause.

FRAGMENT	Students often change their majors. **When they start taking courses.**
REVISED	Students often change their majors when they start taking courses. [joined into one sentence]
REVISED	Students often change their majors. They start taking courses, and realize they are unhappy. [subordinating conjunction dropped to create an independent clause]
FRAGMENT	The chemistry major is looking for a lab partner. **Who is dependable.**
REVISED	The chemistry major is looking for a lab partner who is dependable. [joined into one sentence]

13c Revising phrases punctuated as sentences

To correct a phrase punctuated as a sentence (see the discussions of Questions 1 and 2 in 13a), either you can rewrite it to become an independent clause by adding the missing subject or verb, or you can join it to an independent clause that comes directly before or after.

A **verbal phrase** contains a verbal instead of a verb. **Verbals** are present participles, past participles, and infinitives.

FRAGMENT	The college administration voted last week. **To offer a new program in nursing.**
REVISED	The college administration voted last week to offer a new program in nursing. [joined into one sentence]
REVISED	The college administration voted last week. The members decided to offer a new program in nursing. [rewritten]
FRAGMENT	**Speaking to the students.** The dean explained the new program.
REVISED	Speaking to the students, the dean explained the new program. [joined into one sentence]
REVISED	The dean spoke to the students. She explained the new program. [rewritten]
FRAGMENT	**Seated in the auditorium.** The students listened carefully.
REVISED	Seated in the auditorium, the students listened carefully. [joined into one sentence]
REVISED	The students were seated in the auditorium. They listened carefully. [rewritten]

A **prepositional phrase** contains a preposition (for a complete list see 7g), its object, and any modifiers.

FRAGMENT	She planned to take Biology 102. **During summer session.**
REVISED	She planned to take Biology 102 during summer session. [joined into one sentence]
REVISED	She planned to take Biology 102. It was offered in summer session. [rewritten]

An **appositive** is a word or word group that renames a noun or group of words functioning as a noun.

FRAGMENT	Many students liked the biology professor. **A teacher of great skill and patience.**
REVISED	Many students liked the biology professor, a teacher of great skill and patience. [joined into one sentence]
REVISED	Many students liked the biology professor. She was a teacher of great skill and patience. [rewritten]

Compound predicates contain two or more verbs, plus their objects and modifiers, if any. To be part of a complete sentence, a predicate must have a subject. If the second half of a compound predicate is punctuated as a sentence, it is a sentence fragment.

FRAGMENT	The professor was always available for conferences. **And answered students' questions clearly.**
REVISED	The professor was always available for conferences and answered students' questions clearly. [joined into one sentence]
REVISED	The professor was always available for conferences. And she always answered students' questions clearly. [rewritten]

Revising Fragments

A: Explain what is wrong with each fragment and then rewrite it as a complete sentence.

EXAMPLE   graduating in June
   There is no subject and "graduating" is not a conjugated verb.
   I am graduating in June.

1. and hopes to buy a car

   _____

   _____

2. eating quickly

   _____

   _____

3. behind the door

   _____

   _____

4. the hardest worker in the company

   _____

   _____

5. travels every summer

   _____

   _____

6. if I take out a student loan

   _____

   _____

7. Grace hoping to win the contest

   _____

   _____

8. who dresses in the latest fashions

_____

_____

9. hidden in the closet

_____

_____

B: Write two corrected versions of each fragment. Be sure to use the fragment differently in each and identify how you have used it (as illustrated in the parentheses below).

EXAMPLE   eating an orange

_Eating an orange can be messy. (subject)_____

_Eating an orange, he swallowed a pit. (adjective)_____

1. yelled out the window

_____

_____

2. to afford a color television

_____

_____

3. renting an apartment

_____

_____

4. the manager suspecting theft

_____

_____

5. when the strike ended

_____

_____

6. Aretha Franklin and Stevie Wonder

_____

_____

7. cross the street

_____

_____

8. in the window

_____

_____

9. who stood on line for tickets

_____

_____

10. known for his sense of humor

_____

_____

Revising Fragments
within Passages

There is one fragment in each passage below. Find it and correct it in whatever way you feel is most appropriate.

EXAMPLE   The custom of having a best man at a wedding is a holdover from
second-century Europe. In those days, a man often stole his bride
from a nearby town. Accompanied by a faithful friend. The hopeful
bridegroom would carry off an unprotected girl.
The custom of having a best man at a wedding is a holdover from
second-century Europe. In those days, a man often stole his bride
from a nearby town. Accompanied by a faithful friend, the hopeful
bridegroom would carry off an unprotected girl.

1. Because the job was dangerous. This friend had to be strong and brave.
   He truly was the "best man" the groom could find. His responsibility was
   to stand by the bridegroom throughout the wedding ceremony.

   _____

   _____

2. The best man traditionally was armed. To protect the groom in case the
   bride's family tried to rescue her. In a few societies, clubs and spears were
   even kept under church altars for such emergencies. Sometimes the best
   man also guarded the home of the newlyweds.

   _____

   _____

3. The tradition that the bride stand at the groom's left is related to this
   violent history. Among Northern Europeans, the captured woman stood on
   the left. Leaving the groom's sword hand (the right one) free. Old German
   records exist as evidence of this practice.

   _____

   _____

4. The original meaning of the wedding ring is not known. Some people
   believe that it is a symbol of the chains used to bind a captured bride to
   her new home. These people approve of modern double-ring ceremonies.
   As symbols of equality between husband and wife.

   _____

   _____

5. Other people have studied the actual rings exchanged in past cultures. The first rings were used in ancient Egypt. To the Egyptians, the symbol of eternity was the circle. Which has no beginning or end.

   _____

   _____

6. Young Roman men often went into debt to purchase gold bands for their brides. Most Roman wives had two rings. They wore their gold wedding bands in public. And cheaper iron ones at home.

   _____

   _____

7. Sometimes Roman rings were decorated with a miniature key. The key represented the woman's legal right to half her husband's property. Such as money, grain, rolls of cloth, or whatever else was in his possession. Until very recently, no other culture gave married women this much economic power.

   _____

   _____

8. The custom of the diamond engagement ring dates back to fifteenth-century Italy. Set in costly bands of silver and gold. Diamonds became popular among the wealthy in Venice. These people were among the first to discover the beauty of diamonds.

   _____

   _____

9. Although the history of the diamond engagement ring is easy to trace. The record of earlier types of engagement rings is not as clear. However, exchanging rings to show an engagement was a regular practice long before diamonds became popular. Even today, a diamond ring is not the only way to show an engagement.

   _____

   _____

10. An old English custom required the husband-to-be to break a valuable personal possession in half. One piece was kept by the young man. The other by the bride-to-be's father. A rich man usually broke a piece of gold or silver.

    _____

    _____

11. Breaking a piece of gold or silver later changed to breaking a ring. No one is sure when this happened. Evidence indicates, however, that engagement rings existed before wedding rings. And that the bride received the same ring for a second time during the actual wedding ceremony.

_____

_____

12. Modern traditions concerning the engagement ring began with Pope Nicholas I. Who in 860 ordered that an engagement ring was a required public statement of the wish to marry. The ring had to be expensive, a financial sacrifice. Gold and silver rings thus became required among Roman Catholic couples, and popular with others as well.

_____

_____

13. Breaking an engagement often led to severe punishment. Due to the seriousness with which marriage was regarded in those days. At the least, a man who broke an engagement lost all claim to get the expensive ring back. A woman who broke an engagement had to return the ring.

_____

_____

14. If a woman broke off an engagement for reasons unacceptable to the local priest. He had the power to send her to a convent for life. Basically, her choice was to marry or become a nun. Many women probably entered into terrible marriages because of this pressure.

_____

_____

15. In the West, we place the wedding ring on the finger next to the pinkie. And call it the ring finger. This practice is not the same in all cultures. For example, the early Hebrews placed the wedding ring on the index finger.

_____

_____

16. The wedding cake and the rice thrown at newlyweds are part of one tradition. Both are reminders of old fertility rites. Intended to make sure that the bride had many children. Grain, a symbol of fertility, was thrown at the new bride.

_____

_____

17. Wheat was commonly used in this ceremony. Roman bakers later began making the wedding wheat into small cakes. To be eaten, not thrown at the bride. Wedding guests sometimes threw the cakes anyway.

_____

_____

18. As a compromise, a new ritual developed in which the cakes were crumbled over the bride's head. Then she and the groom ate some of the crumbs to ensure fertility. This Roman practice spread. Throughout Western Europe, all the way to England.

_____

_____

19. The practice of throwing food at the bride changed during the Middle Ages. A time when food was often hard to get. Plain wheat or rice, instead of fancy cakes, was now thrown at the bride. For eating, the small, decorated cakes were replaced with simple biscuits.

_____

_____

20. In Great Britain, guests brought plain cakes and biscuits to the wedding and stacked them up in a high pile. The bride and groom kissed over the pile of cakes for luck. A French chef decided to make an iced, many-layered cake to show the British how beautiful a tall cake ought to be. Beginning the tradition of the modern wedding cake.

_____

_____

Revising Fragments within Paragraphs

Circle the number of any fragments. Then correct each fragment by connecting it to a main clause or by adding words to complete it. Use your own paper.

A.   ¹Rabbits once almost destroyed Australia. ²They are not native to the continent, but in 1850 three pairs of rabbits got loose. ³In the province of New South Wales. ⁴Spreading quickly, within ten years they endangered the country's agriculture. ⁵As millions of rabbits took over farms and ranches. ⁶Seven rabbits eat as much as one sheep, so the cattle-supporting ability of the country was severely damaged. ⁷Many plans were tried to get rid of the rabbits. ⁸In an effort to use natural enemies. ⁹Farmers imported other animals. ¹⁰Such as weasels, ferrets, and mongooses. ¹¹However, they ate more poultry. ¹²Than they did rabbits. ¹³The government offered a reward for dead rabbits. ¹⁴To encourage people to shoot, gas, or poison them. ¹⁵However, the rabbits continued to prosper. ¹⁶Destroying crops and even killing trees. ¹⁷By eating their bark. ¹⁸The only measure that had any success. ¹⁹Was an expensive one. ²⁰Fences, three feet high and sunk deep in the ground. ²¹Surrounded farms and gardens. ²²And in some cases entire districts. ²³One such fence was a thousand miles long. ²⁴At last, the Australians decided to turn the tables on the rabbits. ²⁵And treat them as a crop. ²⁶Now, millions of dollars worth of frozen rabbit meat and rabbit skins. ²⁷Are exported annually. ²⁸Even with the situation now under control. ²⁹You would probably have a hard time convincing an Australian farmer. ³⁰That a rabbit is a harmless, cute little creature.

B.   ¹The striped barber pole is a symbol left over from the times. ²When barbers doubled as surgeons. ³As early as the fifth century. ⁴Roman barbers pulled teeth, treated wounds. ⁵And bled patients. ⁶Records show that in 1461 the barbers of London were the only people practicing surgery. ⁷In the city. ⁸However, under Henry VIII, less than a hundred years later. ⁹Parliament passed a law limiting barbers to minor operations. ¹⁰Such as blood letting and pulling teeth. ¹¹While surgeons were prohibited from "barbery and shaving." ¹²The London barbers and surgeons were considered one group until 1745. ¹³In France and Germany, barbers acted as surgeons. ¹⁴Until even more recent times.

      ¹⁵Barbers usually bled their patients. ¹⁶To "cure" a variety of ailments. ¹⁷Because few people could read in those days. ¹⁸Pictures were commonly used as shop signs. ¹⁹The sign of the barber was a pole painted with red and white spirals. ²⁰From which was suspended a brass basin. ²¹The red represented the blood of the patient. ²²The white the bandage. ²³And the basin the bowl used to catch the blood. ²⁴In the United States, the bowl is often omitted. ²⁵But it is still common on British barber poles. ²⁶Some American barbers added a blue stripe. ²⁷Probably to make the colors match the flag.

14 Comma Splices and Fused Sentences

A **comma splice**, also known as a **comma fault**, occurs when a single comma joins independent clauses. The only time that a comma is correct between two independent clauses is when the comma is followed by a coordinating conjunction (see 7h).

> **COMMA SPLICE**   The car skidded, it hit a mailbox.

A **fused sentence**, also known as a **run-on sentence** or a **run-together sentence**, occurs when two independent clauses are not separated by punctuation nor joined by a comma with a coordinating conjunction.

> **FUSED SENTENCE**   The car skidded it hit a mailbox.

Comma splices and fused sentences are two versions of the same problem: incorrect joining of two independent clauses. Comma splices and fused sentences can be corrected in a variety of ways.

> The car skidded. It hit a mailbox. [period used]
>
> The car skidded; it hit a mailbox. [semicolon used]
>
> The car skidded, and it hit a mailbox. [comma and coordinating conjunction used]
>
> When the car skidded, it hit a mailbox. [the first independent clause revised into a dependent clause]
>
> The car skidded before it hit a mailbox. [the second independent clause revised into a dependent clause]
>
> The car skidded; then it hit a mailbox. [semicolon and conjunctive adverb used]

14a Knowing how to recognize comma splices and fused sentences

To recognize comma splices and fused sentences, you need to be able to recognize an **independent clause**. As explained in 7n-1, an independent clause contains a subject and a predicate. An independent clause can stand alone as a sentence because it is a complete grammatical unit. A sentence may contain two or more independent clauses only if they are joined properly (with a comma and coordinating conjunction *or* with a semicolon).

You can avoid writing comma splices and fused sentences if you realize that most such errors occur for one of three reasons:

LEADING CAUSES OF COMMA SPLICES AND FUSED SENTENCES

1. **Pronouns:** A comma splice or fused sentence often occurs when the second independent clause starts with a pronoun.

   No   Thomas Edison was a productive inventor, **he** held over 1,300 U.S. and foreign patents.

   Yes   Thomas Edison was a productive inventor. **He** held over 1,300 U.S. and foreign patents.

2. **Conjunctive adverbs and other transitional expressions:** A comma splice or fused sentence often occurs when the second independent clause starts with a conjunctive adverb (see 7f for a list) or other transitional expression (see 4b for a list). Remember that these words are *not* coordinating conjunctions, so they cannot work with a comma to join two independent clauses.

   No   Thomas Edison was a brilliant scientist, **however**, his schooling was limited to only three months of his life.

   Yes   Thomas Edison was a brilliant scientist. **However**, his schooling was limited to only three months of his life.

3. **Explanations or examples:** A comma splice or fused sentence often occurs when the second independent clause explains or gives an example of the information in the first independent clause.

   No   Thomas Edison was the genius behind many inventions, the phonograph and the light bulb are among the best known.

   Yes   Thomas Edison was the genius behind many inventions. The phonograph and the light bulb are among the best known.

14b Using a period or semicolon to correct comma splices and fused sentences

A **period** can separate the independent clauses in a comma splice or fused sentence. A **semicolon** can separate independent clauses that are closely related in meaning (see 25a).

COMMA SPLICE   In the 1880s, Sir Francis Galton showed that fingerprints are unique for each person, he was an English anthropologist.

CORRECTED   In the 1880s, Sir Francis Galton showed that fingerprints are unique for each person. He was an English anthropologist.

| FUSED SENTENCE | Mark Twain used fingerprints to solve murders in *Life on the Mississippi* and *Pudd'nhead Wilson* these were popular books. |
| CORRECTED | Mark Twain used fingerprints to solve murders in *Life on the Mississippi* and *Pudd'nhead Wilson*; these were popular books. |

14c Using coordinating conjunctions to correct comma splices and fused sentences

When ideas in independent clauses are closely related, you might decide to connect them with a coordinating conjunction that fits the meaning of the material (see 7h). Two independent clauses joined by a coordinating conjunction and a comma form a compound sentence, also known as a coordinate sentence. ❖ PUNCTUATION ALERT: Use a comma before a coordinating conjunction that links independent clauses. ❖

COMMA SPLICE	In 1901, England began fingerprinting criminals, their prints were kept on file with the police.
CORRECTED	In 1901, England began fingerprinting criminals, **and** their prints were kept on file with the police.
FUSED SENTENCE	Edward Richard Henry, of London's Metropolitan Police, invented a system of classifying fingerprints the FBI uses a version of this original system.
CORRECTED	Edward Richard Henry, of London's Metropolitan Police, invented a system of classifying fingerprints, **and** the FBI uses a version of this original system.

14d Revising one of two independent clauses into a dependent clause to correct a comma splice or fused sentence

You can revise a comma splice or fused sentence by changing one of two independent clauses into a dependent clause. This method is suitable when one idea can be logically subordinated to the other. Sentences composed of one independent clause and one or more dependent clauses are called complex sentences. Inserting an appropriate subordinating conjunction (see 7h) in front of the subject and verb is one way to create a dependent clause.

❖ PUNCTUATION ALERT: Do not put a period after a dependent clause that is not attached to an independent clause, or you will create a sentence fragment (see Chapter 13). ❖

| COMMA SPLICE | Immigrants are fingerprinted, most have done nothing wrong. |
| CORRECTED | Immigrants are fingerprinted **although most have done nothing wrong**. |

FUSED SENTENCE	The government wants to identify dangerous criminals they enter the country.
CORRECTED	The government wants to identify dangerous criminals **before they enter the country**.

A relative pronoun can also be used to correct a comma splice or fused sentence by creating a dependent clause.

COMMA SPLICE	Government employees are also fingerprinted, they work on sensitive projects.
CORRECTED	Government employees **who work on sensitive projects** are also fingerprinted. [restrictive dependent clause]

14e Using a semicolon or a period before a conjunctive adverb or other transitional expression between two independent clauses

Conjunctive adverbs and other transitional expressions link ideas between sentences. Remember, however, that these words are *not* coordinating conjunctions, so they cannot work with commas to join independent clauses. Conjunctive adverbs and other transitional expressions require that the previous sentence end in a period or semicolon.

Conjunctive adverbs include such words as *however, therefore, also, next, then, thus, furthermore*, and *nevertheless* (see 7f for a fuller list).

COMMA SPLICE	Many people object to being fingerprinted, **nevertheless**, fingerprinting remains a requirement for certain jobs.
CORRECTED	Many people object to being fingerprinted. **Nevertheless**, fingerprinting remains a requirement for certain jobs.

Transitional words include *for example, for instance, in addition, in fact, of course*, and *on the other hand* (see 7b for a fuller list).

FUSED SENTENCE	Not everyone disapproves of fingerprinting **in fact**, some parents have their children fingerprinted as a safety measure.
CORRECTED	Not everyone disapproves of fingerprinting. **In fact**, some parents have their children fingerprinted as a safety measure.

A conjunctive adverb or other transitional expression can appear in various locations within an independent cause. In contrast, a coordinating conjunction can appear only between the independent clauses it joins.

Many people object to being fingerprinted. Fingerprinting, **nevertheless**, remains a requirement for certain jobs.

Many people object to being fingerprinted. Fingerprinting remains, **nevertheless**, a requirement for certain jobs.

Many people object to being fingerprinted. Fingerprinting remains a requirement for certain jobs, **nevertheless**.

Many people object to being fingerprinted, **but** fingerprinting remains a requirement for certain jobs.

Revising Comma Splices and Fused Sentences

EXERCISE 14-1
(14a-e)

A: Correct each comma splice or fused sentence in any of the ways shown in this chapter.

EXAMPLE   People get dizzy for many reasons, most dizzy spells are harmless.
People get dizzy for many reasons, but most dizzy spells are harmless.

1. Someone who jumps out of bed quickly may feel faint, however, she will feel fine again soon if she lies down for a while.

_____

_____

2. Young children often like to twirl around until they get dizzy they enjoy the feeling that the earth is moving beneath them.

_____

_____

3. These two different situations are related, they have different causes.

_____

_____

4. Blood rushes away from people's heads when they sit or stand up quickly, as a result their brains do not get enough oxygen.

_____

_____

5. They get dizzy the room seems to spin.

_____

6. Lying down helps the blood go back to the head getting up slowly next time gives the body a chance to adjust to the change.

_____

_____

7. One remedy for dizziness is to place the head lower than the heart, an easy way for someone to do this is to sit with his head between his knees.

_____

_____

B: Correct each comma splice or fused sentence in the way indicated.

EXAMPLE   Placing one's head between one's knees is an effective cure for dizziness it helps oxygen-rich blood to get to the brain.
(Turn one independent clause into a dependent clause.)

Placing one's head between one's knees is an effective cure for dizziness because it helps oxygen-rich blood to get to the brain.

1. The dizziness caused by spinning has a different source than the dizziness caused by getting up too fast it is the result of movement inside the ear.
(Make into two separate sentences.)

_____

_____

2. Feelings of balance are controlled by the ears, inside each ear are three tiny tubes.
(Add a semicolon.)

_____

_____

3. The tubes are filled with fluid tiny hairs stick out into this fluid.
(Turn one part into a dependent clause.)

_____

4. As the head turns, the fluid moves, the hairs do too.
(Add a semicolon and a conjunctive adverb.)

_____

5. The movement of the hairs sends a message to the brain, for example, it might say that the head is moving quickly to the right.
(Add a semicolon.)

_____

6. When someone spins around quickly and then stops suddenly, the fluid does not stop moving immediately, the hairs keep sending the message to the brain that the head is spinning.
(Add a comma and a coordinating conjunction.)

_____

_____

7. The brain is sending unnecessary directions to the body to help it keep balanced the person continues to feel dizzy even after he stops spinning.
(Turn one part into a dependent clause.)

_____

_____

C: Correct each comma splice or fused sentence in four ways: (1) make each into two separate sentences by inserting a period; (2) add a semicolon; (3) add a coordinating conjunction to create a compound sentence—you will also need to add a comma unless the clauses are very short; (4) add a subordinating conjunction or relative pronoun—you may need to drop a word—to create a complex sentence.

EXAMPLE   The first Nobel Peace Prize went to Jean Henri Dunant, he founded the Red Cross.

1. Dunant. He founded the Red Cross.

2. Dunant; he founded the Red Cross.

3. Dunant, for he founded the Red Cross.

4. Dunant because he founded the Red Cross. or Dunant, who founded the Red Cross.

1. Scotland Yard began using fingerprints in 1901, Sir William Henschel developed the first system for their use.

_____

_____

_____

_____

2. The first airplane bought by the U.S. government was a Wright brothers biplane it cost $25,000 in 1909.

_____

_____

_____

_____

3. The first woman to swim the English Channel was American Gertrude Ederle, she was only nineteen at the time.

_____

_____

_____

_____

4. The melody of "Happy Birthday to You" was copyrighted in 1893 it cannot be sung in a public performance without payment to the composers' family.

_____

_____

_____

_____

Revising Comma Splices and Fused Sentences within Passages

Find the comma splice or fused sentence in each passage. Correct each in any way shown in this chapter. You may need to change punctuation or wording, but try to keep the meaning of the original passage.

EXAMPLE One symbol of the United States is a tall man in a top hat, he is known as Uncle Sam. The original Uncle Sam was a meatpacker and politician from New York State. He became the national symbol as the result of a joke.

One symbol of the United States is a tall man in a top hat. He is known as Uncle Sam. The original Uncle Sam was a meatpacker and politician from New York State. He became the national symbol as the result of a joke.

1. For many years, Uncle Sam was considered a myth, the product of someone's overactive imagination. Recently, evidence of the existence of the original man was discovered in an old newspaper. Uncle Sam began life as Samuel Wilson, during the American Revolution he served as a drummer boy and once saved his town from invasion.

_____

_____

_____

2. He warned his neighbors of a British invasion by beating his drum. At fourteen, Sam joined the Revolutionary Army as a soldier, after the war he moved to New York where he opened a meat-packing company. The townspeople called him Uncle Sam because he was pleasant and fair.

_____

_____

_____

3. In 1812 Great Britain again invaded the United States. American troops stayed in the same town as Sam's packing plant. The government heard of his reputation for fairness, Sam got a big contract to supply meat to the troops.

_____

_____

_____

4. Because he was very careful and fair, Sam wanted to make sure the government got everything it paid for. To indicate to the warehouse crew which meat was to be sent to the army, he stamped the boxes with a large *U.S.* He meant it to stand for "United States" it was not a common abbreviation at the time.

_____

_____

_____

5. One day government inspectors came to the plant they asked a worker what the *U.S.* on all the boxes of meat meant. The worker did not know, but he was probably afraid to appear ignorant. He joked that the letters were the initials of his employer, Uncle Sam.

_____

_____

_____

6. The misinformation spread and soldiers began to say that all their food came from Uncle Sam, soon they were saying that all government supplies came from him. They started to refer to themselves as Uncle Sam's men, serving in Uncle Sam's army. Once the joke had gone this far, there was no stopping it.

_____

_____

_____

7. The first drawings of Uncle Sam appeared in New England newspapers eight years later. They showed him wearing a black top hat and a formal black coat, however, he had no beard. The familiar modern version of Uncle Sam took years to develop, as a series of artists added small changes.

_____

_____

_____

8. Solid red pants were the first addition. Next, Uncle Sam grew a beard it was meant to remind people of President Lincoln's beard which was very popular. At the end of the nineteenth century, patriotism led to more, colorful changes.

_____

_____

_____

9. Next, cartoonists decided that Uncle Sam needed to look more American. They added white stripes to his red pants, they added stars and stripes to his hat. He become a walking flag, silly-looking by modern standards.

_____

_____

_____

10. During the Civil War, Uncle Sam changed again, getting still closer to our modern view of him. Cartoonist Thomas Nast made him tall and thin. He was meant to look like President Lincoln, nevertheless, he bore a strange resemblance to Sam Wilson.

_____

_____

_____

11. The most-recognized Uncle Sam appeared during World War I on a poster, a serious-looking, finger-pointing Uncle Sam said, "I Want You for U.S. Army." The poster sold 4 million copies during World War I, and half a million more in World War II. The model this time was not Abraham Lincoln, but the poster's artist himself.

_____

_____

_____

12. During all the years that the poster was popular, Uncle Sam had been considered a legend. The original was finally identified when a researcher found an article about Sam Wilson and the meat inspector in an 1830's New York newspaper. The researcher had been looking through old historical records luckily he knew the value of the article when he came across it.

_____

_____

_____

13. Once Wilson was identified, it was possible to find out more about him for example, he became active in politics and lived to be eighty-eight years old. The proof that Uncle Sam was a real person led to official recognition. Under President John F. Kennedy, Congress formally thanked Wilson for being the original Uncle Sam.

_____

_____

_____

14. Now that the mystery of Uncle Sam has been solved, another mystery remains. The story of the origin of the American flag is even more confused than the origin of Uncle Sam. For starters, it is likely that Betsy Ross had little or nothing to do with the creation of our first flag, her involvement is a myth.

_____

_____

_____

15. The earliest American flag mixed parts of other flags with new details, it included parts of the flags of England and Scotland against a background of thirteen red and white stripes. The colonists claimed to be loyal British subjects fighting to correct bad treatment, so it is not surprising that their flag showed their British roots. This, however, was only a temporary flag.

_____

_____

_____

16. The earliest completely American flag grew out of a proposal in the Continental Congress, the war-time government of the colonies. The Congress authorized a flag with red and white stripes and thirteen stars on a blue background because the government was busy, details, such as size, were not decided upon. Washington's army did not even get these flags until all the major battles of the war were over.

_____

_____

_____

17. For years, most Americans did not think of the flag as a national symbol then in 1814 Francis Scott Key wrote "The Star-Spangled Banner." He was inspired by the endurance of Fort Henry and its troops during a British attack. His new lyrics, set to an old English drinking song, became popular immediately, encouraging interest in the flag.

_____

_____

_____

18. According to legend, Betsy Ross, a seamstress, was visited in her shop by General George Washington in June 1776. They discussed possible designs for the flag, Washington made his selection. When he left, Betsy Ross began work.

_____

_____

_____

19. This story is doubtful for several reasons, first, there is no record of a flag like the one described by Ross being flown during the Revolution. Second, the only source of the story is Ross herself, supported by her grandson, who heard the story only from her. Finally, there is no entry in Washington's appointment book or personal diary about any meeting with Betsy Ross.

_____

_____

_____

20. Information like this can be confusing. Some myths turn out to be true, and some supposedly true stories turn out to be myths. Other surprises are in store for instance, Johnny Appleseed was real, a boyhood friend of Uncle Sam.

_____

_____

_____

15 Sentences That Send Unclear Messages

A sentence can seem correct at first glance but still have flaws that keep it from delivering a sensible message. Sentences may be sending unclear messages because of shifts in person and number, in subject and voice, in tense and mood, and between direct and indirect discourse; misplaced modifiers; dangling modifiers; mixed structures; or incomplete structures.

15a Avoiding unnecessary shifts

Unless the meaning or grammatical structure of a sentence requires it, do not shift person and number, subject and voice, and tense and mood. Also, do not shift from indirect to direct discourse within a sentence without using punctuation and grammar to make the changes clear.

1 Staying consistent in person and number

Person in English includes the **first person** (*I, we*), who is the speaker; the **second person** (*you*), who is the person spoken to; and the **third person** (*he, she, it, they*), who is the person or thing being spoken about. Do not shift person within a sentence or a longer passage unless the meaning calls for a shift.

No	**We** need to select a college with care. **Your** future success may depend upon **your** choice. [*We* shifts to *your*.]
Yes	**We** need to select a college with care. **Our** future success may depend upon **our** choice.

Number refers to one (singular) and more than one (plural). Do not start to write in one number and then shift suddenly to the other.

No	A college **freshman** has to make many adjustments. **They** have to work harder and become more responsible. [The singular *freshman* shifts to the plural *they*.]
Yes	College **freshmen** have to make many adjustments. **They** have to work harder and become more responsible.

A common source of confusion in person and number is a shift to the second-person *you* from the first-person *I* or a third-person noun such as *person,* or *people*. You can avoid this error if you remember to reserve *you* for sentences that directly address the reader (10e) and to use third-person pronouns for general statements.

No	The French **president** serves for seven years. **You** can accomplish much in such a long term. [*President*, third person, shifts to *you*, second person.]
Yes	The French **president** serves for seven years. **He** can accomplish much in such a long term.
No	I would be afraid to give someone such power for so long a time. **You** might decide **you** disliked his policies. [*I*, first person, shifts to *you*, second person.]
Yes	I would be afraid to give someone such power for so long a time. **I** might decide **I** disliked his policies.

2 Staying consistent in subject and voice

The **subject** of a sentence is the word or group of words that acts, is acted upon, or is described: *The **bell** rings.* The **voice** of a sentence is either active (*The bell rings*) or passive (*The bell is rung*). Whenever possible, use the active voice.

No	The chemistry **student lit** a match too near the supplies, and some pure **oxygen was ignited**. [The subject shifts from *student* to *oxygen*, and the voice shifts from active to passive.]
Yes	The chemistry **student lit** a match too near the supplies, and **he ignited** some pure oxygen.
No	When **people heard** the explosion, **the hall was filled**.
Yes	When **people heard** the explosion, **they filled** the halls.
Yes	**People**, hearing the explosion, **filled** the halls.

3 Staying consistent in tense and mood

Tense refers to the ability of verbs to show time. Tense changes are required when time movement is described: *I expect the concert will start late*. If tense changes are illogical, the message becomes unclear.

No	Traffic accidents **kill** between forty and fifty thousand people as they **drove** on U.S. highways each year. [The tense shifts from the present *kill* to the past *drove*.]
Yes	Traffic accidents **kill** between forty and fifty thousand people as they **drive** on U.S. highways each year.
No	India **loses** few people in traffic accidents. Unfortunately, ten thousand people a year **died** of cobra bites. [The shift occurs between sentences. The present tense *loses* shifts to the past tense *died*.]
Yes	India **loses** few people in traffic accidents. Unfortunately, ten thousand people a year **die** of cobra bites.

15b

Mood refers to whether a sentence is a statement or question (**indicative mood**), a command or request (**imperative mood**), or a conditional or other-than-real statement (**subjunctive mood**). Shifts among moods blur your message. The most common shift is between the imperative and indicative moods.

No   Better home security is available to all of us. First, **install** deadbolt locks on all doors. Next, **you can install** inexpensive window locks. [The verb shifts from the imperative *install* to the indicative *you can install*.]

Yes   Better home security is available to all of us. First, **install** deadbolt locks on all doors. Next, **install** inexpensive window locks.

Yes   Better home security is available to all of us. First **you can install** deadbolt locks on all doors. Next, **you can install** inexpensive window locks.

4   Avoiding unmarked shifts between indirect and direct discourse within the same sentence

Indirect discourse *reports* speech or conversation; it is not enclosed in quotation marks. **Direct discourse** *repeats* speech or conversation exactly and encloses the spoken words in quotation marks. Sentences that mix indirect and direct discourse without quotation marks and other markers confuse readers.

No   The recruiter said I could advance in the Air Force, but do you really want to enlist? [The first clause is indirect discourse; the second shifts to unmarked direct discourse.]

Yes   The recruiter said I could advance in the Air Force, but asked whether I really wanted to enlist. [indirect discourse]

Yes   The recruiter said I could advance in the Air Force, but asked, "Do you really want to enlist?" [This revision uses direct and indirect discourse correctly.]

15b   Avoiding misplaced modifiers

A **misplaced modifier** is a description incorrectly positioned within a sentence, resulting in distorted meaning. Always check to see that your modifiers are placed as close as possible to what they describe. The various kinds of misplaced modifiers are discussed below.

An **ambiguous placement** means that a modifier can refer to two or more words in a sentence. Little limiting words (such as *only, just, almost, even, hardly, nearly, exactly, merely, scarcely, simply*) can change meaning according to where they are placed. Consider how the placement of *only* changes the meaning of this sentence: *Scientists say that the space program is important.*

> **Only** scientists say that the space program is important.
> Scientists **only** say that the space program is important.
> Scientists say **only** that the space program is important.
> Scientists say that **only** the space program is important.

Squinting modifiers also cause ambiguity. A squinting modifier appears to describe both what precedes and what follows it.

No   The dock that was constructed **partially** was destroyed by the storm. [What was partial—the construction or the destruction?]

Yes   The dock that was **partially** constructed was destroyed by the storm.

Yes   The **partially** constructed dock was destroyed by the storm.

Yes   The dock that was constructed was **partially** destroyed by the storm.

Wrong placement means that the modifiers are far from the words they logically modify.

No   The British Parliament passed a law forbidding Scots to wear kilts **in 1746**. [This sentence says kilts could not be worn only in 1746.]

Yes   **In 1746**, the British Parliament passed a law forbidding Scots to wear kilts.

No   This was an attempt, **of which the kilt was a symbol**, to destroy Scottish nationalism. [This sentence says the kilt represented the destruction of Scottish nationalism.]

Yes   This was an attempt to destroy Scottish nationalism, **of which the kilt was a symbol**.

An **awkward placement** is an interruption that seriously breaks the flow of the message. A **split infinitive** is a particularly confusing kind of awkward placement. An infinitive is a verb form that starts with *to: to buy, to sell*.

No   The herb sweet basil was thought **to**, in medieval Europe, **have** strange effects on people who ate it.

Yes   In medieval Europe, the herb sweet basil was thought **to have** strange effects on people who ate it.

Generally, avoid interruptions between subject and verb, between parts of a verb phrase, and between verb and object.

15c Avoiding dangling modifiers

A **dangling modifier** modifies what is implied but not actually stated in a sentence. Dangling modifiers can be hard for a writer to spot because the writer's brain tends to supply the missing information, but the reader cannot supply it, and confusion results.

No   **Learning about bamboo, the plant's versatility** amazed me. [This sentence says the plant's versatility is learning.]

You can correct a dangling modifier by revising the sentence so that the intended subject is expressed.

Yes   **Learning about bamboo, I** was amazed by the plant's versatility.

Yes   **I learned about bamboo** and was amazed by its versatility.

No　　When measured, **a Japanese scientist** recorded four feet of growth in one bamboo plant in twenty-four hours. [The scientist was not measured.]

Yes　　When he measured the growth of one bamboo plant, **a Japanese scientist** recorded four feet of growth in twenty-four hours.

15d Avoiding mixed sentences

A **mixed sentence** has two or more parts that do not make sense together. In a **mixed construction**, a sentence starts out taking one grammatical form and then changes, confusing the meaning.

No　　When the Pony Express's riders included Wild Bill Hickok and Buffalo Bill Cody became folk heroes. [The opening dependent clause is fused with the independent clause that follows.]

Yes　　The Pony Express's riders included Wild Bill Hickok and Buffalo Bill Cody, who became folk heroes. [*When* has been dropped, making the first clause independent; and *who* has been added, making the second clause dependent and logically related to the first.]

No　　To novelists, such as Ned Buntline, romanticized their adventures. [A prepositional phrase, such as *to novelists*, cannot be the subject of a sentence.]

Yes　　Novelists, such as Ned Buntline, romanticized their adventures. [Dropping the preposition *to* clears up the problem.]

Yes　　To novelists, such as Ned Buntline, their adventures were romantic. [Inserting a logical subject, *their adventures*, clears up the problem; an independent clause is now preceded by a modifying prepositional phrase.]

In **illogical predication**, sometimes called **faulty predication**, the subject and predicate do not make sense together.

No　　The **job** of the Pony Express riders **delivered** the mail from Saint Joseph, Missouri, to Sacramento, California.

Yes　　The Pony Express **riders delivered** the mail from Saint Joseph, Missouri, to Sacramento, California.

Yes　　The **job** of the Pony Express riders **was to deliver** the mail from Saint Joseph, Missouri, to Sacramento, California.

Illogical predication is the problem in several common, informal constructions: *is when, is where,* and *reason is because.* Avoid these constructions in academic writing.

No　　Across dangerous territory **is where** the riders traveled.

Yes　　The riders traveled across dangerous territory.

No　　**One reason** the Pony Express was so popular **was because** usual mail delivery took six weeks.

Yes　　**One reason** the Pony Express was so popular **was that** usual mail delivery took six weeks.

Yes　　The Pony Express was so popular **because** usual mail delivery took six weeks.

15e | Avoiding incomplete sentences

An **incomplete sentence** is missing words, phrases, or clauses necessary for grammatical correctness or sensible meaning. Do not confuse an incomplete sentence with an elliptical construction. An **elliptical construction** deliberately leaves out words that have already appeared in the sentence: *I have my book and Joan's [book]*. The chief rule for an elliptical comparison is that the words left out must be exactly the same as the words that do appear in the sentence.

No   When migrating, most **birds travel** 25 to 30 miles per hour, but **the goose** 60 miles per hour. [The word *travel* cannot take the place of *travels*, needed in the second clause.]

Yes   When migrating, most **birds travel** 25 to 30 miles per hour, but the **goose travels** 60 miles per hour.

No   Flying **in fog** and **water**, many migrating birds perish.

Yes   Flying **in fog** and **over water**, many migrating birds perish.

In writing a comparison, be sure to include all words needed to make clear the relationship between the items or ideas being compared.

No   Young people learn languages faster. [*Faster* indicates a comparison, but none is stated.]

Yes   Young people learn languages faster than adults do.

No   Some employers value bilingual employees more than people who speak only English. [not clear: Who values whom?]

Yes   Some employers value bilingual employees more than they value people who speak only English.

No   A French speaker's enjoyment of Paris is greater than a nonspeaker. [*Enjoyment* is compared with a *nonspeaker*; a thing cannot be compared logically with a person.]

Yes   A French speaker's enjoyment of Paris is greater than a nonspeaker's.

No   Unfortunately, foreign languages have such a reputation for difficulty. [In academic writing, comparisons begun with *such, so*, and *too* must be completed.]

Yes   Unfortunately, foreign languages have such a reputation for difficulty that many students are afraid to try to learn one.

Small words—articles, pronouns, conjunctions, and prepositions—that are needed to make sentences complete sometimes slip into the cracks. If you tend accidentally to omit words, proofread your work an extra time solely to find them.

No   Naturalists say squirrel can hide as much twenty bushels food dozens of spots, but it rarely remembers where most of food is hidden.

Yes   Naturalists say **a** squirrel can hide as much **as** twenty bushels **of** food **in** dozens of spots, but it rarely remembers where most of **its** food is hidden.

Revising to Eliminate Shifts

A: Revise this paragraph to eliminate shifts in person and number. The first sentence should become "Most people spend more money on clothes than *they* need to." Use your own paper.

Most people spend more money on clothes than you need to. With a little care, you can make the best use of their clothing budget. First, consumers should check her closets before shopping. She may even realize you don't need anything else. More likely she will have a clearer idea of what you need to buy to complement the clothes you already own. An inexpensive shirt is no bargain if nothing else in the closet matches them and a whole new outfit must be purchased to go with it. People who need to shop for a special occasion should begin early, so she can make her choice without pressure. Consumers should never buy an item without trying them on, and if possible they should shop with a friend whose judgment you trust. By shopping during off-season and clearance sales and at factory outlets, I can find quality merchandise at substantial savings. However, you should always try to buy only what you need.

B: Revise this paragraph to eliminate shifts in verb tense. The first sentence should read "No one knows why sailors *wear* bell-bottom pants." Use your own paper.

No one knows why sailors wore bell-bottom pants. However, three theories were popular. First, bell-bottoms will fit over boots and keep sea spray and rain from getting in. Second, bell-bottoms could be rolled up over the knees, so they stayed dry when a sailor must wade ashore and stayed clean when he scrubbed the ship's deck. Third, because bell-bottoms are loose, they will be easy to take off in the water if a sailor fell overboard. In boot camp, sailors were taught another advantage to bell-bottoms. By taking them off and tying the legs at the ends, a sailor who has fallen into the ocean can change his bell-bottom pants into a life preserver.

C: Identify the shift in each passage by writing its code on the line to the right: *1* for a shift in person or number, *2* in subject or voice, *3* in tense, *4* in mood, or *5* in discourse (confusing direct and indirect quotation). Then revise each sentence to eliminate the shift.

EXAMPLE My doctor told me that immunization is an important public health measure and you are due for a tetanus booster shot. _____5_____
My doctor told me that immunization is an important public health
measure and that I was due for a tetanus booster shot.

or
My doctor told me, "Immunization is an important public health
measure, and you are due for a tetanus booster shot."

1. Immunizations have a great effect on health in developed countries; in fact, it has changed the way we live. _____

_____

2. Until recently, smallpox, cholera, and diphtheria killed thousands every year, and many others were killed by tetanus and yellow fever. _____

_____

3. Now immunization keeps these diseases under control in the United States, and cases were rare. _____

_____

4. My doctor said, "You do not need a yellow fever vaccination unless a person is traveling in certain undeveloped nations." _____

_____

5. If you are traveling to an area where yellow fever is still active, see your doctor. You should get an immunization shot. _____

_____

6. Flu shots are available, but it is only partially effective. _____

_____

7. Experts agree that the flu shot can have side effects, and you should not risk taking it unless you are elderly or have breathing problems. _____

_____

8. Do not needlessly get flu shots, but you should be immunized for diphtheria, whooping cough, tetanus, polio, and smallpox. _____

_____

9. All of us should have the basic series of three tetanus shots while we are young. Then booster shots are required by us every ten years. _____

_____

10. It is hard for a person to know when you need an emergency tetanus shot.

_____

11. Minor wounds that are made by sharp, clean objects, such as knives, are usually not problems, but if dirt penetrated deep under the skin, tetanus can result.

_____

12. The tetanus germ can grow only where there is no air. They may flourish if a person has received a deep cut or puncture wound. _____

_____

13. If you have had three or more tetanus shots and if you had the last one less than five years ago, another shot is not needed by you if you are wounded. _____

_____

14. If you have had three or more shots but you had the last one more than five years ago, people should get a booster shot. _____

_____

15. If you do not have some immunity to tetanus from the three basic shots, you had to get a "supershot"—tetanus immune globulin—which is expensive and painful. _____

_____

Eliminating Misplaced
and Dangling Modifiers

A: Underline each misplaced modifier. Then revise the sentence, placing the modifier where
it belongs.

EXAMPLE   Humans <u>approximately</u> use the same amount of energy to walk as to
run.
*Humans use **approximately** the same amount of energy to walk*
as to run.

1. Contrary to popular belief, moderate exercise increases appetite scarcely.

   _____

2. Kim walked quickly going to exercise class.

   _____

3. Jogging nearly puts pressure on the feet equal to three times the body's
   weight.

   _____

4. Mostly the human body is hydrogen (63%) and oxygen (25.5%).

   _____

5. A smashed fingernail takes four to five months to grow about back.

   _____

6. The stomach's lining renews itself in less than a week, which is subject to
   corrosive digestive fluid.

   _____

7. I heard recently there are 206 bones in the human body.

   _____

8. Men have twice as much blood almost as women.

   _____

9. We are asked repeatedly to donate blood.

   _____

10. The largest bone in the human body located in the thigh is the femur.

    _____

11. People who wear glasses often do not need them as they get older.

    _____

12. One-third of Americans all the time wear glasses.

    _____

13. Hardening is a disease of the arteries that contributes to heart attacks and strokes.

   _____

14. It is a disease in the United States that leads to 850,000 deaths a year.

   _____

15. Many people don't realize it who have high blood pressure.

   _____

16. A little red meat added only to a vegetarian's diet can increase his or her risk of heart disease.

   _____

B: Revise each sentence to eliminate dangling modifiers. You may have to add or change a few words. If a sentence is acceptable as written, write *correct* on the line.

EXAMPLE   Advising a group of young women in his neighborhood, many discussions focusing on love problems were led by Samuel Richardson.
   Advising a group of young women in his neighborhood, Samuel
   Richardson led many discussions focusing on love problems.

1. Playing the role of a caring and wise father, the girls were told by Richardson how to handle various situations.

   _____

   _____

2. To help the girls, letters to their suitors were sometimes written for them by Richardson.

   _____

   _____

3. After writing a number of successful letters, the idea of writing a book of model letters occurred to Richardson.

   _____

   _____

4. To prepare the book, it included letters written as if from adults to sons, daughters, nieces, and nephews.

   _____

   _____

5. When ready to send advice, a letter was copied out by a parent, and just the names changed.

   _____

   _____

6. Bought by many, Richardson was a successful author.

   _____

   _____

7. While working on one letter, enough ideas for a whole book occurred to Richardson.

   _____

   _____

8. By writing a series of letters between a girl and her faraway parents, young readers would be entertained and instructed.

   _____

   _____

9. Upon finishing *Pamela, or Virtue Rewarded* in 1740, a new form of literature had been invented by Richardson.

   _____

   _____

10. After years of development, we call this form the novel.

    _____

11. Being a nasty person, Horace Walpole's only novel wasn't very attractive either.

    _____

12. Imitated by others for over 200 years, his *The Castle of Otranto* was the first gothic novel.

    _____

13. Although badly written, Walpole invented the themes, atmosphere, mood, and plots that have filled gothic novels ever since.

    _____

    _____

14. Featuring gloomy castles filled with dark secrets, people are entertained by gothic movies too.

    _____

    _____

C: Underline all misplaced and dangling modifiers in this paragraph. Then revise the paragraph to eliminate them. You can change or add words and otherwise revise to make the material sensible.

[1]Finding them very entertaining, the newspaper comics are popular with people today. [2]The newspaper comics got their start as a weapon in the New York war between publishers William Randolph Hearst and Joseph Pulitzer. [3]The color strip appeared in January 1894 first in Pulitzer's *New York World*. [4]Much like today's Sunday's comics, the first weekly full-color comic section came out two years later in Hearst's *Morning Journal*. [5]Seeming to have a good influence on newspaper sales, the publishers looked for more comics. [6]Away from Pulitzer, Hearst hired the cartoonist Richard Outcault. [7]The Yellow Kid was created by Outcault, the first continuous comic character to in American papers appear. [8]"The Yellow Kid" that used speech balloons was the first strip. [9]The first to incorporate all the features of modern comics, our great-grandparents enjoyed "The Katzenjammer Kids." [10]Along with replacing the larger single scene of most early comics with small panels, readers saw such modern traits as speech balloons and a continuous group of characters.

Eliminating Mixed Constructions, Faulty Predication, and Incomplete Sentences

A: Revise these mixed sentences to eliminate faulty predication and mixed constructions. It may be necessary to change, add, or omit words.

EXAMPLE   A furlong is when you measure 280 yards.
A furlong is 280 yards.

1. Beavers spend a great deal of time in the water, but did you know they do not eat fish?

2. Although pewter is traditionally made of four parts tin to one part lead, but the modern version also includes traces of zinc and copper.

3. The reason bananas are picked while green is because if left on the tree to ripen they rot before becoming edible.

4. By using the terms "dove" and "pigeon" to refer to the same bird confuses some people.

5. Because a seashell picks up and magnifies the sounds around it, so it seems to contain the roar of the sea.

6. A lake that is easy to swim in is where there is a high salt content because the salt makes the water more buoyant.

7. The fact that ducks have oil glands that waterproof their coats is the reason ducks do not get wet.

8. The reason the common housefly does not bite is because it lacks hard jaws.

_____

9. Although sugar cane and sugar beets are very different kinds of plants, but their sugars do not taste any different.

_____

10. Aldus Manutius, a late fifteenth-century Italian scholar and printer, is who invented the modern system of punctuation.

_____

11. In processing canned fish at high heat softens the bones.

_____

12. After La Paz, Bolivia, revolted when Sucre was made the official capital in 1898, so La Paz was made the co-capital.

_____

B: Revise these incomplete sentences to supply any carelessly omitted words or to complete compound constructions and comparisons clearly. Write *correct* if the sentence has no errors.

EXAMPLE   Guerrilla warfare refers the tactics used in a "small war."
          *Guerrilla warfare refers **to** the tactics used in a "small war."*

1. Dry ice is carbon dioxide; its temperature is 140° lower than regular ice.

_____

2. The custom of calling government inaction "red tape" goes back to nineteenth century and refers to the custom of tying bundles of legal documents with red ribbon.

_____

3. Because the male mosquito never bites, it is less of a pest.

_____

4. Moonbows are rare and most likely seen after showers on nights when the moon is bright and close to the horizon.

_____

5. There is more lightning in summer.

_____

6. Because it has large fat particles that easily clump, cow's milk makes butter more easily than camels.

   _____

7. A weed uses more soil nutrients than any plant.

   _____

8. Checking my apartment for loose change, I looked under the sofa, between the cushions, and the ashtrays.

   _____

9. Cormorants, large sea birds, are better at catching fish than hawks.

   _____

10. The Grateful Dead sounds better to me than Barry Manilow.

    _____

11. A puppy's paw is a more reliable indication of adult size than a human baby.

    _____

12. The Rolling Stones were more popular.

    _____

13. Always signal when making turn in traffic.

    _____

14. Opening nights on Broadway are harder to get into than plays.

    _____

C: Revise these paragraphs, changing, adding, or deleting words as you see best, in order to eliminate mixed and incomplete sentences. Circle the number of the one sentence that contains no errors.

¹The Phoenicians were who first made soap in 600 B.C. ²They discovered it from goat's fat blended with wood ash. ³They sold their soap to the Greeks and Romans as a cleanser, and it was bought by the Gauls as a laxative. ⁴With their elaborate public baths were the main place the Romans used soap.

⁵However, soap has not always been seen such a positive light. ⁶During the Middle Ages, bathing more than once a month was considered potentially fatal. ⁷Even after soap manufacturing became a big business in eleventh-century Italy and twelfth-century London, but Central Europeans were suspicious of it. ⁸The Germans seem to have been more suspicious of it than any people. ⁹In fact, when a German nobleman sent Lady von Schleinitz a gift of Venetian soap in 1672, he assumed she had little knowledge but maybe some curiosity about it. ¹⁰So he included directions on use.

16 | Conciseness

Conciseness refers to writing that is direct and to the point. In concise writing, every word contributes to the clear presentation of the author's message.

16a Eliminating wordy sentence structures

1 Revising unnecessary expletive constructions

An **expletive** postpones the subject by putting *it* or *there* plus a form of the verb *be* before the subject. If you remove the expletive and revise slightly, you place the subject in a position of greater impact—the beginning of the sentence.

> **No**   It is fun to taste foods from other cultures.
> **Yes**   Tasting foods from other cultures is fun.
>
> **No**   There is a new Greek restaurant opening in town.
> **Yes**   A new Greek restaurant is opening in town.

2 Revising unnecessary passive constructions

For most writing, the active voice (see 8j) adds liveliness as well as conciseness. When a passive construction (see 8j) names the doer of an action, it does so in a phrase starting with *by*. To change a passive sentence into an active sentence, make the noun or pronoun in the *by* phrase the subject of the sentence.

> **No**   The cafeteria was boycotted by students to protest high prices.
> **Yes**   Students boycotted the cafeteria to protest high prices.

You can also revise a sentence from passive to active by finding a new verb. In this technique you keep the same subject but change the verb voice.

> **Passive**   Clint Eastwood **was elected** mayor of Carmel, California.
> **Active**   Clint Eastwood **won** the mayoral election in Carmel, California.

3 | Combining sentences, reducing clauses to phrases, and reducing phrases to words when possible

Often when you revise you can combine sentences or reduce a clause to a phrase or a phrase to a single word, making your writing more concise and your original idea clearer.

Combining sentences: Look carefully at sets of sentences in your draft. You may be able to reduce the information in an entire sentence to a group of words that you can include in another sentence.

TWO SENTENCES	In 1985, Mel Fisher found *Nuestra Señora de Atocha* 40 miles west of Key West, Florida. The *Atocha* was a Spanish treasure ship.
COMBINED SENTENCE	In 1985, Mel Fisher found the Spanish treasure ship *Nuestra Señora de Atocha* 40 miles west of Key West, Florida.
TWO SENTENCES	The *Atocha* was heading for Spain in 1622 when it sank in a hurricane. It was loaded with gold and silver.
COMBINED SENTENCE	The *Atocha* was heading for Spain in 1622 when it sank in a hurricane, along with its load of gold and silver.

Reducing clauses: You can often reduce adjective clauses (see 7n-2) to phrases, sometimes just by dropping the relative pronoun and its verb.

Earlier, Fisher had found the *Santa Margarita*, **which was the *Atocha*'s sister ship**.

Earlier, Fisher had found the *Santa Margarita*, **the *Atocha*'s sister ship**.

Sometimes you can reduce the clause to a single word.

Fisher's find will make **people who invested in his company** rich.
Fisher's find will make **investors** rich.

Creating elliptical constructions (7n-2) is another way to reduce clauses, but be sure to omit only strongly implied words.

While they were searching for the *Atocha*, Fisher's son and daughter-in-law drowned.
While searching for the *Atocha*, Fisher's son and daughter-in-law drowned.

Reducing phrases: You may be able to shorten phrases or reduce them to single words.

In 1966, Fisher had begun to search for **the fleet that the *Atocha* was leading**.
In 1966, Fisher had begun to search for **the *Atocha* fleet**.

In twenty years, Fisher found more than a hundred **ships that had been wrecked**.
In twenty years, Fisher found more than a hundred **shipwrecks**.

4 Using strong verbs and avoiding nouns formed from verbs

Your writing will have more impact when you choose strong verbs—verbs that directly convey action—instead of forms of *be* or *have*. Using strong verbs also reduces the number of words in your sentences.

No	The city council **has a plan** to build a new stadium.
Yes	The city council **plans** to build a new stadium.

No	Being home to a professional baseball team **is a way to promote** civic pride.
Yes	Being home to a professional baseball team **promotes** civic pride.

When you look for weak verbs to revise, look too for **nominals**—nouns created from verbs, often by adding suffixes such as *-ance, -ment*, or *-tion*. For clear, concise writing, turn nominals back into verbs.

No	The company **was involved in the importation** of catchers' mitts.
Yes	The company **imported** catchers' mitts.

16b Eliminating unneeded words

Imprecise and showy language creates wordiness. See 21d for advice on recognizing and avoiding showy (pretentious) language. When a writer tries to write very formally or tries to reach an assigned word limit, **padding** usually results. Sentences are loaded down with **deadwood**—empty words and phrases that add nothing but confusion.

Padded	The lifeguards, who watch out for the safety of beachgoers, closed the beach near the water when a shark was sighted and seen.
Concise	The lifeguards closed the beach when a shark was sighted.

Padded	After two hours, a fishing boat full of fishermen reported seeing the shark leave the local area of the shore, so the beach was declared reopened to the public.
Concise	Two hours later, a fishing boat reported seeing the shark leave the area, so the beach was reopened.

On the next page is a chart showing a few of the most common empty phrases. For a more complete list, refer to the *Simon & Schuster Handbook for Writers*, Chapter 16.

RECOGNITION AND REVISION LIST OF EMPTY WORDS AND PHRASES

EMPTY WORD OR PHRASE	WORDY EXAMPLE	REVISION
as a matter of fact	**As a matter of fact**, statistics show that many marriages end in divorce.	Statistics show that many marriages end in divorce.
because of the fact that	**Because of the fact that** a special exhibit is scheduled, the museum will be open until ten o'clock.	Because of a special exhibit, the museum will be open until ten o'clock.
in fact	**In fact**, the physicist published her results yesterday.	The physicist published her results yesterday.
in view of the fact that	**In view of the fact that** the rainfall was so heavy, we may have flooding.	Because the rainfall was so heavy, we may have flooding.
seems	It **seems** that the union called a strike over health benefits.	The union called a strike over health benefits.
tendency	The team had a **tendency** to lose home games.	The team often lost home games.

16c Revising redundancies

Intentional repetition can create a powerful effect, but unplanned repetition of words or ideas (known as **redundancy**) can make an essay boring.

No The college is building a new **parking lot** to provide more **parking space.**

YES The college is building a new **lot** to provide more **parking space.**

No The model was **slender in shape** and **tall in height**.

YES The model was **slender** and **tall**.

Eliminating Wordy Sentence Structures

Revise these sentences to eliminate wordy sentence structures. You may need to delete expletives, change passive sentences to the active voice, reduce clauses to phrases or phrases to words, and/or replace weak, heavily modified verbs with strong direct verbs.

EXAMPLE   There was a Spanish expedition to the west coast of Florida led by Pánfilo de Narvaéz in 1528.
In 1528 Pánfilo de Narvaéz led a Spanish expedition to the west
coast of Florida.

1. The environment, which was hostile, and the native inhabitants, namely Indians, soon led to most of the expedition members becoming dead.

   _____

2. One of the survivors and the leader of the others was Alvar Núñez Cabeza de Vaca, who had been the expedition's treasurer.

   _____

3. The men who were the surviving members of the crew built barges, hoping to sail across the waters of the Gulf of Mexico to Mexico City.

   _____

4. There was an accident on the way, and the barges were sunk.

   _____

5. Cabeza and the three other survivors were put into slavery by the local Indian inhabitants of the area.

   _____

6. It was after four and a half years of slavery that they made their escape and left.

   _____

7. They walked over a thousand miles across the desert of the American Southwest, which was unexplored.

   _____

8. It took them three years to walk, going across Texas, New Mexico, and Arizona.

   _____

9. Amazingly, they were without any clothing for most of the walk.

_____

10. A Spanish outpost in northern Mexico was finally reached in 1536.

_____

Eliminating Unneeded Words

Revise these sentences to eliminate unneeded words and phrases.

EXAMPLE Monster movies have always been popular for the reason that most people like being scared.
Monster movies have always been popular because most people like being scared.

1. In spite of the fact that _Frankenstein_ was written in 1818, movie versions of the novel are still immensely popular.

_____

2. The first case of a sound version of _Frankenstein_ was the 1931 movie starring Boris Karloff.

_____

3. Movie critics have a tendency to claim this is the best film version of the tale.

_____

4. Up to this point in time there have been about thirty Frankenstein movies and about forty Dracula movies.

_____

5. The best Dracula movies are not of a gruesome nature.

_____

6. Instead, Dracula, starting with actor Bela Lugosi, has been portrayed in a sophisticated and even sexy manner.

_____

7. Movie makers got clues to the character and appearance of the Wolfman by means of studying earlier films, such as _Dr. Jekyll and Mr. Hyde._

_____

8. The first sound version of *Dr. Jekyll and Mr. Hyde*, made in 1931, for all intents and purposes is the best ever, as can be confirmed by the fact that critics agree.

_____

9. Frederic March received the Best Actor Oscar for this movie due to the fact that his performance was brilliant in a very real sense.

_____

10. He became the only performer ever to win for a film in the nature of a horror movie.

_____

Eliminating Redundancies

EXERCISE 16-3
(16c)

Revise these passages to eliminate unnecessary repetition of words and redundant ideas. Retain helpful repetition.

EXAMPLE   Greek plays were connected to religious ceremonies, so the men who performed and acted in them had high social status.
Greek plays were connected to religious ceremonies, so the men _____
who performed in them had high social status. _____

1. In Rome, however, the usual custom was for actors to be slaves.

_____

2. The first professional actors acted in sixteenth-century Europe.

_____

3. There were no female actresses until the sixteenth century.

_____

4. The first genuine indoor public theater was opened in the city of Paris in the middle of the sixteenth century in the year 1548.

_____

5. It had a pit for standing patrons to stand in.

   _____

6. It also had expensive seats that cost more money in raised rows and boxes.

   _____

7. Earlier, before this time, plays had been performed in churches, homes, and schools.

   _____

8. In 1566 an Italian architect wrote suggestions for stage lighting. He said that lights of different colors could be made by shining light through bottles of wine. Shining a light through a bottle of red wine would produce red light. A light passing through white wine would create amber light. And using aqua vitae would make blue light.

   _____

   _____

   _____

   _____

9. Genuine American theater began in New York in 1787 with a production at the John Street Theater. The group produced *The Contrast*, the first production of a play by an American author with an American setting.

   _____

   _____

10. The first true musical play was *Showboat* (1927), a musical based on an Edna Ferber novel with music by Jerome Kern, the composer.

    _____

    _____

Revising for Conciseness

Revise these paragraphs to eliminate wordiness, pointless repetitions, and redundancies. Combine sentences as necessary.

A: The deadly bubonic plague was a disease that killed one-third of Europe's population of people. It was in the fourteenth century. This Asian disease came from Asia. It began this way. To begin with, there was a group of merchants from Genoa. They were attacked by infected bandits while they were at a Crimean trading outpost. They became infected. Diseased corpses were thrown over the outpost walls by the bandits, and this was a factor in the merchants catching the plague. Many of the merchants got the disease. They had a tendency to die from the disease. Those who were survivors of the disease went home. The plague was brought back with them. The first European city to have an outbreak was Constantinople in Europe. This happened in 1334. The disease had symptoms of a horrible nature. The disease then spread to the rest of Europe.

B: There is bleeding when a blood vessel is damaged or hurt. If the vessel that is carrying the blood is on the inside of the body in question, blood tends to ooze and seep into the tissue which is nearby, and a bruise is formed. Where blood vessels of a delicate nature are near the surface instead of down inside the skin or the body, even a small and little injury can cause bleeding to take place. This is why a nosebleed from the nose may occur after an event that is usually more or less harmless, such as when a person sneezes. Minor bleeding is almost always, that is in most cases, harmless. It seems that the body of the person who is bleeding automatically takes three steps to stop the bleeding. Here are the three steps the body takes. First, blood vessels near the area of the wound get narrow. This action causes a reduction of the flow of blood to the area that is bleeding. Second, small cells in the blood, which are called platelets, gather at the damaged area. They stick at the damaged area. They form a plug there. Third, strands of another material form in the area. This material is called fibrin. The fibrin traps blood cells in its strands. Because of the fact that enough cells are stuck together by fibrin, a clot is formed and the bleeding stopped. This usually doesn't take much time at all. It usually occurs in ten minutes or even less.

17 | Coordination and Subordination

Coordination and subordination make it possible for your writing style to work together with your meaning. **Coordination** of sentences gives equal weight to your ideas, and **subordination** emphasizes one idea over others.

COORDINATION

A **coordinate** (or **compound**) **sentence** consists of independent clauses (7n) joined by a semicolon or a coordinating conjunction (*and, but, for, nor, or, so*, or *yet*). ✤ PUNCTUATION ALERT: Always put a comma before a coordinating conjunction that joins two independent clauses. ✤

COORDINATE (COMPOUND SENTENCE

	, and	
	, but	
	, for	
	, nor	
Independent clause	, or	independent clause.
	, so	
	, yet	
	;	

Each coordinating conjunction has a specific meaning that establishes the relationship between the ideas in a coordinate sentence.

MEANING OF THE COORDINATING CONJUNCTIONS

CONJUNCTION	MEANING	FUNCTION
and	also, in addition to	to join
but	however	to contrast
for	because	to show cause
nor	an additional negative	to make the second element negative
or	an alternative	to show more than one possibility
so	therefore	to show result
yet	nevertheless	to contrast

Tuition was increasing, **and** the price of the meal plan was going up even more. Her schedule was tight, **but** she knew she needed to get a job.

17a Using coordinate sentences to show relationships

Coordinate sentences communicate that the ideas in each independent clause carry equal weight. At the same time, they explain the relationships among those ideas more effectively than a group of separate sentences would.

UNCLEAR RELATIONSHIPS	We planned a picnic. It rained. We had brought a lot of food. We had to make other arrangements. The food would spoil. We went to the ballfield in the park to use the dugout. It was full of water. We all went home.
CLEAR RELATIONSHIPS	We planned a picnic, **but** it rained. We had brought a lot of food, **so** we had to make other arrangements, **or** the food would spoil. We went to the ballfield in the park to use the dugout, **but** it was full of water, **so** we all went home.

17b Using coordinate sentences for occasional effect

Coordination can be used to pile up details for dramatic effect. Consider this passage, in which coordinate sentences present an unfolding of events.

> Scott woke up before the alarm went off. He was hungry, **but** he skipped breakfast. He raced to the showroom, **and** then he had to stand in the cold for fifteen minutes waiting for the place to open. Finally, the manager arrived, **but** before he could put the key in the lock, Scott blurted out, "I got this card; it says my car has arrived."

17c Avoiding misusing coordination

Coordination is illogical when ideas in the joined independent clauses are not related and when ideas do not unfold in a purposeful sequence. Avoid illogically coordinated sentences.

No   Bicycles are becoming a popular means of transportation, **and** they are dangerous on city streets. [Each independent clause is true, but the ideas are not related.]

Yes   Bicycles are becoming a popular means of transportation, **yet** the crowded conditions on city streets can make riding them dangerous.

Like all good techniques, coordination can be used too often. Overused coordination can result from writing down whatever comes into your head and not revising later. Avoid overusing coordination.

No   Hawaii is famous for its coral, **and** some of it is very shiny and hard, **so** it can last indefinitely. Some Hawaiian coral is black, **and** some is gold or pink, **and** Hawaii has $10 million a year in coral sales, **but** worldwide sales are $500 million a year.

Yes   Hawaii is famous for its coral. Some of it is very shiny and hard enough to last indefinitely. Hawaiian coral comes in black, gold, and pink. Although Hawaii has $10 million a year in coral sales, worldwide sales are $500 million a year.

No   Laughter seems to help healing, so many doctors are prescribing humor for their patients, and some hospitals are doing the same. Comedians have donated their time to several California hospitals, and the nurses in one large hospital in Texas have been trained to tell each patient a joke a day.

Yes   Laughter seems to help healing. Many doctors and hospitals are prescribing humor for their patients. Comedians have donated their time to several California hospitals, and the nurses in one large hospital in Texas have been asked to tell each patient a joke a day.

SUBORDINATION

A sentence that uses subordination contains at least two clauses: (1) an **independent clause** (7n), which can stand on its own as a sentence, and (2) a **dependent clause**, which cannot stand alone. Subordination joins related but separate items so that one is featured—the one in the independent clause.

Some dependent clauses start with **subordinating conjunctions**, words such as *after, before, until, when, so that* and *although*. ✣ PUNCTUATION ALERTS: (1) When a dependent clause that starts with a subordinating conjunction occurs before the independent clause, separate the clauses with a comma. (2) When such a clause follows the independent clause, separate the clauses with a comma *unless* the dependent clause is essential to the meaning of the independent clause (24e). ✣

While tuition had increased, the price of the meal plan had gone up even more.

Although her schedule was tight, she knew she needed to get a job.

Some dependent clauses start with **relative pronouns**, such as *who, which,* and *that*. Dependent clauses that begin with relative pronouns are called **relative clauses** (or **adjective clauses**). They either follow or interrupt the independent clauses they modify. ✣ PUNCTUATION ALERT: When an adjective clause is nonrestrictive—that is, when the clause is not essential to the meaning of the sentence—separate it from the independent clause with commas. ✣

Tuition, **which was high**, increased again.

The student, **who was already on a tight schedule**, needed to get a job.

17d Using subordination to show relationships

Subordination directs your reader's attention to the idea in the independent clause, while using the ideas in the dependent clause to provide context and support. Subordination communicates relationships among ideas more effectively than a group of separate sentences does.

UNCLEAR RELATIONSHIPS	I waited at the bus station. I thought I saw Marcia. She was my baby-sitter fifteen years ago. I was gathering the courage to approach her. She boarded a bus and was gone.
CLEAR RELATIONSHIPS	As I waited at the bus station, I thought I saw Marcia, who was my baby-sitter fifteen years ago. While I was gathering the courage to approach her, she boarded a bus and was gone.

17e Choosing the subordinating conjunction appropriate to your meaning

Each subordinating conjunction expresses a different relationship between the major and minor ideas in the subordinate sentences.

SUBORDINATING CONJUNCTIONS AND THE RELATIONSHIPS THEY IMPLY	
Time	*after, before, once, since, until, when, whenever, while*
Reason or Cause	*as, because*
Result or Effect	*in order that, so that*
Condition	*if, even if, provided that, unless*
Concession	*although, even though, though*
Location	*where, wherever*
Choice	*rather than, than, whether*

Notice how a change in the subordinating conjunction can change your meaning.

After you have been checked in, you cannot leave the security area without a pass. [time limit]

Because you have been checked in, you cannot leave the security area without a pass. [reason]

Unless you have been checked in, you cannot leave the security area without a pass. [condition]

Although you have been checked in, you cannot leave the security area without a pass. [concession]

17f Avoiding misusing subordination

Subordination is illogical when the subordinating conjunction does not make clear the relationship between the independent and dependent clauses. Avoid illogical subordination.

No   Before some states made wearing seat belts mandatory, the number of fatal automobile accidents fell. [illogical: The fatality rate fell as a result of, not prior to, the seat belt laws.]

Yes   After some states made wearing seat belts mandatory, the number of fatal automobile accidents fell.

No   Because he was deaf when he wrote them, Beethoven's final symphonies were masterpieces. [illogical: It was not Beethoven's deafness that led to his writing symphonic masterpieces.]

Yes   Although Beethoven was deaf when he wrote his final symphonies, they are musical masterpieces.

Like all good writing techniques, subordination can be overused. Overusing subordination means crowding together too many images or ideas, so that readers become confused and lose track of the message. Avoid overusing subordination.

No   As a result of water pollution, many shellfish beds, which once supported many families that had lived in the areas for generations, are being closed, which is causing hardships for these families.

Yes   As a result of water pollution, many shellfish beds are being closed. This is causing hardships for the many families that have supported themselves for generations by harvesting these waters.

No   A new technique for eye surgery, which is supposed to correct near-sightedness, which previously could be corrected only by glasses, has been developed, although many doctors do not approve of it because it can create unstable eyesight.

Yes   A new technique for eye surgery, which is supposed to correct near-sightedness, has been developed. Previously, nearsightedness could be corrected only by glasses. Because it can create unstable eyesight, many doctors do not approve of it, however.

17g Achieving a balance between subordination and coordination

Coordination and subordination are not always used in separate sentences. **Compound-complex sentences**, combine coordination with subordination to make sentences that flow.

Since only a few people are supposed to have this mathematical mind, part of what makes us so passive in the face of our difficulties in learning mathematics is that we suspect all the while we may not be one of "them," and we spend our time waiting to find out when our nonmathematical minds will be exposed.

—Sheila Tobias, *Overcoming Math Anxiety*

Combining Sentences
with Coordination

Combine these sentences using coordination. For the first five sentences, use the coordinating conjunction given; for the rest, use whatever coordinating conjunction you feel is most appropriate. It may be necessary to add or change a few words, but major rewriting is not needed.

EXAMPLE   *TV Guide* was not the first television magazine with local listings.
It has become the most popular. (but)
TV Guide *was not the first television magazine with local listings,*
but it has become the most popular.

1. In 1952 publisher Walter H. Annenberg heard that someone was considering starting a national television magazine.
He became interested in the idea himself. (and)

_____

2. He wanted to learn about his competition.
He had one of his assistants find out if such magazines already existed. (so)

_____

3. The assistant found local television magazines being published in New York, Philadelphia, Chicago, and Los Angeles.
Annenberg bought them all. (;)

_____

4. Articles to appear in the first issue were written quickly.
There was no supply of already completed work to rely on. (for)

_____

5. One of the first people hired was sportswriter Red Smith.
This was before he won a Pulitzer Prize for sports reporting. (but)

_____

6. Starting the magazine was hard work.
One decision was not hard at all.

_____

7. *I Love Lucy* was the most popular show on the air in 1953.
   The star, Lucille Ball, had just given birth to a baby boy.

   _____

8. The whole country had followed Lucy's pregnancy.
   The editors decided to take advantage of this interest and to feature the baby, Desi Arnaz, Jr.

   _____

9. They could not ignore the baby's popularity.
   They could not ignore Lucy's popularity.

   _____

10. The cover had a big picture of Desi, Jr.
    It had a smaller picture of Lucy in the upper right-hand corner.

    _____

11. From the beginning *TV Guide* has been a national magazine.
    It has different editions, giving local listings.

    _____

12. Sales fell soon after the first, successful issue.
    Summer had come.
    People preferred to sit outside in the cool night air rather than watch television in their hot living rooms.

    _____

13. The editors had to have a sudden great idea.
    The magazine would fail.

    _____

14. They needed to increase interest in their subject.
    They decided to devote one issue to the new shows scheduled for the 1953–54 season.

    _____

15. That first Fall Preview issue sold out.
    It started a tradition that is repeated at the start of every new television season.

    _____

Combining Sentences with Subordination

EXERCISE 17-2
(17d-f)

Combine these sentences using subordination. For the first five sentences, use the subordinating conjunction or relative pronoun given; for the rest, use whatever subordinating conjunction or relative pronoun you feel is most appropriate. Some items have more than one correct answer, but most make sense only one way, so decide carefully which sentence comes first and where to place the subordinating conjunction or relative pronoun. It may sometimes be necessary to add or change a few words, but major rewriting is not needed.

EXAMPLE   Readers in the 1920s wanted to be well-informed. No one had the time or money to read all the popular magazines. (although)

Although readers in the 1920s wanted to be well-informed, no one had the time or money to read all the popular magazines.

1. DeWitt Wallace was a minister's son.
   He had an idea for a new magazine. (who)

   _____

2. Wallace planned to select the most important articles in all the magazines, condense them, and gather them in one place.
   People could keep up-to-date. (so that)

   _____

3. He prepared a sample issue without knowing something.
   He could get a publisher. (whether)

   _____

4. He sent two hundred copies of his magazine to possible financial backers.
   None of them offered to help him. (after)

   _____

5. Wallace and his fiancée got married.
   They continued to work on the magazine. (before)

   _____

6. They prepared for their wedding.
   They continued to condense magazine articles.

   _____

7. They printed a notice offering subscriptions.
   They mailed it to thousands of people.

   _____

8. They returned from their honeymoon two weeks later.
   They found 1,500 people had sent in money for subscriptions.

   _____

9. They now had plenty of customers.
   They got to work immediately on the first issue of *Reader's Digest*.

   _____

10. They found success.
    They had a new problem.

    _____

11. In the beginning other magazines were glad to have their articles reprinted.
    The Wallaces did not pay them for the articles.

    _____

12. The other magazines considered a reprinted article good publicity.
    Reader's Digest became successful enough to be competition.

    _____

13. The *Reader's Digest* began to take away readers and advertising fees.
    Many magazines refused to give permission for any more reprints.

    _____

14. For a while, Wallace paid for articles to be written for other small
    magazines with the understanding that he would be able to reprint them.
    He needed articles, and some of his best sources had been cut off.

    _____

15. The practice was stopped in the 1950s.
    Many people complained, saying the policy was dishonest.

    _____

Expanding Sentences with
Coordination and Subordination

Add to each sentence below in two ways. First add an independent clause, using a coordinating conjunction. Then add a dependent clause beginning with either a subordinating conjunction or a relative pronoun.

EXAMPLE   Traveling by balloon is exciting.
           Traveling by balloon is exciting, and I hope to do it again soon.
           Traveling by balloon is exciting because the wind is unpredictable.

1. Wrestling is popular.

   _____

   _____

2. Dogs are smarter than cats.

   _____

   _____

3. Cooking can be creative.

   _____

   _____

4. Practicing the drums can drive the neighbors crazy.

   _____

   _____

5. The camel is a strange animal.

   _____

   _____

6. Baby-sitting is not easy.

   _____

   _____

7. Always read a contract before you sign it.

   _____

   _____

8. The condition of the roads is terrible.

_____

_____

9. Some people do not like miniskirts.

_____

_____

10. The car battery was dead.

_____

_____

Using Coordination and Subordination in a Paragraph

These paragraphs are full of choppy sentences. Revise them using coordinating and subordinating conjunctions so that the sentences are smoother and more fully explain the relationships between ideas. Many correct versions are possible. Take the time to try several, and select the version you like best.

Growing seasons are short. Food is likely to spoil. Spoilage occurs after just a short time. For centuries people have used various methods of preserving food. There were several early methods. The most popular included pickling and smoking. Then in 1795, the French government offered a reward. The reward was to be given to someone. This someone had to develop a means of preserving food. The food had to be preserved conveniently for long periods of time. The French wanted to send the food to troops in the field. Nicholas Appert was a chef. He spent fourteen years perfecting his method.

His method was based on a theory. Appert believed that spoilage could be prevented. Food had to be sealed in airtight bottles. Appert did this. He plunged jars filled with food into boiling water for several hours. He plugged the jars with cork. He sealed them with wax. The food was sampled months later. It tasted fresh. The government panel was shocked. It gave Appert the reward. He took the prize money. He opened a bottlery. It remained open until 1933.

18 Parallelism

Parallelism is related to the concept of parallel lines in geometry. In writing, parallelism calls for the use of equivalent grammatical forms to express equivalent ideas. Parallel forms match words with words in the same form, phrases with similar phrases, or clauses with other clauses composed of the same verb forms and word orders.

Parallelism helps you communicate that two or more items in a group are equally important and makes your writing more graceful. For this reason, it is a good idea to avoid the error of faulty **parallelism**—using nonequivalent grammatical patterns.

PARALLEL WORDS	A triathlon includes **running, swimming**, and **cycling**. [The -ings are parallel in form and equal in importance.]
PARALLEL PHRASES	Training requires **an intense exercise program** and **a carefully regulated diet**. [The phrases are parallel in structure and equal in importance.]
PARALLEL CLAUSES	Most people prefer to watch the triathalon rather than participate **because the triathalon is so difficult** and **because their couches are so comfortable**. [The clauses starting with because are parallel in structure and equal in importance.]

18a Using words in parallel form

Words in lists or other parallel structures must occur in the same grammatical form. Be sure to use such matching forms for parallel items.

No	The warm-up includes **stretches, sit-ups**, and **sprinting**.
YES	The warm-up includes **stretches, sit-ups**, and **sprints**.
YES	The warm-up includes **stretching, doing sit-ups**, and **sprinting**.
No	The strikers had tried **pleading, threats**, and **shouting**.
YES	The strikers had tried **pleading, threatening**, and **shouting**.
YES	The strikers had tried **pleas, threats**, and **shouts**.

18b Using phrases and clauses in parallel form

Phrases and clauses in parallel structures must occur in the same grammatical form. Be sure to use such matching forms for parallel items.

No   The kitchen crew **scraped the grill, the salt shakers were refilled,** and **were taking out the trash**.

Yes   The kitchen crew **scraped the grill, refilled the salt shakers,** and **took out the trash**.

18c Being aware that certain words call for parallel structures

Whenever you join words, phrases, or clauses with coordinating conjunctions or correlative conjunctions (7h), be sure that they occur in parallel form.

> Absence *diminishes little passions* **and** *increases great ones*, as wind *extinguishes candles* **and** *fans a fire*.
>
> —François de La Rochefoucauld

> We are the carriers of health and disease—**either** *the divine health of courage and nobility* **or** *the demonic disease of hate and anxiety*.
>
> —Joshua Loth Liebman

To strengthen the effect of parallelism, repeat words that begin parallel phrases or clauses. Such words include prepositions (7g), articles (*a, an, the*), and the *to* of an infinitive (7d).

> **To** *find* a fault is easy; **to** *do* better may be difficult.
>
> —Plutarch

Use parallel clauses beginning with *and who, and whom,* or *and which* when they follow clauses beginning with *who, whom* or *which*.

> I have in my own life a precious friend, a woman of 65 **who has** lived very hard, **who is** wise, **who listens** well, **who has** been where I am and can help me understand it; **and who represents** not only an ultimate ideal mother to me but also the person I'd like to be when I grow up.
>
> —Judith Viorst, "Friends, Good Friends—and Such Good Friends"

18d Using parallel sentences in longer passages for impact

Parallel sentences in longer passages provide coherence (4b). The carefully controlled repetition of words and word forms creates a pattern that enables readers to follow ideas more easily.

18e Using parallel structure for formal outlines and lists

Items in formal outlines and lists should be in parallel structure. Without parallelism, the information may not be clear to the reader and may not communicate that the items are equally important. (For information about developing outlines, see 2e).

Outline not in parallel form

TYPES OF FIRE EXTINGUISHERS

   I.   The Class A Type
       A.   Contains water or water-chemical solution
       B.   For fighting wood, paper, or cloth fires
  II.   Class B
       A.   Foam, dry chemicals, or carbon dioxide "snow"
       B.   Use against grease or flammable-liquid fires
 III.   C
       A.   Containing dry chemicals
       B.   Electrical fires

Outline in parallel form

TYPES OF FIRE EXTINGUISHERS

   I.   **Class** A
       A.   **Contains** water or water-chemical solution;
       B.   **Fights** wood, paper, or cloth fires
  II.   **Class** B
       A.   **Contains** foam, dry chemicals, or carbon dioxide "snow"
       B.   **Fights** grease or flammable-liquid fires
 III.   **Class** C
       A.   **Contains** dry chemicals;
       B.   **Fights** electrical fires

18e

List not in parallel form

HOW TO ESCAPE A FIRE

1. Feel the door for heat, and don't open it if it is hot.
2. You should open the door slowly.
3. Smoke?
4. If there is smoke, close the door and leave by another door or window.
5. If there is no other exit—try crawling under the smoke.
6. Be sure to use the stairs; the elevator should be avoided.
7. The fire department.
8. Reenter the building? No!

List in parallel form

HOW TO ESCAPE A FIRE

1. **Feel** the door for heat; **do** not **open** it if it is hot.
2. **Open** the door slowly.
3. **Check** the hall for smoke.
4. **If there is** smoke, **close** the door and **leave** by another door or window.
5. **If there is** no other exit, **crawl** under the smoke.
6. **Use** stairs, never an elevator.
7. **Call** the fire department.
8. **Do** not **reenter** the building.

Identifying Parallel Elements

Underline parallel words, phrases, and clauses.

EXAMPLE   Many ancient writers <u>in Greece</u> and <u>in Rome</u> wrote about underwater ships.

1. They hoped these ships would be used for exploration and travel.

2. Leonardo Da Vinci felt that humanity would be destroyed by a great flood because of its proud and evil ways.

3. Therefore, just as earlier he had made plans for a helicopter, he made plans for an underwater ship.

4. However, the first working submarine was designed by a British mathematician and built by a Dutch inventor.

5. It was designed in 1578, built in 1620, and successfully tested from 1620 to 1624.

6. This submarine was equipped with oars, so it could be used either on the surface or below the surface.

7. King James I of England actually boarded the submarine and took a short ride.

8. James's praise soon made submarines the talk of the town and the focus of scientific investigation.

9. A much later model featured goatskin bags attached to holes in the bottom of the ship. When the vessel was to submerge, the bags would fill with water and pull the ship downward; when the vessel was to rise, a twisting rod would force water from the bags, and the lightened ship would surface.

10. David Bushnell, a student at Yale during the American Revolution, designed and built a war-submarine, the *Turtle*.

11. It was intended to sneak up on British warships and attach explosives to their hulls.

12. Despite successful launching and steering, the *Turtle* failed on its only mission when the pilot was unable to attach the explosives to the British target ship.

13. The first successful wartime submarines were developed by the South in the Civil War: small, four-person ships called ''Davids'' and a full-sized submarine called the ''Hunley.''

14. New submarines were designed throughout the nineteenth century, but providing dependable power and seeing to navigate remained problems for years.

15. The development of the gasoline engine and the invention of the periscope solved these problems before the beginning of World War I.

Writing Parallel Elements

Fill in the blanks with words, phrases, or clauses, as appropriate.

EXAMPLE   Her hobbies include *hiking, playing tennis,* and *listening to jazz.*

1. He keeps gaining weight because he loves _____ but hates _____ .

2. Many Americans would like to travel to both _____ and _____ .

3. _____ a television is easier than _____ one.

4. After graduation, I plan to get a good job, _____ , and _____ .

5. A new factory, which will _____ and _____ , is opening across town.

6. A successful picnic has no _____ and no _____ .

7. The best food in town is found at _____ and _____ .

8. The student who _____ and _____ will speak at graduation.

9. It is better to _____ than never _____ .

10. I'll take math at either _____ or _____ .

11. She is on the run all day, _____ , _____ , and _____ .

12. After the _____ and _____ received a pay raise, the ambulance drivers demanded one too.

13. When her child wandered off in the department store, the woman looked for him _____ , _____ , and _____ .

14. Professional dancers have to be _____ and _____ .

15. I want to marry someone who _____ and _____ .

19 Variety and Emphasis

Your writing style has **variety** when your sentence lengths and patterns vary. Your writing style has **emphasis** when your sentences are constructed to reflect the relative importance of your ideas. Variety and emphasis are closely related. They represent the joining of form and meaning.

19a Varying sentence length

If you vary your sentence length, you signal distinctions among your ideas so that your readers can understand the focus of your material. Also you avoid the monotony created by an unvarying rhythm.

Strings of too many short sentences rarely establish relationships and levels of importance among ideas. Such strings suggest that the writer has not thought through the material and decided what to emphasize.

No   Ants are much like human beings. It is embarrassing. They farm fungi. They raise aphids as livestock. They launch armies into wars. They use chemical sprays to alarm and confuse enemies. They capture slaves.

Yes   Ants are so much like human beings as to be an embarrassment. They farm fungi, raise aphids as livestock, launch armies into wars, use chemical sprays to alarm and confuse enemies, capture slaves.

—Lewis Thomas, "On Societies as Organisms"

Too often, compound sentences are only short sentences strung together with *and* or *but*, without consideration of the relationships among the ideas. Consider this passage, which babbles along.

No   Sodium is an element and some people think it is the same as salt, but sodium is just one element in salt, and it also contains chlorine.

Yes   Sodium is an element. Some people think it is the same as salt; however, sodium is just one element in salt. In fact, salt also contains chlorine.

As can be seen in the passage below, you can emphasize one idea among many others by expressing it in a sentence noticeably different in length or structure from the sentences surrounding it.

> Mistakes are not believed to be part of the normal behavior of a good machine. **If things go wrong, it must be a personal, human error, the result of fingering, tampering, a button getting stuck, someone hitting the wrong key.** The computer, at its normal best, is infallible. **I wonder whether this can be true.**
>
> —Lewis Thomas, "To Err Is Human"

19b Using an occasional question, mild command, or exclamation

To vary your sentence structure and to emphasize material, you can call on four basic sentence types. The most typical English sentence is **declarative:** it makes a statement—it declares something. A sentence that asks a question is called **interrogative**. Occasional questions help you involve your reader. A sentence that issues a mild or strong command is called **imperative**. Occasional mild commands are particularly helpful for gently urging your reader to think along with you. A sentence that makes an exclamation is called **exclamatory**.

Consider the following examples from *Change!* by Isaac Asimov.

Question   The colonization of space may introduce some unexpected changes into human society. **For instance, what effect will it have on the way we keep time?** Our present system of time keeping is a complicated mess that depends on accidents of astronomy and on 5,000 years of primitive habit.

Mild Command   **Consider the bacteria.** These are tiny living things made up of single cells far smaller than the cells in plants and animals.

Exclamation   **The amazing thing about the netting of the coelacanth was that till then zoologists had been convinced the fish had been extinct for 60 million years!** Finding a living dinosaur would not have been more surprising.

19c Choosing the subject of your sentence according to your intended emphasis

Because the subject of a sentence establishes the focus for that sentence, choose a subject that corresponds to the emphasis you want to communicate. The following sentences, each of which is correct grammatically, contain the same information. Consider, however, how changes of the subject (and its verb) influence meaning and impact.

Our **poll shows** that most voters prefer Jones. [emphasis on the poll]

Most **voters prefer** Jones, according to our poll. [emphasis on the voters]

Jones is preferred by most voters, according to our poll. [emphasis on Jones]

19d Adding modifiers to basic sentences for variety and emphasis

Sometimes you may want a very short sentence for its dramatic effect, but you usually need to modify simple subjects and verbs.

BASIC SENTENCE	Traffic stopped.
ADJECTIVE (7E, 12)	**Rush-hour** traffic stopped.
ADVERB (7F, 12)	Traffic stopped **suddenly**.
PREPOSITIONAL PHRASE (7M)	**In the middle of rush hour**, traffic stopped **on the bridge**.
PARTICIPAL PHRASE (7M)	**Blocked by an overturned tractor-trailer**, traffic stopped, **delaying hundreds of travelers**.
ABSOLUTE PHRASE (7M)	**The accident blocking all lanes**, traffic stopped.
ADVERB CLAUSE (7N-2)	**Because all lanes were blocked**, traffic stopped **until the trailer could be removed**.
ADJECTIVE CLAUSE (7N-2)	Traffic, **which was already slow**, stopped.

19e Repeating important words or ideas to achieve emphasis

Repeating carefully chosen words can help you to emphasize your meaning, but choose for repetition only those words that contain a main idea or that use rhythm to focus attention on a main idea.

> **Happiness** is never more than partial. There are no pure states of mankind. Whatever else **happiness** may be, it is neither in having nor in being, but in becoming. What the Founding Fathers declared for us as an inherent right, we should do well to remember, was not **happiness** but the *pursuit* of **happiness**.
>
> —JOHN CIARDI, "Is Everybody Happy?"

Varying Sentence Beginnings
by Varying Subjects

Revise each sentence so that it begins with the word or words given.

EXAMPLE A look at our history shows that Americans have enjoyed following the latest fads.

Americans: *Americans have enjoyed following the latest fads* _____
throughout our history. _____

1. Parents usually think the dances their teenagers like are strange.

   The dances: _____

2. In the early 1900s, fifteen women were fired by the management of the magazine where they worked.

   In the early 1900s, the management: _____

3. They had offended management by dancing the Turkey Trot during their lunch hour.

   Their offense: _____

4. Other popular dances of the period included the Grizzly Bear, the Kangaroo Dip, and the Bunny Hug.

   The Grizzly Bear: _____

5. Alvin "Shipwreck" Kelly invented flagpole sitting.

   Flagpole sitting: _____

6. No one knows the source of his nickname.

   The source: _____

7. Pie plates from the Frisbee Baking Company were the first Frisbees.

   The first Frisbees: _____

8. A Harvard student began a goldfish swallowing fad in 1939.

   The goldfish swallowing fad: _____

9. Reporters saw him swallow a live three-inch fish.

   He: _____

10. Australians invented the Hula Hoop for use in gym classes.

    The Hula Hoop: _____

Expanding Sentences with Modifiers

A: Expand these simple sentences in the ways stated in parentheses.

EXAMPLE   The moon was shining.
          (prepositional phrase) _The moon was shining through the trees._

1. The bus was crowded.

   (adjective) _____

   (adverb clause) _____

   (participial phrase) _____

2. The student transferred.

   (adverb) _____

   (adjective clause) _____

   (absolute phrase) _____

3. Practice is necessary.

   (prepositional phrase) _____

   (adjective) _____

   (adverb clause) _____

4. The cat crossed the street.

   (participial phrase) _____

   (adverb) _____

   (adjective clause) _____

5. He decided to buy the jacket.

   (absolute phrase) _____

   (prepositional phrase) _____

   (adjective) _____

B: Add the several elements given to each of the following sentences.

EXAMPLE   The astronaut was welcomed home.
(adjective modifying *astronaut*; adverb modifying was *welcomed*;
prepositional phrase modifying *home*)
The *brave* astronaut was *warmly* welcomed home *from space.*

1. The celebration included a parade.
(adjectives modifying *celebration* and *parade*; prepositional phrase
modifying *parade*)

_____

2. The crowd was dressed in shorts and shirts.
(absolute phrase; adjective modifying *shirts*)

_____

3. The mayor stopped traffic.
(adjective clause modifying *mayor*; adverb clause)

_____

4. The astronaut rode in a car.
(adjectives modifying *astronaut* and *car*; adverb modifying *rode*)

_____

5. Youngsters tried to get autographs.
(adverb clause; adjective clause modifying *youngsters*)

_____

6. The mayor gave a speech.
(absolute phrase; two adjectives modifying *speech*)

_____

7. Everyone cheered.
(two adverb clauses)

_____

8. The celebration ended.
(prepositional phrase modifying *ended*)

_____

9. Everyone headed home.
(participial phrase modifying *everyone*)

_____

10. The street cleaners came out.
(prepositional phrase modifying *came out*; adverbial clause)

_____

Revising to Emphasize the Main Idea

Using sentence combining, revise each passage into one or two sentences that emphasize its main idea. To do this, select the most effective subject for the sentence, stay in the active voice whenever possible, use a variety of sentence types (simple, compound, complex, compound-complex) and modifiers, and change clauses into phrases where practical.

EXAMPLE   Elizabeth Blackwell was a teacher. She was bored with teaching. She wanted to become a doctor. She had trouble qualifying for medical school.

Elizabeth Blackwell was bored with teaching and wanted to become a doctor, but she had trouble qualifying for medical school.

1. There was only one way to gain the knowledge she needed. She became a governess for doctors' families. She used her spare time. She studied their medical books.

_____

_____

2. She was turned down by eleven medical schools. She was finally accepted by Geneva Medical College in New York in 1848. The faculty let the students vote whether or not to accept her. They voted her in as a joke.

_____

_____

3. Blackwell was a good student. She received her degree in 1849. She could not find work in U.S. hospitals. She went to Europe to work.

_____

_____

4. She returned to New York in 1851. She wanted to open her own practice. No one would rent her office space. She bought her own house. It became the New York Infirmary for Women and Children.

_____

_____

5. The infirmary had an all-female staff. It was the first all-female hospital in the world. It offered internships to women medical students. It was the first to do this too.

_____

_____

20 Understanding the Meaning of Words

20a **Learning to use dictionaries**

Good dictionaries show how language has been used and is currently being used. Such dictionaries give not only a word's meaning, but also much additional important information.

An individual dictionary entry usually includes the following information: spelling; word division into syllables (syllabication); pronunciation; parts of speech; grammatical forms (plurals, parts of verbs including irregular forms, etc.); word origin; meanings; related words (nouns, adjectives); synonyms; words used in sample sentences; usage labels; and idioms that include the word.

The spelling is given first, with the word usually divided into syllables by centered dots. The pronunciation follows. Here you will sometimes see unusual symbols, such as /ə/, the **schwa** or "uh" sound. These symbols are explained in a pronunciation key, usually located in the dictionary's introduction or at the bottom of each page. The part of speech comes next. It is usually abbreviated, such as *n* for *noun* or *vt* for *transitive verb*. The dictionary also gives the principal parts of each word (for regular verbs, the *-ed* form for past tense and past participle, the *-ing* form for the present participle). The word's history (known as the etymology) usually follows. The word's meanings come next. If a word can be used as more than one part of speech, the meanings are grouped according to the parts of speech. Usage labels give additional important information, indicating which words are *slang, poetic,* or *dialect.*

Dictionaries come in several varieties. **Unabridged** ("unshortened") dictionaries have the most in-depth, accurate, complete, and scholarly entries of the various kinds of dictionaries. They give many examples of a word's current uses and changes in meanings over time. They also include infrequently used words that other dictionaries may omit.

Abridged ("shortened") dictionaries contain only the most commonly used words. They are convenient in size and economical to buy. These are the most practical reference books for writers and readers.

A number of specialized dictionaries focus on single areas, such as slang, word origins, synonyms, usage, or almost any other aspect of language. Whatever your interest, a specialized dictionary is probably available. Ask your reference librarian to point out what you need.

20b Choosing exact words

Careful writers pay close attention to **diction**—word choice. To choose the most appropriate and accurate word, a writer must understand the word's denotation and connotation.

When you look up a new word in the dictionary to find out exactly what it means, you are looking for its **denotation**. Words with the same general definition may have subtle differences of meaning. These differences enable you to choose precisely the right word, but they also obligate you to make sure you know what meanings your words convey. For example, describing someone as *lean* or *slender* is far different from calling that person *skinny*.

Connotation refers to the ideas implied but not directly indicated by a word. Connotations convey emotional overtones beyond a word's direct definition. What first comes to mind when you see the word *blood*? To some people *blood* represents war or injury while to others it is a symbol of family or ethnic identity; to people in the healing professions, *blood* may be interpreted as a symbol of life. Good writers understand the additional layer of meaning connotations deliver to specific audiences.

Specific words identify individual items in a group (*grape, orange, apple, plum*), whereas **general** words relate to an overall group (*fruit*). **Concrete** words identify persons and things that can be detected by the senses—seen, heard, tasted, felt, smelled (the *crisp, sweet red apple*). **Abstract** words denote qualities, concepts, relationships, acts, conditions, or ideas (*delicious*). Writers must use all these types of words. Effective writers, however, make sure to supply enough specific, concrete details to breathe life into generalizations and abstractions.

20c Increasing your vocabulary

Here are a few techniques you can use to make new words you encounter part of your vocabulary.

TECHNIQUES FOR BUILDING YOUR VOCABULARY

1. Using a highlighter pen, mark all unfamiliar words in your textbooks and other reading material. Then define the words in the margin so you can study the meaning in context. Copy new words onto index cards or into a special notebook.

2. Listen carefully to learn how speakers use the language. Jot down new words and later look them up. Write each new word and its definitions on an index card or in a special notebook.

3. Set aside time each day to study the new words. You can carry your cards or notebook in your pocket to study in spare moments during the day.

4. Use mnemonics to memorize words (see 22b). Set a goal of learning *and using* eight to ten new words a week.

5. Every few weeks go back to the words from previous weeks. Make a list of any words you do not still remember and study them again.

---

1 Knowing prefixes and suffixes

Prefixes are syllables in front of a **root** (base) word that modify its meaning. *Per (thoroughly)* placed before the root *form (to make or do)* gives *perform* ("to do thoroughly"). **Suffixes** are syllables added to the end of a root word that modify its meaning. For example, *ice* has the various forms of adjective, adverb, and noun when suffixes are added: *icy, icily, icicle, icing.*

Roots are the central parts of words to which prefixes and suffixes are added. Once you know, for example, the Latin root *bene (well, good)*, you can decode various forms: **bene**factor, **bene**diction.

Knowing common prefixes and suffixes is an excellent way to learn to figure out unfamiliar words. The following charts list some of the most common prefixes and suffixes.

PREFIXES

PREFIX	MEANING	EXAMPLE
anti-	against	*antiballistic*
contra-	against	*contradict*
extra-	more	*extraordinary*
hyper-	more	*hyperactive*
super-	more	*supernatural*
ultra-	more	*ultraconservative*
dis-	not	*disagree*
il-	not	*illegal*
im-	not	*immoral*
in-	not	*inadequate*
ir-	not	*irresponsible*
mis-	not	*misunderstood*
non-	not	*noninvolvement*
un-	not	*unhappy*
semi-	half	*semicircle*
mono-	one	*monopoly*
uni-	one	*uniform*
multi-	many	*multitude*
poly-	many	*polygamy*
ante-	before	*antebellum*
pre-	before	*prehistoric*
post-	after	*postscript*
re-	back	*return*
retro-	back	*retroactive*
sub-	under	*submissive*
trans-	across	*transportation*
inter-	between	*interpersonal*
intra-	inside	*intravenous*
auto-	self	*autobiography*
mal-	poor	*malnutrition*
magni-	great	*magnificent*
omni-	all	*omnipotent*
ab-	from	*abstain*

NOUN SUFFIXES

SUFFIX	MEANING	EXAMPLE
-tion	act of	*integration*
-hood	state of	*childhood*
-ness	state of	*kindness*
-ship	state of	*friendship*
-tude	state of	*solitude*
-dom	state of	*freedom*
-eer	a doer of	*auctioneer*

VERB SUFFIXES

SUFFIX	MEANING	EXAMPLE
-ate	to make	*integrate*
-ify	to make	*unify*
-ize	to make	*computerize*
-en	to cause to be	*broaden*

ADJECTIVAL SUFFIXES

SUFFIX	MEANING	EXAMPLE
-able	able to be	*comfortable*
-ible	able to be	*compatible*
-ate	full of	*fortunate*
-ful	full of	*tactful*
-ous	full of	*pompous*
-y	full of	*gloomy*
-less	without	*penniless*
-like	characteristic of	*doglike*
-ly	characteristic of	*saintly*

2 Using context clues to deduce word meanings

The familiar words that surround an unknown word can give you hints about the new word's meaning. These **context** clues include four main types.

1. **Restatement** context clue: You can figure out an unknown word when a word you know repeats the meaning: *The dieter was* **enervated**. *He was even too weakened to do his exercises. Enervated* means "weakened."

2. **Contrast** context clue: You can figure out an unknown word when an opposite or contrast is presented: *We expected Uncle Roy to be* **omnivorous***, but he turned out to be a picky eater. Omnivorous* means "eating any sort of food." The explanatory contrast is *but he turned out to be a picky eater.*

3. **Example** context clue: You can figure out an unfamiliar word when an example or illustration relating to the word is given: *The Board of Directors made the vice-president the* **scapegoat***, saying that the pollution was a result of her policies. Scapegoat* means "one who bears the blame for mistakes of others."

4. **General sense** context clue: An entire passage can convey a general sense of a new word. For example, *After a series of victories, the tennis star came to think of herself as invincible*. You can figure out that *invincible* has something to do with winning consistently.

Keep in mind that a specific context will reveal only one of many possible meanings of a word. Once you have deciphered a meaning from context clues, check the exact definition of the word in a dictionary.

Name _____ Date _____

Using the Dictionary

A: Using a college-level dictionary, rewrite each word to indicate capitalization, syllabication, hyphens, and spaces between words; use a dot to represent a break between syllables. Then rewrite the word to show pronunciation.

	Spelling	**Pronunciation**
EXAMPLE salami	*sa · la · mi*	*sə lä' mē*
1. dirge	_____	_____
2. leanto	_____	_____
3. outclass	_____	_____
4. phlegm	_____	_____
5. seabee	_____	_____
6. seagirt	_____	_____
7. seadog	_____	_____
8. gargoyle	_____	_____
9. lycanthropy	_____	_____
10. defenestration	_____	_____

B: Give the meaning of these abbreviations and symbols. Consult your college-level dictionary if you are unsure.

EXAMPLE adj. _____*adjective*_____

1. *Afr.*	_____	11. *cf.*	_____
2. *alt.*	_____	12. *Colloq.*	_____
3. *AmInd.*	_____	13. *exc.*	_____
4. *art.*	_____	14. *ff.*	_____
5. *Celt.*	_____	15. *G.*	_____
6. *ger.*	_____	16. *L.*	_____
7. *Gr.*	_____	17. *ME.*	_____
8. <	_____	18. *	_____
9. *IE.*	_____	19. *pp.*	_____
10. *i.e.*	_____	20. *var.*	_____

C: Give the past and past participle forms of these irregular verbs.

	Past	Past Participle
EXAMPLE send	sent	sent
1. have		
2. do		
3. break		
4. hear		
5. begin		
6. go		
7. spend		
8. know		
9. become		
10. buy		

D: Give the comparative and superlative forms of these adjectives and adverbs.

	Comparative	Superlative
EXAMPLE kind	kinder	kindest
1. kindly		
2. good		
3. well		
4. bad		
5. badly		
6. attractive		
7. attractively		
8. swiftly		
9. important		
10. inky		

Name _____ Date _____

E: Give the plural forms of these nouns. If your dictionary gives more than one form, list them all in the order given.

EXAMPLE alligator _____ *alligators, alligator* _____

1. scarf _____   6. phenomenon _____

2. llama _____   7. index _____

3. salmon _____   8. kibbutz _____

4. nucleus _____   9. bandit _____

5. formula _____   10. château _____

F: Carefully read the etymologies of these words in your dictionary. Then list (a) each word's original language and (b) its original meaning. Do not use abbreviations.

EXAMPLE house a. *Old English hus*
               b. *house*

1. wife   a. _____
               b. _____

2. husband   a. _____
               b. _____

3. son   a. _____
               b. _____

4. daughter   a. _____
               b. _____

5. marry   a. _____
               b. _____

6. house   a. _____
               b. _____

7. kitchen   a. _____
               b. _____

8. parlor   a. _____
               b. _____

9. foyer   a. _____
               b. _____

10. hall   a. _____
               b. _____

269

G: Find out what you can about the origin of each of these words.

EXAMPLE   sandwich

after John Montagu, fourth Earl of Sandwich (1718–1792), who was
said to have eaten these in order not to leave the gambling table
for meals

1. cardigan _____
2. quixotic _____
3. pants _____
4. bedlam _____
5. saxophone _____
6. pasteurize _____
7. dunce _____
8. guillotine _____
9. hamburger _____
10. mentor _____

H: List all the parts of speech that each word below can serve as. How many meanings does each part of speech have? Do not count the meanings of idiomatic expressions using these words.

EXAMPLE   nest   *noun, 6 meanings; intransitive verb, 3 meanings; transitive*
verb, 3 meanings

1. orange _____
2. period _____
3. practice _____
4. go _____
5. turn _____

I: What usage label does your dictionary assign to each of these words? If no label is given, write *no label*.

EXAMPLE   prithee   *archaic* _____

1. into (meaning *involved in*) _____
2. hot (meaning *stolen*) _____
3. rare (meaning *scattered*) _____
4. lift (meaning *elevator*) _____
5. ere (meaning *before*) _____

270

Understanding Differences in Denotation and Connotation

A: Underline the most appropriate word from the pair given in parentheses. If you are unsure, consult your dictionary's synonymy. (A synonymy is a paragraph comparing and contrasting words.)

EXAMPLE The sky was (clear, transparent), with not a cloud in sight.

1. The sergeant (instructed, commanded) his men to clean the barracks.
2. The plane remained (complete, intact) after passing through the severe storm.
3. The dictator was (conquered, overthrown) by his own brother.
4. Astronomy calls for great (accuracy, correctness).
5. After he fell into the cesspool, his suit was so (soiled, foul) it could not be cleaned.
6. The inheritance was (divided, doled out) among her sisters.
7. The crowd (dissipated, dispersed) once the ambulance took away the accident victim.
8. The tenants (withheld, kept) their rent in protest over the long-broken boiler.
9. Most fashion models are (lofty, tall).
10. The patient was (restored, renovated) to health by physical therapy.
11. Because of his (immoderate, exorbitant) behavior, the young man was thrown out of the restaurant.
12. The committee voted to (eliminate, suspend) voting on the budget until the missing members could be located.
13. The coach talked to the team in the (capacity, function) of a friend.
14. The family (donated, bestowed) its time to help restore the fire-damaged day-care center.
15. The practical joker (tittered, guffawed) as his victim slipped on a banana peel.
16. The professor (praised, eulogized) the class for its good work on the midterm examination.
17. Sometimes people offer (premiums, rewards) to help capture dangerous criminals.
18. The guest wondered if it would be (impolite, boorish) to ask for a third piece of pie.
19. The man (clandestinely, secretly) took his wife's birthday present into the attic.
20. The lifeguard's (skin, hide) was dry from overexposure to the sun.

B: The following words are synonymous, but not all are equally appropriate in every situation. Check the precise meaning of each word, and then use each in a sentence. Your dictionary may have a synonymy (a paragraph comparing and contrasting all the words) listed under one of the words, so check all the definitions before writing your sentences.

EXAMPLE laughable *The travel book was laughable because the author had never left the tour bus.*

amusing *We spent an amusing afternoon riding in an old, horse-drawn carriage.*

droll *The political commentator had a droll sense of humor.*

comical *The clowns in the circus were truly comical.*

1. danger _____

peril _____

hazard _____

risk _____

2. rich _____

wealthy _____

affluent _____

opulent _____

3. speak _____

talk _____

converse _____

discourse _____

4. think _____

reason _____

reflect _____

speculate _____

deliberate _____

5. irritable _____

choleric _____

touchy _____

cranky _____

cross _____

Using Concrete, Specific Language

A: Reorder the words in each list so they move from most general to most specific.

EXAMPLE cola   _____*beverage*_____

       soda   _____*soda*_____

       Coca Cola   _____*cola*_____

       beverage   _____*Coca Cola*_____

1. sandwich _____

    food _____

    cheese sandwich _____

    Swiss cheese on rye _____

2. A&P _____

    store _____

    business _____

    supermarket _____

3. bill _____

    record club charges _____

    letter _____

    mail _____

4. clothing _____

    jeans _____

    pants _____

    stone-washed jeans _____

5. land _____

    tropical paradise _____

    islands _____

    Hawaii _____

6. cookbook _____

    The Joy of Cooking _____

    how-to book _____

    book _____

7. lion _____

    hunter _____

    cat _____

    animal _____

8. television show _____

    entertainment _____

    family comedy _____

    The Cosby Show _____

9. *The Blue Boy* _____

    painting _____

    art _____

    portrait _____

10. sports _____

    100-yard dash _____

    running _____

    track _____

B: The italicized word or phrase in each sentence below is too abstract or general. Replace it with a word (or words) that is more specific or concrete. Use the lines to the right.

EXAMPLE   The *beast* escaped from the zoo.   *ferocious*
                                                            leopard

1. He's very proud of his new *car*.   _____
2. They planted *bushes* along the edge of the walk.   _____
3. The milk tasted *funny*.   _____
4. Proudly, she *walked* onto the stage.   _____
5. My aunt lives in *the South*.   _____
6. *Somebody* asked me to deliver these roses to you.   _____
7. She wrote a book about *history*.   _____
8. A *bird* flew into the classroom.   _____
9. To be successful, an accountant must be *good*.   _____
10. The Coast Guard chased the *criminals*.   _____
11. The dancer *hurt* her ankle.   _____
12. He received *jewelry* as a birthday present.   _____
13. The engine made a *strange* sound.   _____
14. He thought Economics class was *a pain*.   _____
15. The nurse was very *nice* to the patients.   _____
16. After practice, we went to *a movie*.   _____
17. His new dining room set was delivered *damaged*.   _____
18. The building is a *mess*.   _____
19. I want to get a *good* job after graduation.   _____
20. The doctor gave *everyone* a booklet about how to quit _____
    smoking.

Using Prefixes and Suffixes

A: Add a prefix to each of these roots to form a synonym of the word or phrase in parentheses.

EXAMPLE   (away)   *ab*sent

1. (use incorrectly)   _____apply

2. (without pausing)   _____stop

3. (coming before)   _____ceding

4. (make over)   _____model

5. (move something from one place to another)   _____fer

6. (immortal)   _____dying

7. (a person's own signature)   _____graph

8. (make something appear greater than it is)   _____fy

9. (knowing only one language)   _____lingual

10. (having many parts)   _____ple

11. (in all places at the same time)   _____present

12. (having more than one husband or wife)   _____gamy

B: Add a suffix to each of these roots to form a synonym of the word or phrase in parentheses. Indicate any necessary changes in spelling.

EXAMPLE   (state of being a child)   child*hood*

1. (state of being happy)   happy_____

2. (resembling a wolf)   wolf_____

3. (act of expanding)   expan_____

4. (act of being dedicated)   dedica_____

5. (resembling heaven)   heaven_____

6. (one who climbs mountains)   mountain_____

7. (one who flies)   aviat_____

8. (to make hard)   hard_____

9. (state of having the skill of a leader)   leader_____

10. (state of being wise)   wis_____

11. (to make larger)   magn_____

12. (able to be afforded)   afford_____

Using Context Clues

Using context clues, write the probable meaning of each italicized word. Then check the definitions in the dictionary. Finally, revise any of your definitions that are inaccurate.

EXAMPLE   According to folklore, coffee has been popular since the ninth century. Supposedly, an Ethiopian goatherd found his flock jumping around after eating coffee beans, and when he tried some he began *gamboling* along with them.
jumping around _____

1. Of all the natural *commodities* in world trade, coffee ranks second in dollar value, coming after petroleum.

   _____

2. Twenty-five million people in fifty exporting countries rely on coffee for their *sustenance*.

   _____

3. This is *singular*, as coffee has almost no nutritional value.

   _____

4. Except for Brazil, which consumes a third of its own crop, coffee-producing nations are *loath* to encourage coffee drinking at home.

   _____

5. There are greater *fiscal* benefits in exporting coffee.

   _____

6. Coffee prices rose *precipitously* in 1975 and 1979, when killing frosts destroyed many of Brazil's coffee trees.

   _____

7. The custom of *imbibing* coffee instead of eating it probably began in Yemen about 1000 A.D.

   _____

8. Coffee had an *invigorating* effect: helping people stay awake all night when they needed to.

   _____

9. For *teetotal* Muslims, coffee provided a lift they were forbidden to get from alcohol.

_____

10. Coffee was considered so *requisite* that old Turkish law allowed a wife to sue for divorce if her husband did not keep the home supplied with coffee.

_____

21 Understanding the Effect of Words

To use words well, you have to make careful choices. Your awareness of your purpose in writing, your audience, and the situation in which you are writing should influence your choice of words.

21a Using appropriate language

Good writers pay special attention to **diction** (word choice), making certain that the words they use communicate their meaning as clearly and convincingly as possible.

Informal levels and highly formal levels of writing use different vocabulary and sentence structures, and the two differ clearly in **tone**. Tone reflects the attitude of the writer toward the subject and audience. It may be highly formal, informal, or in between. Different tones are appropriate for different audiences, subjects, and purposes. An **informal** tone occurs in casual conversation or letters to friends. A highly **formal** tone, in contrast, occurs in public and ceremonial documents, such as proclamations and treaties. Informal language, which creates an informal tone, may use slang, colloquialisms, and regionalisms. In addition, informal writing may include sentence fragments, contractions, and other casual forms. Medium-level language uses general English—not too casual, not too scholarly. Unlike informal language, medium-level language is acceptable for academic writing. This level uses standard vocabulary (for example, *learn* instead of the informal *wise-up*), conventional sentence structure, and few or no contractions. Highly formal language uses many long words derived from Latin and a flowery style. Academic writing and most writing for general audiences should range from medium to somewhat formal levels of language.

The language standards you are expected to use in academic writing are those of a book like this workbook. Such language is called **standard English**, because it follows established rules of grammar, sentence structure, punctuation, and spelling. This language is also called **edited American English**. Standard English is not a fancy dialect for the elite. It is a practical set of rules about language use that most educated people observe.

Slang consists of newly created words and new meanings attached to established words. Slang words and phrases usually pass out of use quickly: *hip, cool, fresh.* **Colloquial language** is characteristic of casual conversation and informal writing: *The pileup on Route 23 halted traffic.* **Regional (dialectal) language** is specific to some geographic areas: *They had nary a dime to their name.* These usages are not appropriate for academic writing.

To communicate clearly, choose words that demonstrate your fairness as a writer. When you are talking about a subject on which you hold strong opinions, do not slip into biased or emotionally loaded language. Suppose you were arguing against a proposed increase in tuition. If you write that the president of the college is "a blood-sucking dictator out to destroy the lives of thousands of innocent young people," a neutral audience will doubt your ability to think rationally and write fairly about the subject.

21b Avoiding sexist language

Sexist language assigns roles or characteristics to people on the basis of sex. Such practices unfairly discriminate against both sexes. Sexist language inaccurately assumes that all nurses and homemakers are female (and therefore refers to them as "she") and that all physicians and wage earners are male (and therefore refers to them as "he"). One of the most widespread occurrences of sexist language is the use of the pronoun *he* to refer to someone of unidentified sex. Although traditionally *he* has been correct in such a general situation, using only masculine pronouns to represent the human species excludes females. You can avoid this problem by using the techniques suggested in the following chart.

HOW TO AVOID SEXIST LANGUAGE

1. Avoid using only the masculine pronoun to refer to males and females together:
   a. Use a pair of pronouns, but try to avoid strings of pairs in a sentence or in several consecutive sentences.

      No A doctor cannot read much outside **his** specialty.

      Yes A doctor cannot read much outside **his or her** specialty.

   b. Revise into the plural.

      No A successful doctor knows that **he** has to work long hours.

      Yes Successful doctors know that **they** have to work long hours.

   c. Recast the sentence to omit the gender-specific pronoun.

      No Everyone hopes **that he will** win the scholarship.

      Yes Everyone hopes **to win** the scholarship.

2. Avoid using *man* when men and women are clearly intended in the meaning.

      No **Man** is a social animal.

      Yes **People** are social animals.

HOW TO AVOID SEXIST LANGUAGE *(continued)*

3. Avoid stereotyping jobs and roles by gender when men and women are included.
   No chairman; policeman; businessman; statesman
   Yes chair, chairperson; police officer; businessperson, business executive; diplomat, prime minister, etc.

   No teacher . . . she; principal . . . he
   Yes teachers . . . they; principals . . . they

4. Avoid expressions that exclude one sex.
   No mankind; the common man; man-sized sandwich; old wives' tale
   Yes humanity; the average person; huge sandwich; superstition

5. Avoid using degrading and insulting labels.
   No lady lawyer; gal Friday; career girl; coed
   Yes lawyer; assistant; professional woman; student

21c Using figurative language

Figurative language uses one idea or image to explain another by creating comparisons and connections. The most common figures of speech are similes and metaphors.

A **simile** states a direct comparison between two otherwise dissimilar things. It sets up the comparison by using the words *like* or *as*. A disagreeable person might be said to be *as sour as unsweetened lemonade*.

A **metaphor** implies a comparison between otherwise dissimilar things without using *like* or *as: The new tax bill bled lower-income families of their last hope.*

Be careful not to create an inappropriate and silly image, such as in *The rush hour traffic bled out of all the city's major arteries.* Cars are not at all like blood and their movement is not similar to the flow of blood, so the metaphor ends up confusing rather than explaining. Also be careful not to create **mixed metaphors**, illogical combinations of images: *Milking the migrant workers, the supervisor bled them dry.* Here the initial image is of taking milk from a cow, but the final image is of blood, not milk.

21d Avoiding clichés

A **cliché** is an overused, worn-out expression that has lost its ability to communicate effectively. Some comparisons that were once clever have grown old and worn out: *dead as a doornail, gentle as a lamb.* Do not take the easiest phrase, the words that come immediately to mind. If you have heard them over and over again, so has your reader. Rephrasing clichés will improve your writing.

21e Avoiding artificial language

Always try to make what you are saying as clear as possible to your readers. Extremely complex ideas or subjects may require complex terms or phrases to explain them, but in general the simpler the language, the more likely it is to be understood.

Pretentious language is too showy and sometimes silly, calling unsuitable attention to itself with complex sentences and long words: *I had a portion of an Italian comestible for the noontime repast* [Translation: I had a slice of pizza for lunch]. Plain English that communicates clearly is far better than fancy English that makes the reader aware that you are showing off.

Jargon is specialized vocabulary of a particular group—words that an outsider would not understand. Whether or not the word is considered jargon depends on purpose and audience. For example, when a sportswriter uses words such as *gridiron* and *sacked*, a football fan understands them with no difficulty. Specialized language evolves in every field: professions, academic disciplines, business, even hobbies. However, using jargon unnecessarily or failing to explain it is showy and artificial.

Euphemisms attempt to avoid harsh reality by using pleasant-sounding, "tactful" words. Although they are sometimes necessary to spare someone's feelings, euphemisms drain meaning from truthful writing. People use unnecessary euphemisms to describe socially unacceptable behavior: *Barry bends the rules* instead of *Barry cheats*. They use euphemisms to hide unpleasant facts: *She really likes her liquor* instead of *She is a drunk*. Euphemisms like these fool no one. Except in the rare cases where delicate language is needed—to soften the pain of death, for example—keep your language free of euphemisms.

Doublespeak is artificial, misleading language. For example, people who strip and sell stolen cars might call themselves "auto dismantlers and recyclers" selling "predismantled previously owned parts." Such language is distorting and dishonest. To use doublespeak is to use words that hide the truth, a highly unethical practice that tries to control people's thoughts. For example, in 1984 the U.S. State Department announced it would no longer use the word *killing* in its official reports about human rights in other countries. *Killing* was replaced with *unlawful or arbitrary deprivation of life*. This practice forces readers into thinking inaccurately. Such misuses of language have terrible social and political effects.

Like doublespeak, **bureaucratic language** is confusing. Unlike doublespeak, it is not intended to mislead. Rather, it is carelessly written, stuffy, overblown language, as shown by the following memo:

> You can include a page that also contains an Include instruction. The page including the Include instruction is included when you paginate the document but the included text referred to in its Include instruction is not included.

EXERCISE 21-1
(21a)

Recognizing Levels of Formality

Different levels of formality are appropriate in different situations. Decide which level (informal, medium, between medium and formal, and formal) best fits each of these situations.

Level of Formality

EXAMPLE   a letter requesting the list of winners in a
sweepstakes   *medium*

1. a note to a friend asking him or her to take a package to   _____
   the post office for you
2. a lab report for chemistry   _____
3. a petition to have a candidate's name added to the   _____
   election ballot
4. an invitation to a veteran to speak to your daughter's   _____
   sixth grade class about his experiences in Viet Nam
5. the valedictorian's speech at a college graduation   _____
   ceremony

Now select three of these documents, each calling for a different level of formality, and write them. Use your own paper.

EXERCISE 21-2
(21a)

Avoiding Slang, Colloquial, and Overly Formal Language

Underline the word in each sentence that best suits an academic style. You may need to check your dictionary for usage labels.

EXAMPLE   That academic advisor fails to motivate students because she is
(stuck-up, <u>aloof</u>).

1. My anthropology professor is a brilliant (guy, man).
2. The food in the main dining hall is barely (edible, comestible).
3. (Prithee, Please) shut off the lights when leaving classrooms.
4. The Dean of Faculty will (address, parley with) the audience at graduation.
5. (Regardless, Irregardless) of the weather, the honors and awards ceremony will be held on Thursday evening.
6. All students must wear skirts or (britches, slacks) under their graduation robes.

7. The elevator is reserved for faculty and (educands, students) with passes.

8. Remind your guests to park their (cars, wheels) in the visitors' lot.

9. Anyone parking a (motorcycle, chopper) on campus should chain it to the rack in the parking field.

10. Relatives may stay overnight in the (dormitories, dorms) provided they have written in advance and (check in, touch base) with the house parents before 10 P.M.

Revising Sentences for Appropriate Language

EXERCISE 21-3

(21a)

Revise these sentences using language appropriate for academic writing.

EXAMPLE   William Burke and William Hare were these murderers who hung around Edinburgh, Scotland, during the prior century.
William Burke and William Hare were murderers who preyed on the
people of Edinburgh, Scotland, during the last century.

1. At that time, the docs and med students in Scotland needed bodies to cut up in order to figure out how to handle diseases.

_____

2. However, mighty tough laws made it hard to procure enough bodies.

_____

3. Copping stiffs from boneyards to sell to the medicos was an easy way to make a buck, but risky.

_____

4. Hare ran a boarding house, and when one of his roomers kicked the bucket, he and Burke sold the body.

_____

5. It was a cinch.

_____

6. These guys took to luring travelers to their pads, getting them cock-eyed on booze, and then wringing their necks.

_____

7. In nine months, they packed off fifteen suckers at up to £14 a pop.

_____

8. However, the fadeaway of the sixteenth victim was ascertained.

_____

9. Burke, Hare, and their cronies were nabbed.

_____

10. Hare ratted on his mate and got off; Burke was the guest of honor at a necktie party.

_____

Revising Slanted Language

Here is the opening paragraph of a very slanted letter to the editor. Revise it, using moderate language. Try to convince the reader that you are a reasonable person with a valid argument.

The Morning Telegram
Anytown, U.S.A. 00001

Dear Editor:
    I just read your ridiculous article on the proposed opening of a hazardous waste storage depot just outside town. Are you crazy? Anyone who would propose such a deadly project has no soul. Those city council members who are sponsoring this monstrous facility obviously have the brains of fruit flies. If they had bothered to do a little research, they would have discovered that dreadful things can happen to any poor community that lets such a depot be forced upon it.

Revising for Appropriate Figurative Language

Revise these sentences by replacing clichéd, inappropriate, or mixed metaphors with fresh, appropriate figures of speech. You may want to reduce the number of figures of speech in a sentence, or you may sometimes feel a message is best presented without any figurative language.

EXAMPLE   The police set up a statewide dragnet, certain the killer could not drop through the cracks.
        The police set up a statewide dragnet, certain that the killer could not escape. [A net cannot have cracks.]

1. My uncle has a grip like a vise.

_____

2. He held her in an embrace as inescapable as flypaper.

   _____

3. The fingers of the waves danced on the shore.

   _____

4. As soon as she entered her studio, the flames of creativity swept over her like an advancing iceberg.

   _____

5. They talked us into going to an expensive restaurant, so we went, reluctantly, like lambs going to the slaughter.

   _____

6. Having no backbone is his Achilles heel.

   _____

7. Like a vise, he caught her eye, turned her head, and swept her off her feet.

   _____

8. I burned the midnight oil studying until 6 A.M.

   _____

9. The train rushed at us like a scared rabbit.

   _____

10. After I painted myself in the corner, I felt like a trapped rat.

    _____

11. The situation came to a head, so an investigation was set afoot.

    _____

12. The mailman licked the prowler and held him for police.

    _____

13. He wore his heart on his sleeve and bared his soul to her.

    _____

14. This painting is pretty as a picture.

    _____

15. The meteorologist's explanation of what causes mist was foggy.

    _____

Using Figurative Language

Using new, appropriate figures of speech, write a sentence describing each of the following.

EXAMPLE   a fast train
Disappearing like the vapor trail of a jet, the train sped into _____
the distance. _____

1. a graceful horse

_____

2. a run-down shack

_____

3. a terrible dance band

_____

4. greasy french fries

_____

5. being awakened by your alarm clock

_____

6. a professor who requires too much work

_____

7. a salesperson with a phony smile

_____

8. a hot day in the city

_____

9. something that is very late

_____

10. an unpleasant singing voice

_____

Eliminating Artificial Language

A: "Translate" these sentences into standard academic English by eliminating inappropriate jargon and euphemisms. You may need to refer to your dictionary.

EXAMPLE We received two inches of precipitation last night.
We got two inches of rain (or snow) last night.

1. After falling, the child sustained a severe hematoma of the patella.

2. Operators of automotive vehicles should be sure to utilize their seat belts before engaging engines.

3. Although she was in a family way, she continued in the fulfillment of her familial and employment responsibilities.

4. The municipal public-thoroughfare contamination controllers are on unauthorized, open-ended leave.

5. The dean has asked department heads to interface with him.

B: Find a piece of published writing that you feel uses pretentious language, unnecessary jargon, unnecessary euphemisms, doublespeak, and/or bureaucratic language. Likely sources are newsletters, business memos and reports, political mailings, solicitations for charity, and sales brochures. Be prepared to say in what ways the language is artificial and what problems that language can create for readers. Then rewrite the piece using appropriate language. Submit the original and your revision to your instructor.

22 Spelling and Hyphenation

One reason English spelling can be difficult is that our words have come from many sources. We have borrowed words from Latin, Greek, French, Spanish, and many other languages. Because of these various origins, plus differences in the ways English-speaking people pronounce words, it is unwise to rely on pronunciation in spelling a word.

What we can rely on, however, is a system of proofreading, studying, and learning spelling rules. With a little time and effort, English spelling can be mastered.

22a Eliminating careless errors

Many spelling errors are not *spelling* errors at all. They are the result of illegible handwriting, slips of the pen, or typographical errors ("typos"). While you may not be able to change your handwriting completely, you can make it legible enough so that readers know what words you are writing. Careful proofreading is required to catch typos. When you reread your papers, you are likely to read what you meant to write rather than what is actually on the page because the brain tends to "read" what it expects to see. When proofreading for typos, then, try reading the page backwards, from the last sentence to the first. Using a ruler to help you focus on one line at a time is also effective.

22b Training yourself to improve your spelling

If you are unsure how to spell a word but you do know how it starts, look it up in the dictionary. If you do not know how to spell the beginning of a word, think of a synonym, and look that word up in a thesaurus.

When you come across unfamiliar words in a textbook, highlight or underline them as you read. Then, after you have finished reading, go back and memorize the correct spelling.

As you discover words you frequently misspell, print each carefully on a card, highlighting the problem area by using larger print, a different-colored ink, or a highlighter.

Mnemonic devices, techniques to improve memory, can also help you to remember the spelling of difficult words:

> The princi**pal** is your **pal**. A princi**ple** is a ru**le**.

> The w**ea**ther is cl**ea**r. **Wh**ether is **wh**at.

22c Recognizing homonyms and commonly confused words

Many words sound similar to or exactly like others (*its/it's, morning/mourning*). Words that sound alike are called **homonyms**. To avoid using the wrong word, look up unfamiliar homonyms in the dictionary, and then use mnemonic devices to help you remember their meanings.

Some expressions may be written either as one word or two, depending on meaning:

> An **everyday** occurrence is something that happens **every day**.

> The guests were there **already** by the time I was **all ready**.

> When we were **all together** there were five of us **altogether**.

> We were there for **a while** when the host said dinner would be **awhile** longer.

> **Maybe** the main course will be sushi, but it **may be** tofuburgers.

> When we went **in to** dinner, he walked **into** the table.

Two expressions, however, are *always* written as two words: *all right* (not *alright*) and *a lot* (not *alot*).

HOMONYMS AND NEAR SOUNDALIKES

accept / except
advice / advise
affect / effect
aisle / isle
already / all ready
altar / alter
altogether / all together
angel / angle
are / hour / our
ascent / assent
assistance / assistants
bare / bear
board / bored
brake / break
breath / breathe
buy / by
capital / capitol
choose / chose
cite / sight / site
clothes / cloths
coarse / course
complement / compliment
conscience / conscious
council / counsel
dairy / diary
dessert / desert
device / devise
dominant / dominate
die / dye
dying / dyeing
fair / fare
formally / formerly
forth / fourth
gorilla / guerrilla
hear / here
heard / herd

hole / whole
human / humane
its / it's
know / no
later / latter
lead / led
lessen / lesson
lightning / lightening
loose / lose
maybe / may be
meat / meet
miner / minor
of / off
our / hour
passed / past
patience / patients
peace / piece
personal / personnel
plain / plane
principal / principle
quiet / quite / quit
rain / reign / rein
right / rite / write
road / rode
scene / seen
sense / since
stationary / stationery
than / then
there / they're / their
through / threw / thorough
to / too / two
weak / week
weather / whether
where / were / wear
which / witch
whose / who's
your / you're / yore

22d

22d Solving spelling problems within words

1 Spelling suffixes (word endings) carefully

A **suffix** is an ending added to the basic form of a word, to change either the tense (*-d, -ed*) or the part of speech. Spelling problems arise when different suffixes sound alike or when changes must be made in the base word before the suffix is added.

-d ending: When the *-d* ending is not clearly pronounced at the end of past-tense verbs and adjectives, the wrong form of the word may be written. Watch out for incorrect forms such as *prejudice person* (instead of *prejudiced person*) and *use to* (instead of *used to*).

-able, -ible: These two suffixes cause problems because there are no reliable rules for their use. More words end in *-able: comfortable, probable, treatable*. Still, some common words end in *-ible: irresistible, audible*. The best rule to follow with these two endings is when in doubt, look up the word.

-ally/-ly: Both endings turn words into adverbs: *-ally* is added to words ending in *ic (logically, tragically); -ly* is added to words not ending in *ic (quickly, slowly)*.

-ance, -ence, -ant, -ent: These endings do not occur according to any rules. Some words end in *-ance: observance, reluctance*. Some words end in *-ence: convenience, correspondence*. Once you know whether a noun ends in *-ance* or *-ence*, you will know whether its adjective form ends in *-ant* or *-ent: observant, reluctant, convenient, correspondent*.

-cede, -ceed, -sede: Only one word ends in *-sede: supersede*. Only three words end in *-ceed: exceed, proceed, succeed*. The rest end in *-cede: precede, recede, secede*.

Final e: Drop the final *e* before a suffix beginning with a vowel (*arrange + -ing = arranging*), but keep it if the suffix begins with a consonant (*arrange + -ment = arrangement*). Often a final *e* "softens" the sound of a preceding *c* or *g* (soft *c* sounds like *s*, soft *g* like *j*). In such cases, the final *e* is retained with suffixes beginning with *a* or *o*, in order to retain the soft sound of the consonant: *service + able = serviceable; outrage + ous = outrageous*. Some words retain final *e* to prevent confusion with other words: *dye + -ing = dyeing*, to avoid confusion with *dying*. For the few exceptions to the basic rule for final *e*, simply memorize their spelling: *argument, awful, truly, wisdom*.

Final y: If the final *y* is preceded by a consonant, change the *y* to *i* before adding a suffix unless the suffix begins with *i; try + -ed = tried; try + -ing = trying.* If the final *y* is preceded by a vowel, retain the *y* when adding any suffix: *employ + -ed = employed; employ + -ing = employing; employ + -er = employer.* Common exceptions to this rule are the past tenses of *lay, pay,* and *say: laid, paid,* and *said.*

Doubling final consonants: If a one-syllable word ends in a consonant preceded by a single vowel, double the final consonant before adding a suffix: *flip + -ing = flipping.* With two-syllable words, an additional rule applies: double the final consonant only if the last syllable of the stem is accented. Thus, adding *-ing* to the word *refer* produces *referring* (final *r* doubled), but adding *-ence* produces *reference* (final *r* not doubled) because in *referring* the accent is on the last syllable of *refer,* while in *reference* the accent is on the first syllable.

2 Knowing the *ie, ei* rule and exceptions

Generally, you can rely on the old rhyme: "*i* before *e*, except after *c*, or when sounded like *ay*, as in *neighbor* and *weigh*": *field, believe, grief; receive, ceiling, conceit; neigh, vein, eight.* There are, however, a few common exceptions that are worth memorizing: *counterfeit, foreign, forfeit, either, neither, leisure, seize, weird, height, sleight, ancient.*

3 Knowing how to use prefixes

Prefixes are syllables placed in front of base words, either changing or adding to the word's meaning. Prefixes do not alter the spelling of the base word: *un + reliable = unreliable; re + locate = relocate.* For a list of prefixes and their meanings, see 20c-1.

4 Knowing how to form plurals

Regular plurals: In general, add *-s* to form a plural: *desks, tables.* If a word ends in *-ch, -s, -sh, -x,,* or *-z*, add *-es: patches, dresses, flashes, waxes, buzzes.* Words ending in *-o* preceded by a consonant take the *-es* plural: *heroes, tomatoes.* Words ending in *-o* preceded by a vowel take the *-s* plural: *ratios, videos.* There are exceptions to these two rules, many of which are music terms taken from Italian: *contraltos, solos, pianos, tobaccos.* A few words ending in *-o* may take either the *-s* or *-es* plural: *cargoes/cargos, volcanoes/volcanos, zeroes/zeros.*

Words ending in -f or -fe: In general, change the *f* to *ve* before adding *-s: leaf/leaves, wife/wives.* There are three exceptions to this rule: *belief/beliefs, motif/motifs, safe/safes.* These exceptions avoid confusion with the singular verbs *believes* and *saves* and the plural noun *motives.* When the words ends in *-ff* or *-ffe*, simply add *-s: giraffe/giraffes, staff/staffs.*

Compound nouns: In general, place the *-s* or *-es* at the end of a compound noun: *attorney generals, capfuls, nurse-midwives*. If, however, the major word in the compound is the first word, add the *-s* or *-es* to the first word: *professors emeritus, passersby, sisters-in-law*.

Internal changes: Some words change internally to form the plural: *man/ men, child/children, mouse/mice, foot/feet, ox/oxen*.

Foreign plurals: Words borrowed from other languages usually form their plurals according to the rules of that language. Latin words ending in *-um* or *-on* usually form their plurals by changing the *-um* or *-on* to *-a: curriculum/curricula, medium/media, datum/data, criterion/criteria*. For Latin words ending in *-us*, the plural is *-i: alumnus/alumni, syllabus/syllabi*.

Plurals retaining singular form: Some words are spelled the same in both singular and plural forms. Usually these are the names of animals or grains: *deer, elk, fish, rice, wheat*.

22e Using hyphens correctly

1 Learning when and how to divide a word at the end of a line

Try not to divide words at the end of a line, but when you must do so, follow these guidelines.

GUIDELINES FOR DIVIDING WORDS AT END OF LINE

1. Never divide short words, and never divide single-syllable words at the end of a line, no matter how long the word: *cleanse*, not *cle-anse*.

2. Always divide words between syllables. The dictionary listing of a word shows its syllables clearly: *helicopter*, for example, appears in the dictionary as *he li cop ter*.

3. Never leave or carry over only one or two letters on a line: *alive*, not *a-live*.

4. Follow rules for double consonants. Suffixes usually create added syllables. If a base word ends in a double consonant, divide the word *after* the double consonant: *success-ful*, not *succes-sful*. If a single consonant is doubled when the suffix is added, then divide the word *between* the double consonants: *omit-ting*, not *omitt-ing*.

5. Never violate pronunciation when dividing words. Not all word endings create syllables. The *-ed* ending, for example, often simply adds the sound of the consonant *d* to a word. If you divide such a word before the *-ed* ending, you create a new syllable: *com-pelled*, not *compell-ed*.

---

2 Dividing words with prefixes and suffixes correctly

Most prefixes form **closed words**, or words written as one (*semi + sweet = semisweet*). When you divide a word with a prefix, it is preferable to divide after the prefix (unless the prefix has only one or two letters) rather than between other syllables: *mis-understood* not *misunder-stood*.

A few prefixes require hyphens. When you divide a word with a prefix attached by a hyphen, always divide after the prefix.

all-, ex-, quasi-, **and** *self-:* These prefixes usually come before complete words and require hyphens: *all-inclusive, ex-husband, quasi-judicial, self-assured.*

Proper nouns and numbers: When the main word is a proper noun or number, the prefix is followed by a hyphen: *all-American, pre-1950.*

Compound main words: When the main word is a compound, the prefix is followed by a hyphen: *anti-gun control.*

Avoiding confusion: Sometimes it is necessary to hyphenate a prefix in order to avoid confusion, either in meaning or pronunciation. If a prefix added to a word causes it to look exactly like another word, the prefix must be followed by a hyphen: *re-creation* vs. *recreation.*

3 Spelling compound words correctly

When a compound acts as a modifier *before* a noun, it is usually hyphenated: *fast-paced lecture, long-term commitment.* When the same modifier comes after the noun, however, there is no hyphen: *The lecture was fast paced.* Some terms have become clear enough that they do not require hyphens: *genetic engineering laboratory, health insurance policy, junior high school, state sales tax.*

The hyphen is omitted in several other situations: when the first word in the compound ends with *-ly,* when the first word is a comparative or superlative, or when the compound is a foreign phrase: *happily married couple, lowest common denominator, ad hoc committee.*

A hyphen is placed between the two parts of a combined unit of measurement: *kilowatt-hours, light-years.*

Most compound titles are not hyphenated (*state senator, vice principal*), but many are. Hyphenated titles usually are national names, actual double titles, or three-word titles: *Italian-American, father-in-law, director-producer.*

22e

4 Using hyphens correctly in spelled-out numbers

Fractions: Hyphens are used between the numerator and the denominator of fractions, unless a hyphen already appears in either or both: *three-hundredths (3/100),* but *two three-hundredths (2/300).*

Double-digit numbers: Hyphens are used between the two parts of all double-digit numbers, whether those numbers are written alone or as part of larger numbers: *sixty-two, five hundred sixty-two.*

Combined numbers and words: When numbers and words are combined to form one idea or modifier, a hyphen is placed between the number and the word: *50-minute class.* If the word in the modifier is possessive, omit the hyphen: *one week's work.*

Recognizing Homonyms and Commonly Confused Words

Underline the word within parentheses that best fits each sentence.

EXAMPLE   When (your, <u>you're</u>) in New York, be sure to visit the Museum of Natural History.

1. The winners of the World Series (road, rode) down Main Street in a parade.
2. After reading murder mysteries all summer, she decided to (right, write) one herself.
3. While I was cleaning, I found some (loose, lose) change under the sofa cushions.
4. Thunder and (lightning, lightening) kept the campers awake all night.
5. The young woman put a lock on her (dairy, diary) when she realized her roommate had been reading it.
6. A square has four right (angels, angles).
7. The runners stood (altogether, all together) near the starting line, waiting for the signal to take (their, there) places.
8. The trip was great, (accept, except) for the day the car broke down in the (dessert, desert).
9. The broken-hearted man wrote to the (advice, advise) columnist.
10. Going to college can (altar, alter) a person's view about many things.
11. The play was an (hour, our) long.
12. The neighborhood (counsel, council) agreed to patrol the park at night.
13. Professional bakers have special (devices, devises) that help them make (peaces, pieces) of pastry easily.
14. The amount of oxygen in the air (lessens, lessons) as climbers reach higher levels.
15. Scott Kamiel (maybe, may be) the best pitcher we have ever had.
16. Prince Charles will (reign, rein) as the next King of England.
17. Do you know (whose, who's) car is blocking the driveway?
18. The last (scene, seen) of the movie was filmed from a helicopter.
19. He hid the last chocolate bar (where, were) his brothers could not find it.
20. Everything costs more now (than, then) it used (to, too).

Writing Sentences with Homonyms and Commonly Confused Words

Use each word below in a sentence that clearly demonstrates its meaning.

EXAMPLE its *Every plan has its disadvantages.*

it's *It's too late to go out for pizza.*

1. already _____

    all ready _____

2. its _____

    it's _____

3. than _____

    then _____

4. they're _____

    their _____

    there _____

5. to _____

    two _____

    too _____

6. your _____

    you're _____

7. passed _____

    past _____

8. quiet _____

    quite _____

9. through _____

    threw _____

    thorough _____

10. whose _____

    who's _____

Adding Suffixes

A: Combine these suffixes and roots. If in doubt about the spelling, look up the word in your dictionary.

EXAMPLE awake + ing _____*awaking*_____

1. supervise + ion _____
2. endure + ance _____
3. peace + ful _____
4. peace + able _____
5. sure + ly _____
6. true + ly _____
7. dye + ing _____
8. argue + able _____
9. outrage + ous _____
10. love + ing _____

What basic rules govern the combining of roots ending in *e* and suffixes?

_____

_____

B: Combine these suffixes and roots. If in doubt about the spelling, look up the word in your dictionary.

EXAMPLE carry + ing _____*carrying*_____

1. beauty + ful _____
2. delay + ing _____
3. cry + er _____
4. carry + ing _____
5. pushy + est _____
6. destroy + ed _____
7. marry + ing _____
8. rely + s _____
9. droopy + ness _____
10. toy + ing _____

What basic rules govern the combining of roots ending in *y* and suffixes?

_____

_____

C: Combine these suffixes and roots. If in doubt about the spelling, look up the word in your dictionary.

EXAMPLE trap + ed   _____trapped_____

1. clip + ing   _____
2. read + able   _____
3. shop + ed   _____
4. plan + er   _____
5. spend + ing   _____
6. hot + er   _____
7. paint + ed   _____
8. rip + ing   _____
9. prefer + ing   _____
10. prefer + ence _____

What basic rules govern the doubling of final consonants when a suffix is added?

_____

_____

Distinguishing Between ei *and* ie

Fill in the blanks with *ei* or *ie*. Because there are frequent exceptions to the rule, check your dictionary whenever you are in doubt.

EXAMPLE   anc_*ie*_nt

1. bel_____ve
2. rec_____ve
3. n_____ther
4. c_____ling
5. for_____gn

6. f_____ld
7. counterf_____t
8. w_____rd
9. fr_____ght
10. n_____ce

Adding Prefixes

Combine these prefixes and roots.

EXAMPLE   re + start   _____*restart*_____

1. un + able   _____
2. mis + spell   _____
3. anti + freeze   _____
4. pre + determine _____
5. extra + ordinary _____
6. super + human   _____
7. trans + form   _____
8. sub + marine   _____
9. re + appear   _____
10. uni + cycle   _____

What rule governs the combining of prefixes and roots? _____

_____

_____

Writing Plural Nouns

Write the plural forms of these nouns.

EXAMPLE lamp   _____*lamp*_____

          attorney at law   *attorneys at law*

1. orange   _____

2. kiss   _____

3. stray   _____

4. life   _____

5. radio   _____

6. pair   _____

7. speech   _____

8. fly   _____

9. monkey   _____

10. piano   _____

11. mother-in-law   _____

12. datum   _____

13. ice skate   _____

14. herself   _____

15. echo   _____

16. half   _____

17. child   _____

18. woman   _____

19. phenomenon   _____

20. mouse   _____

Correcting Common
Spelling Errors

Underline the misspelled word in each sentence, and spell it correctly on the line to the right. If a sentence has no misspellings, write *correct* on the line.

EXAMPLE   Some exceptions to spelling rules are <u>wierdly</u> irregular.   *weirdly*

1. The letter carrier retired after being biten by the same dog for the seventh time.   _____

2. The counterfeiter pleaded innocent, saying he had been frammed.   _____

3. In the committee's judgment, the fair succeeded because of extremely efficient managment.   _____

4. The scientists received news from a reliable source about an important foriegn discovery.   _____

5. We had hoped to buy a new dinning room set with our winnings from the quiz show we competed on last month.   _____

6. It seems incredable that, after trailing in the polls for weeks, our candidate managed finally to win the election.   _____

7. Running, swimming, and jumpping rope are all ways to increase the heart's endurance.   _____

8. Many undocumented aliens have little liesure time because they often hold two or even three jobs, all paying illegally low salaries.   _____

9. Because we did not think the payments were affordable, we reluctantly postponed repairing the leaky ceiling.   _____

10. The disatisfied customers tried to return the chipped benches to the manufacturer, but the factory was permanently closed.   _____

11. The young man received a commendation from the community for his incredibly couragous performance in rescuing disabled children from an overturned bus.   _____

12. When he was layed off from work, he filed a grievance with his union representative and then proceeded to the unemployment office.   _____

13. After carefully painting the attic stairs, my brother-in-law realized he had closed off his route of escape, and he was traped upstairs until the paint dried. _____

14. When I was younger, I use to want to take drum lessons until I realized how tiring practicing the drums could be. _____

15. The professor stated that she would return illegable papers without commenting on them, and she encouraged students to type all work carefully. _____

16. Although the street was usually gloomy, every New Year's Eve it magicly transformed itself into a joyful scene for a few hours. _____

17. According to some philosophies, the world is constantly changing and it is pointless to expect anything to be permanant. _____

18. The neighborhood children voted to coordinate a carwash and use the procedes to buy durable playground equipment. _____

19. The chef advertised in the classified section of the newspaper for a relieable dessert-maker. _____

20. The school aide was payed a bonus for her invaluable assistance during the hurricane. _____

21. In some cultures, it is beleived that the ghosts of ancestors take up residence in the family home. _____

22. One of the most appealing aspects of watching team sports is seeing the interraction among the players on the field. _____

23. The most boring part of working in a department store is taking part in periodic inventorys of the available merchandise. _____

24. Each autumn, people tragically injure themselves in avoidable falls on rain-soaked leafs. _____

25. *Star Wars* was a very well-received and profitible movie, and it set the pattern for many imitations. _____

Dividing Words
at the Ends of Lines

Using your dictionary, rewrite each word on the line to its right. Use a slash to indicate the best place to divide the word at the end of a line. Some words may be broken in more than one place. Pick the best place, and use dots to indicate all other syllable breaks. If the word cannot be divided, write it out as one unit.

EXAMPLES signaled   *sig/naled*
                brake   *brake*
                sledgehammer   *sledge/ham·mer*

1. sleepless _____
2. slenderize _____
3. referee _____
4. phlegm _____
5. palate _____
6. muscle-bound _____
7. indecent _____
8. Hollywood _____
9. expiration _____
10. echo _____
11. cuckoo _____
12. cough _____
13. butte _____
14. avocado _____
15. avoirdupois _____
16. loose _____
17. cattail _____
18. enroll _____
19. grouch _____
20. progressing _____

21. sleeve _____
22. sapsucker _____
23. Polynesia _____
24. palace _____
25. nonresident _____
26. increase _____
27. however _____
28. gesticulate _____
29. emerge _____
30. cubic _____
31. colorless _____
32. caretaker _____
33. buttermilk _____
34. await _____
35. antacid _____
36. mother-in law _____
37. trousseau _____
38. midget _____
39. controlling _____
40. farther _____

Writing Compound Nouns and Adjectives

Using your dictionary, rewrite each of these compound words as a single word, as a hyphenated word, or as two separate words. If more than one form is correct, be prepared to explain.

EXAMPLE   foot ball   _____football_____

1. open heart surgery   _____
2. free for all   _____
3. high school   _____
4. pear shaped   _____
5. bird house   _____
6. accident prone   _____
7. pot hole   _____
8. bathing suit   _____
9. bread winner   _____
10. hand made   _____

11. head ache   _____
12. head cold   _____
13. head phone   _____
14. head to head   _____
15. head stone   _____
16. free agent   _____
17. free hand   _____
18. free form   _____
19. free spoken   _____
20. free style   _____

Using Hyphens in Numbers

Formal usage in the humanities requires that numbers, including common fractions, be written in words. Write out each of these numbers, using hyphens as needed.

EXAMPLE   2102   _____twenty-one hundred and two_____

1. 35 _____
2. ½ _____
3. ⅘ _____
4. 101 _____
5. 1st _____
6. 3457 _____
7. 495 _____

23 The Period, Question Mark, and Exclamation Point

23a Using a period at the end of a statement, a mild command, and an indirect question

Most sentences end with a period.

STATEMENT   Those who cannot remember the past are condemned to repeat it.

—GEORGE SANTAYANA

MILD COMMAND   Be ready at 6:00.

INDIRECT QUESTION   I wondered how to select a deserving charity. [Compare with direct question (23c).]

23b Using periods with most abbreviations

Most abbreviations call for periods, but some do not. Typical abbreviations with periods that are acceptable in academic writing include *Dr., Mr., Mrs., Ms., Ph.D., M.D., R.N.*, and *a.m.* and *p.m.* with exact times such as *2:15 p.m.* Abbreviations not requiring periods include postal abbreviations for states, such as *CA* and *NY*; names of some organizations and government agencies, such as *CBS* and *FBI*; and acronyms (initials pronounced as words), such as *NASA* and *CARE*.

❖ PUNCTUATION ALERT: (1) Abbreviations of academic degrees should usually be set off with commas. When they follow city names, abbreviations of states are set off by commas. (2) When the period of an abbreviation falls at the end of a sentence, the period also serves to end the sentence. ❖

23c Using a question mark after a direct question

In contrast to an **indirect question**, which *reports* a question and ends with a period, a **direct question** *asks* a question and ends with a question mark.

What is the capital of Georgia?

How do I select a deserving charity? [Compare with indirect question (23a).]

✣PUNCTUATION ALERT: Do not combine a question mark with a comma, a period, or an exclamation point. ✣

No   She asked, "How are you?."

Yes   She asked, "How are you?"

23d Using an exclamation point to issue a strong command or an emphatic declaration

A strong command gives a very firm order, and an emphatic declaration makes a shocking or surprising statement.

Wait!   Sit down!   He lost the rent money!

✣PUNCTUATION ALERT: Do not combine an exclamation point with a comma, a period, or a question mark. ✣

No   "Halt!," shouted the guard.

Yes   "Halt!" shouted the guard.

23e Avoiding overuse of the exclamation point

In academic writing your choice of words, not exclamation points, is expected to communicate the strength of your message. Overusing exclamation points can make your writing appear hysterical.

No   Any head injury is potentially dangerous! Go to the doctor immediately in case of bleeding from the ears, eyes, or mouth! Go if the patient has been unconscious!

Yes   Any head injury is potentially dangerous. Go to the doctor immediately in case of bleeding from the ears, eyes, or mouth, or if the patient has been unconscious.

Supplying Appropriate End Punctuation

A: Circle all inappropriate end punctuation: periods, exclamation marks, and question marks. Then on the line to the right, copy the final word of the sentence and add the appropriate end punctuation. If the end punctuation is correct as is, write *correct* on the line.

EXAMPLE   Many people wonder why nurses wear white(?)   *white.*

1. Have you ever wondered why doctors wear blue or green while operating.   _____

2. White is the traditional symbol of purity!   _____

3. It is also easier to keep clean because it shows dirt.   _____

4. Surgeons wore white during operations until 1914?   _____

5. Then one surgeon decided that the sight of red blood against the white cloth was disgusting!   _____

6. He preferred—would you believe?—a spinach green that he felt reduced the brightness of the blood?   _____

7. After World War II, surgeons began using a different shade of green!   _____

8. Called minty green, it looked better under the new lighting used in operating rooms.   _____

9. The latest color is a blue-gray!   _____

10. Why did the doctors change again.   _____

11. Do you believe they did it because this blue shows up better on television than green does.   _____

12. Believe it or not.   _____

13. The surgeons appear on in-hospital television demonstrating new techniques to medical students!   _____

B: Add end punctuation to this paragraph as needed.

Do you know who Theodor Seuss Geisel is Sure you do He's Dr Seuss, the famous author of children's books After ten years as a successful advertising illustrator and cartoonist, Seuss managed to get his first children's book published *And to Think That I Saw It on Mulberry Street* was published in 1937 by Vanguard Press It had been rejected by 27 other publishers I wonder why They certainly were foolish What's your favorite Dr Seuss book Mine is *The Cat in the Hat*, published in 1957 Everyone has a favorite And I do mean *Everyone* His books have been translated into 17 languages, and by 1984 over a hundred million copies had been sold worldwide In fact, in 1984 Seuss received a Pulitzer Prize for his years of educating and entertaining children How fitting

Writing Sentences with Appropriate End Punctuation

Write a sentence to illustrate each of these uses of end punctuation.

EXAMPLE   an emphatic command
          Wipe that grin off your face!

1. an indirect question

2. a mild command

3. a direct question

4. an abbreviation

5. a declarative sentence containing a direct quotation

6. an exclamation

7. a declarative statement

8. an emphatic command

9. a declarative sentence containing a quoted direct question

10. a declarative sentence containing an indirect quotation

11. a declarative sentence containing a quoted exclamation

24 The Comma

24a Using a comma before a coordinating conjunction that links independent clauses

The coordinating conjunctions—*and, but, for, or, nor, yet*, and *so*—can link two or more independent clauses to create compound sentences. Use a comma before the coordinating conjunction ♣ COMMA CAUTION: Do not put a comma *after* a coordinating conjunction that links independent clauses. ♣

Independent clause,	**and** **but** **for** **or** **nor** **yet** **so**	independent clause.

Tea contains caffeine, **but** herbal tea does not.
Caffeine makes some people jumpy, **and** it may even keep them from sleeping.
Caffeine is found in colas, **so** heavy cola drinkers may also have trouble sleeping.

♣ COMMA CAUTION: Don't use a comma when a coordinating conjunction links words, phrases, or dependent clauses. ♣

No   More restaurants now carry decaffeinated coffee, and fruit juice.
Yes   More restaurants now carry decaffeinated coffee and fruit juice.

♣ COMMA CAUTION: To avoid creating a comma splice, do not use a comma to separate independent clauses unless they are linked by a coordinating conjunction. ♣

No   Caffeine occurs naturally in many foods, it is even found in chocolate.
         [These independent clauses have no linking word. The comma cannot substitute for a linking word.]
Yes   Caffeine occurs naturally in many foods, and it is even found in chocolate.
         [A coordinating conjunction and comma link the two independent clauses.]

When independent clauses containing other commas are linked by a coordinating conjunction, use a semicolon before the coordinating conjunction.

Some herbal teas, such as orange flavored, have become very popular; yet some people, afraid to try anything new, refuse to taste them.

24b Using a comma after an introductory clause, phrase, or word

When a clause, phrase, or word introduces an independent clause, use a comma to signal the end of the introductory element and the beginning of the independent clause.

Introductory clause,

Introductory phrase,   independent clause.

Introductory word,

An adverb clause, one type of dependent clause, cannot stand alone as an independent unit. Although it contains a subject and verb, it begins with a subordinating conjunction (7h, 7n-2). Use a comma to set off an adverb clause that introduces an independent clause.

Whenever it rains, the lake floods local streets.

Because federal loans are hard to get, the community will have to get private help.

When an adverb clause comes after the independent clause, do not use a comma.

The lake floods local streets whenever it rains.

The community will have to get private help because federal loans are hard to get.

A **phrase** is a group of words that cannot stand alone as an independent unit because it lacks a subject, a verb, or both. Use a comma to set off a phrase that introduces an independent clause.

Inside even the cleanest homes, insects thrive. [prepositional phrase]

Carefully using insecticides, we can safely drive the insects out of our homes again. [participial phrase]

Introductory transitional words (see 4b) indicate relationships between ideas in sentences and paragraphs. Use a comma to set off a transitional word or phrase that introduces an independent clause (Some writers prefer to omit the comma after single word transitions).

First, an exterminator must clear the area of open containers of food, pets, and fragile plants.

In addition, he must be careful not to transport insects to new areas when he moves these items.

24c Using commas to separate items in a series

A series is a group of three or more elements—words, phrases, or clauses—that match in grammatical form and have the same importance within a sentence. Use commas between items in a series and before *and* when it is used between the last two items.

> **word, word**, and **word**
>
> **word, word, word**
>
> **phrase, phrase**, and **phrase**
>
> **phrase, phrase, phrase**
>
> **clause, clause**, and **clause**
>
> **clause, clause, clause**

Citrus fruits include **oranges, tangerines** and **grapefruits**.

There are many varieties or oranges: **the sweet orange, the Jaffa orange, the navel orange, the mandarin.**

Lemons are good for **flavoring cakes, decorating platters**, and **removing stains**.

When the items in a series contain commas or other punctuation, or when the items are long and complex, separate them with semicolons instead of commas.

Oranges are probably native to tropical Asia, but they spread quickly centuries ago because of the Roman conquest of Asia, Europe, and North Africa; the Arab trade routes; the expansion of Islam throughout the Mediterranean, except for France and Italy; and the Crusades.

24d Using a comma to separate coordinate adjectives

Coordinate adjectives are two or more adjectives that equally modify a noun or noun group. Separate coordinate adjectives with commas or coordinating conjunctions.

> **coordinate adjective, coordinate adjective** noun

The sweet orange has **broad, glossy** leaves.

Adjectives are coordinate if *and* can be inserted between them or if their order can be reversed without damaging the meaning of the sentence. Meaning does not change when the example sentence says *broad and glossy leaves or glossy, broad leaves.* ✤ COMMA CAUTIONS: (1) Don't put a comma after a final coordinate adjective and the noun it modifies—note that no comma comes between *glossy* and *leaves* in the above example. (2) Don't put a comma between adjectives that are not coordinate: *Six large oranges cost two dollars.* ✤

24e Using commas to set off nonrestrictive (nonessential) elements

Restrictive and nonrestrictive elements are kinds of modifiers. A **nonrestrictive modifier** is also called a **nonessential modifier** because the information it provides about the modified term is "extra." If a nonrestrictive modifier is dropped, a reader can still understand the full meaning of the modified word. Nonrestrictive modifiers are set off with commas.

Nonrestrictive element, independent clause.

Beginning of independent clause, **nonrestrictive element**, end of independent clause.

Independent clause, **nonrestrictive element**.

Believe it or not, the first daily newspaper was a Roman invention.

The *Acta Diurna*, **whose title means "daily events,"** was available every day.

Scribes made multiple copies of each day's political and social news, **which included senate action and the results of gladiatorial games**.

When the nonrestrictive information in these examples is eliminated, the meaning of the modified terms does not change.

The first daily newspaper was a Roman invention.

The *Acta Diurna* was available every day.

Scribes made multiple copies of each day's political and social news.

In contrast, a **restrictive modifier** (also known as an **essential modifier**) cannot be omitted without creating confusion. No commas are used because the information in these passages is part of the basic message of the sentence. ♣ COMMA CAUTION: A restrictive modifier is not extra. Do not use commas to set it off from the rest of the sentence. ♣

Whoever invented paper is unknown.

The Chinese printed **what are considered the first books**.

They invented a white paper **that was made of wood** and a way to transfer a carved image from stone to paper.

Compare the pairs of restrictive and nonrestrictive modifiers that follow.

NONRESTRICTIVE CLAUSE	The world's oldest surviving book printed from wood blocks was published in A.D. 868 by Wang Chieh, **who followed an already long Chinese printing tradition.** [*Who followed an already long Chinese printing tradition* adds information about Wang Chieh, but it is not essential to the sentence.]
RESTRICTIVE CLAUSE	Students **who wish to imitate the woodblock method** do not need many materials. [The clause clarifies which students, so it is essential.]

NONRESTRICTIVE PHRASE	**Before carving**, the student should sketch out a preliminary version of the page. [*Before carving* is a prepositional phrase that explains when to act. However, the sentence is clear without it.]
RESTRICTIVE PHRASE	Marco Polo introduced woodblock printing **to Europe**. [Prepositional phrase is essential to the message.]

An **appositive** is a word or group of words that renames the noun or noun group preceding it. Most appositives are nonrestrictive. Once the name of something is given, words renaming it are not usually necessary to specify or limit it even more.

> Johann Gutenberg, **a German printer living in France**, was the first European to use movable type.

Some appositives, however, are restrictive and are not set off with commas.

> Mr. Jones **the rare book collector** would pay a fortune to own a Gutenberg Bible. [The appositive is essential for distinguishing this Mr. Jones from other Mr. Joneses.]

24f | Using commas to set off parenthetical and transitional expressions, contrasts, words of direct address, and tag questions

Words, phrases, or clauses that interrupt a sentence but—like nonrestrictive elements—do not change its basic meaning should be set off, usually with commas. (Parentheses or dashes also set material off.)

Parenthethetical expressions are "asides," additions to sentences that the writer thinks of as extra.

> The Spanish brought the first printing press in the New World to Mexico City in 1534, but, **surprisingly**, the earliest surviving pieces of work are from 1539. [parenthetical expression]

Transitional words (such as *however, for example, in addition, therefore*) sometimes express connections within sentences. When they do, they are set off with commas.

> The oldest surviving document, **in fact**, of a news event is a report of a storm and earthquake in Guatemala in 1541. [transitional expression]

♣ COMMA CAUTION: When a transitional expression links independent clauses, use a semicolon or a coordinating conjunction. A comma alone will create a comma splice: *Few old documents survive;* **in fact**, the oldest surviving news report is from 1541. ♣

Expressions of contrast are set off with commas.

An early printing press at Lima turned out Indian- and Spanish-language religious material, **not political or news pamphlets**. [words of contrast]

The roots of the extensive modern Spanish-language press go back to these two printing centers, **rather than to Spain itself**. [words of contrast]

Words of direct address and tag questions should be set off with commas.

Did you know, **Rosa**, that your daily Spanish newspaper is part of a 400-year-old tradition? [direct address]

You are bilingual, **aren't you?** [tag question]

24g **Using commas to set off quoted words from explanatory words**

Use a comma to set off quoted words from short explanations in the same sentence, such as *she said, they replied*, and *he answered*.

According to a Chinese proverb, "A book is like a garden carried in the pocket."

"When I stepped from hard manual work to writing," said Sean O'Casey, "I just stepped from one kind of hard work to another."

"I can't write five words, but that I change seven," complained Dorothy Parker.

❖ COMMA CAUTION: When quoted words end with a question mark or an exclamation point, keep that punctuation and do not add a comma even if explanatory words follow. ❖

24h **Using commas in dates, names, addresses, and numbers according to accepted practice**

RULES FOR COMMAS WITH DATES

1. Use a comma between the date and the year: **November 24, 1859**.
2. Use a comma between the day and the date: **Thursday, November 24.**
3. Within a sentence, use commas after the day *and* the year in a full date.
    November 24, 1859, was the date of publication of Charles Darwin's *The Origin of Species*.

4. Don't use a comma in a date that contains only the month and year or only the season and year.
    Darwin's *The Origin of Species* was published in **winter 1859**.

5. An inverted date takes no commas.
    Charles Darwin's *The Origin of Species* was first published on **24 November 1859**.

24h

RULES FOR COMMAS WITH NAMES, PLACES, AND ADDRESSES

1. When an abbreviated title (Jr., M.D., Ph.D.) comes after a person's name, set the abbreviation off with commas.

    The company celebrated the promotion of **Susan Cohen, M.B.A.**, to senior vice president.

2. When you invert a person's name, use a comma to separate the last name from the first: **Cohen, Susan.**

3. Use a comma between a city and state: **Cherry Hill, New Jersey**. In a sentence, use a comma after the state as well.

    Cherry Hill, New Jersey, is not far from Philadelphia.

4. When you write a complete address as part of a sentence, use a comma to separate all the items but the zip code, which follows the state. A comma does not follow the zip code.

    The check from U.R. Stuk, **1313 Erewhon Lane, Englewood Cliffs, New Jersey 07632** bounced.

RULES FOR COMMAS WITH LETTERS

1. For the opening of an informal letter, use a comma: **Dear Betty,**
2. For the close of a letter, use a comma: **Sincerely yours, Love, Best regards, Very truly yours,**

RULES FOR COMMAS WITH NUMBERS

1. Counting from the right, put a comma after every three digits in numbers over four digits: **72,867 156,567,066**
2. In a number of four digits, a comma is optional.

    $1776 or **$1,776**   **1776 miles** or **1,776 miles**

3. Don't use a comma for a four-digit year—**1990** (but **25,000 B.C.**); or in an address—**12161 Dean Drive**; or in a page number—**see page 1338**
4. Use a comma to separate related measurements written as words: **five feet, four inches**
5. Use a comma to separate a play's scene from an act: **Act II, scene iv**
6. Use a comma to separate a reference to a page from a reference to a line: **page 10, line 6**

24i Using commas to clarify meaning

Sometimes you will need to use a comma to clarify the meaning of a sentence, even though no other rule calls for one.

No   In his will power to run the family business was divided among his children.

YES   In his will, power to run the family business was divided among his children.

No   People who want to register to vote without being reminded.

YES   People who want to, register to vote without being reminded.

24j Avoiding misuse of the comma

Do not overuse commas by inserting them where they do not belong. Comma misuses are discussed throughout this chapter, signaled by ❖ COMMA CAUTION. ❖

Besides the misuses of commas discussed earlier, writers sometimes use commas to separate major sentence parts.

No   Snowfalls over the last 20 million years, have created the Antarctic ice sheet. [Do not separate a subject from its verb with a single comma.]

YES   Snowfalls over the last 20 million years have created the Antarctic ice sheet.

No   The massive ice sheet is, 16,000 feet deep. [Do not separate a verb from its complement with a single comma.]

YES   The massive ice sheet is 16,000 feet deep.

No   The weight of the ice has pushed, the continent 2,000 feet into the water. [Do not separate a verb from its object with a single comma.]

YES   The weight of the ice has pushed the continent 2,000 feet into the water.

No   Therefore, most of the continent lies below, sea level. [Do not separate a preposition from its object with a single comma.]

YES   Therefore, most of the continent lies below sea level.

Using Commas in Compound Sentences

EXERCISE **24-1**
(24a)

A: Rewrite the following sentences, inserting commas wherever coordinating conjunctions are used to join sentences. If a sentence does not need any additional commas, write *correct* on the line."

EXAMPLE   The Pilgrims' Thanksgiving was the first one in the New World but it was not the first in the whole world.
The Pilgrims' Thanksgiving was the first one in the New World, but it
was not the first in the whole world.

1. The ancient Greeks, Romans, and Hebrews had festivals of thanksgiving to celebrate the annual harvest and this custom was still followed in the days of the Pilgrims.

   _____

   _____

2. The Pilgrims landed in December 1620 and they immediately faced terrible cold weather and disease.

   _____

3. Forty-six Pilgrims died that first winter but the situation was much better by the fall.

   _____

4. A new crop had been gathered so for the first time the Pilgrims had enough food.

   _____

5. They were alive mainly because of the help of one Indian.

   _____

6. Squanto had been sold into slavery in Spain but he had escaped to England.

   _____

7. Luckily he had returned to America just six months before the Pilgrims came for they never could have survived without him.

_____

_____

8. The Pilgrims did not know how to build suitable housing nor did they know how to grow corn and barley.

_____

9. In the fall, the Pilgrims elected a new governor and declared a day of Thanksgiving to celebrate living through the winter.

_____

_____

10. The Pilgrims invited the local Indian chief and his braves yet they did not plan very well.

_____

11. Thirteen women had died during the terrible winter so the job of preparing everything for 147 people fell on the six women survivors.

_____

_____

12. The first American Thanksgiving had all the basic features of our modern holiday but everything was just a bit different.

_____

_____

13. The most typical part of the modern Thanksgiving feast was probably not served that first fall for "turkey" was a general word that referred to many kinds of birds.

_____

_____

14. The Pilgrims may have caught some wild turkeys or they may have caught other birds.

_____

15. We know the feast featured venison for one of the Pilgrims wrote that the Indians killed and brought five deer to the celebration.

_____

320

B: Combine the following sentences by using the coordinating conjunctions given in parentheses. Remember to use a comma before each coordinating conjunction used to join two sentences.

EXAMPLE   The first Thanksgiving celebrated by all the colonies took place in
           October 1777.
           It was a one-time event. (but)
           The first Thanksgiving celebrated by all the colonies took place in _____
           October 1777, but it was a one-time event. _____

1. The colonists believed they had good reason to celebrate.
   They had just defeated the British in a major battle. (for)

   _____

   _____

2. George Washington proclaimed a national Thanksgiving holiday in 1789.
   Quarrels among the colonies interfered. (but)

   _____

   _____

3. Some people felt that the sufferings of one small group of settlers should
   not matter to the whole country.
   They wanted to find a more suitable national event to celebrate. (and)

   _____

   _____

   _____

4. President Jefferson spoke against national celebration of the Pilgrims'
   Thanksgiving.
   He agreed with those who felt the event was unimportant. (for)

   _____

   _____

5. Early popular opinion against the holiday was strong.
   Thanks to the efforts of one woman, we celebrate Thanksgiving. (yet)

   _____

   _____

6. Sarah Josepha Hale was editor of a woman's magazine with 150,000 readers.
   She used her position to support a national Thanksgiving holiday. (and)

   _____

   _____

7. She wrote lively, patriotic articles.
   She urged her readers to write letters to local politicians. (and)

   _____

   _____

8. She was afraid this might not be enough.
   She also wrote hundreds of letters herself over a period of forty years. (so)

   _____

   _____

9. One of Mrs. Hale's most passionate articles appeared during a point late in the Civil War when people were tired of bloodshed.
   President Lincoln was convinced to proclaim Thanksgiving a holiday for the whole nation. (so)

   _____

   _____

   _____

10. Since then no one has dared to challenge Thanksgiving.
    No one has been able to change the date of celebration. (nor)

    _____

    _____

Using Commas After
Introductory Elements

A: Applying the rules regarding commas and introductory elements, rewrite these sentences, inserting commas as needed. If any sentence does not need an additional comma, write *correct* on the line.

EXAMPLE As you have probably noticed houses are often painted white.
As you have probably noticed, houses are often painted white.

1. In fact white is the most common color for houses.

   _____

2. For starters white is associated with classic Greek and Roman buildings.

   _____

3. Also the Puritans thought colorful houses were foolish.

   _____

4. In contrast they thought of white as serious.

   _____

5. In the mid-nineteenth century white color for houses was attacked.

   _____

6. According to some experts at the time white houses clashed with the soft green of surrounding trees and bushes.

   _____

7. Earth tones were said to be the most attractive colors for houses.

   _____

8. Especially after the invention of premixed color paints white houses became less popular.

   _____

9. By the late nineteenth century white houses were back in style.

   _____

10. Although fashions have come and gone since then white has remained one of the most popular colors for homes.

_____

11. Because he was puzzled by the popularity of white houses a researcher asked a group of paint experts for theories.

_____

12. In the opinion of one expert white is easy to use because it suits any style home.

_____

13. When another expert was asked she said that people like white because of its connections with cleanliness and purity.

_____

14. Another expert simply said that white is classic.

_____

15. Finally white matches all other colors, so it goes with any color roof and house trim.

_____

B: Applying the rules governing commas and introductory elements, insert commas as needed in this paragraph.

[1]If farmers have pest problems nonchemical controls may be the safest and least expensive solution. [2]For a pest population to succeed it must have its particular food. [3]When crops are rotated (grown in different fields each season) each crop's pests may starve to death in the spring because their food source has been replaced. [4]Also planting, fertilizing, and watering schedules can be adapted to prevent pests. [5]As many home gardeners already know nearby plants can help by attracting pests away from crops or by driving them away altogether. [6]The common marigold is popular because it works in this way. [7]All in all simple measures such as these can make gardening or farming safer and more profitable.

Using Commas in Series and with Coordinate Adjectives

EXERCISE 24-3
(24c-d)

A: In each sentence, first underline all items in series and all coordinate adjectives. Then rewrite each sentence, adding any necessary commas. If no commas are needed, explain why.

EXAMPLE   Many famous people have been superstitious, including <u>Napoleon</u>
<u>Caesar</u> and <u>Henry VIII.</u>
Many famous people have been superstitious, including Napoleon,
Caesar, and Henry VIII.

1. Even many rational intelligent people believe in some superstitions, such as lucky numbers.

   _____

2. Some lucky numbers are based on birthdays anniversaries and family "firsts."

   _____

3. Superstition prevents some people from walking under ladders opening umbrellas indoors or starting new jobs on Friday the thirteenth.

   _____

   _____

4. Most superstitions do not seem logical, but originally every superstition had a purpose a cultural setting and a practical explanation.

   _____

   _____

5. Superstitions arose as people looked for explanations of natural events, such as thunder lightning eclipses birth and death.

   _____

   _____

6. Looking for protection in a dangerous world, people placed their faith in a rabbit's foot a four-leaf clover or a magic spell.

   _____

   _____

7. Such charms seemed to make the world safer more understandable and friendlier.

_____

8. Think about your own behavior on a typical busy day.

_____

9. During lunch in a crowded noisy restaurant, you spill some salt.

_____

10. Are you the kind of person who will throw some of the spilled salt over your shoulder even if you risk getting it on a large angry man at the next table?

_____

_____

B: Write complete sentences as described below. Take special care to follow the rules governing the use of commas in lists and between coordinate adjectives.

EXAMPLE   Mention three places you would like to visit someday.
          Someday I would like to visit Ireland, Israel, and Nigeria.

1. In a complete sentence, list your three least-liked foods.

_____

_____

2. Describe the worst food in a complete sentence, using two or three adjectives in series.

_____

_____

3. In a complete sentence, list your four favorite movie stars (or singers).

_____

_____

4. Describe your favorite movie star (or singer) in a complete sentence, using three adjectives in series.

_____

_____

5. In a complete sentence, list three places you can hide something. Use prepositions.

_____

_____

6. In one sentence, describe why one of these hiding places is effective. Give at least three reasons.

_____

_____

7. In a complete sentence, list the steps of a simple process. Begin "In order to _____, you must _____, _____, . . ."

_____

_____

8. Using at least two adjectives in series, write a complete sentence describing what is made in the process described in number 7.

_____

_____

Using Commas with Nonrestrictive, Parenthetical, and Transitional Elements

Rewrite these sentences to punctuate nonrestrictive clauses, phrases, appositives, and transitional expressions.

EXAMPLE   Although bulls are almost colorblind many people believe that they are attracted by the color red.
Although bulls are almost colorblind, many people believe that they are attracted by the color red.

1. The bull's attention of course is attracted by bright colors such as red, orange, and royal blue.

   _____

2. However it is the brightness that catches his eye not the color itself.

   _____

3. The idea that fish is especially good brain food dates back to a scientific error of the nineteenth-century German scientists' belief that the element phosphorus was good for the brain.

   _____

   _____

4. Because fish are high in phosphorus they soon had a reputation for being necessary to thought.

   _____

5. Actually phosphorus is only one of many nutrients required by the brain.

   _____

6. Fish is good for us as good as any other high-protein, low-fat food.

   _____

7. The owl who is not really especially smart has long been a symbol of wisdom.

   _____

8. The owl was believed to be the favorite bird of Athena the Greek goddess of wisdom.

_____

9. The owl's wide-eyed, alert look is the result really of its being unable to move its eyes in their sockets.

_____

10. If it wants to see something off to the side the owl must move its entire head.

_____

11. Its excellent night vision made it an object of envy especially in the days before electric light.

_____

12. Dogs and cats just like people are either right-handed or left-handed preferring to use one paw more than the other.

_____

Expanding Sentences with Restrictive and Nonrestrictive Elements

EXERCISE **24-5**
(24e-f)

Expand each sentence twice: first with a restrictive word, phrase, or clause, and then with a nonrestrictive word, phrase, or clause. Place commas as needed.

EXAMPLE   Spring is beautiful.
   1. (restrictive) *Spring in the Rockies is beautiful.*
   2. (nonrestrictive) *Spring, with all the flowers in bloom, is beautiful.*

1. Apartments are hard to find.

_____

_____

2. Travel can be nerve-wracking.

_____

_____

3. Dogs usually make good pets.

   _____

   _____

4. My neighbor hates loud music.

   _____

   _____

5. Sidewalks can be dangerous.

   _____

   _____

6. I want to buy an air-conditioner.

   _____

   _____

7. The roof leaked.

   _____

   _____

8. The truck made an illegal U-turn.

   _____

   _____

Using Commas with Quotations

Using the rules governing the use of commas to attach quotations to their speaker tags, place commas in these sentences.

EXAMPLE   According to Herbert Samuel, "It takes two to make a marriage a success and only one to make it a failure."

1. "Marriage" said Joseph Barth "is our last, best chance to grow up."
2. Peter De Vries was right when he said "The difficulty with marriage is that we fall in love with a personality, but must live with a character."
3. According to André Maurois "A successful marriage is an edifice that must be rebuilt every day."
4. "Heaven" said Andrew Jackson "will be no heaven to me if I do not meet my wife there."
5. "Marriage resembles a pair of shears, so joined that they cannot be separated; often moving in opposite directions, yet always punishing any one who comes between them" observed Sydney Smith.
6. "Chains do not hold a marriage together" said Simone Signoret. "It is threads, hundreds of tiny threads which sew people together through the years."
7. An anonymous wise person said "If there is anything better than to be loved it is loving."
8. "The way to love anything is to realize that it might be lost" advised Gilbert K. Chesterton.
9. "Love gives itself; it is not bought" observed Longfellow.
10. "Love does not consist in gazing at each other" said Antoine de Saint-Exupéry "but in looking outward together in the same direction."

Using Commas in Dates, Names, Addresses, and Numbers

Rewrite the following sentences, inserting commas to punctuate dates, names, addresses, and numbers. If a sentence is correct as written, write *correct* on the line.

EXAMPLE   The world's record distance for a hot-air balloon flight is 2804 miles.
The world's record distance for a hot-air balloon flight is 2,804 miles.
or correct (2804 miles)

1. This record-setting flight across the Atlantic Ocean began on July 2 1987 and ended July 3.

   _____

2. Two British men took off from Sugarloaf Mountain Maine in a 200-foot-high balloon.

   _____

3. Major league baseball showed its increasing popularity when total attendance passed the 50000000 mark for the first time during the 1987 season.

   _____

   _____

4. History was made on October 17 1987 when the first indoor World Series game was played at the Hubert H. Humphrey Metrodome in Minneapolis Minnesota.

   _____

   _____

5. In basketball that year, seven-foot two-inch Kareem Abdul-Jabbar helped lead the Los Angeles Lakers to National Basketball Association victory.

   _____

   _____

6. On Saturday August 13 1987 I began weight training.

   _____

7. I expect to be able to compete by spring 1990.

   _____

8. Alexa Perlmutter M.D. is the local sports medicine specialist.

   _____

9. She is listed in the phone book as "Perlmutter Alexa."

   _____

10. Her office is at 9876 Main Street Port Jefferson New York 11776.

    _____

Adding Commas

A: Rewrite the following sentences, inserting commas as needed. If a sentence is correct as written, write *correct* on the line.

EXAMPLE   Have you ever wondered why traffic lights are red yellow and green?
Have you ever wondered why traffic lights are red, yellow, and
green?

1. Surprisingly traffic signals existed before the automobile.

   _____

2. One perhaps the first was erected in London in 1868.

   _____

3. This signal which was imitated in America had arms like the gate at a railroad crossing that came down to block traffic.

   _____

4. Rather than controlling automobile traffic these early signals directed walkers.

   _____

5. Because people walking at night could not see the device's arms lights were attached.

   _____

6. The designer adopted the color system already in use for railroad signs red to stop and green to go.

   _____

7. The first signal was not a complete immediate success.

   _____

8. The gas lights on the signal's arms blew up one day killing a police officer.

   _____

9. Salt Lake City St. Paul and Cleveland all claim to be the home of the first signal used to control automobile traffic.

_____

10. The signal on Euclid Avenue in Cleveland Ohio is believed by most authorities to be the oldest.

_____

11. Although the colors were originally placed in random order concern with safety led to the regularization of the colors and the design of the lights.

_____

12. As recently as thirty years ago many traffic signals displayed their colors horizontally.

_____

13. Color-blind people unfortunately were frequently confused by such designs.

_____

14. The design has been regularized and now people can count on the red light being on top the green at the bottom and the yellow in the center.

_____

15. As an additional aid to the color-blind the red has a bit of orange in it and the green has a bit of blue.

_____

B: Add commas as needed. You will not need to add any words or other marks of punctuation.

[1]In spite of the lion's reputation for fierceness every year more people are killed in Africa by crocodiles than by lions. [2]The crocodile is a large flesh-eating reptile that lives in and near tropical waterways. [3]Crocodiles have long tails and thick tough skin. [4]Their heads end in long heavy triangular jaws. [5]A crocodile weighing 120 pounds a rather small one can shut its jaws with a pressure of 1540 pounds. [6]In contrast a human's jaws exert only 40 to 80 pounds of pressure. [7]The largest crocodiles generally grow to be about 20 feet long but there are rumors of 30-foot crocodiles. [8]Crocodiles are cannibals eating their own young as willingly as they eat other animals. [9]Crocodiles do not chew their food but swallow it whole. [10]Although they may appear clumsy crocodiles are very fast on land. [11]If a person is chased by a crocodile the best plan is to run in a zigzag pattern for the crocodile cannot make sudden changes of direction.

[12]The crocodile is related to the alligator the caiman and the gavial. [13]The alligator is found in tropical rivers and swamps in the United States and China. [14]Its snout the nose and jaws is shorter and blunter than the crocodile's. [15]The caiman is a South American relative of the alligator and crocodile and the gavial is found in northern India Borneo and Sumatra.

Eliminating Unnecessary Commas

Rewrite this paragraph, omitting any unnecessary commas. You will not need to add any words or marks of punctuation.

[1]The Victoria Falls, were discovered by Dr. David Livingstone in 1855. [2]The waterfall is part of, the Zambezi River in Africa. [3]The falls are 355 feet high, and 4,495 feet wide. [4]Depending upon the time of year, up to 140 million cubic feet of water may pass over the falls each day. [5]The falls are, the result of an unusual geological condition. [6]The river bed abruptly funnels, into a deep crack. [7]The trapped water can escape, under great pressure, only through a narrow, crevice. [8]The rapidly moving water is divided by a number of small islands, and, each of the falls is named separately: the Devil's Cataract, the main falls, the Rainbow Falls, and the Eastern Cataract. [9]Once water has passed over the falls, it continues through narrow, savage, Batoka Gorge, and flows under the railroad bridge that joins Zimbabwe and Zambia. [10]The area has changed very little since, Livingstone's day. [11]Herds of wild animals live protected in the nearby, national parks, and the area is largely, undeveloped.

Adding and Deleting Commas

Rewrite this paragraph, adding or deleting commas as needed. You will not have to change any words or other marks of punctuation. Number each change you make, and on the lines below indicate the reason for each addition or omission.

Mount Everest, the highest mountain in the world is located in the Himalayas on the border of Tibet, and Nepal. It is surrounded, by glaciers formed from the ice, and snow that fall from its peak. The first, successful climb up that peak was made by Edmund Hillary, and Tenzing Norgay a Sherpa
5 guide in 1953. Everest had been a challenge to, all climbers ever since 1852 when its height was first recorded, 29028 feet. The attempt to climb Everest began, in earnest in 1924, and continued right through 1952. On the first attempt two climbers Mallory and Irvine disappeared, leaving only an ice axe behind. Almost thirty years later the Royal Geographical Society team led by
10 Sir John Hunt, succeeded. As members of this team Hillary and Tenzing fulfilled a hundred-year-old dream. Since then there have been successful climbs by Indian Japanese United States and Swiss teams. Advanced equipment and the knowledge of the Hunt expedition have made them possible but climbing Everest still remains only for the strong the brave and the lucky.

Commas Added	*Commas Deleted*
_____	_____
_____	_____
_____	_____
_____	_____
_____	_____
_____	_____
_____	_____
_____	_____
_____	_____
_____	_____
_____	_____
_____	_____

25 The Semicolon

25a Using a semicolon between closely related independent clauses

When independent clauses are related in meaning, you can separate them with a semicolon instead of a period. ❖ COMMA CAUTION: Do not use only a comma between independent clauses, or you will create a comma splice (see Chapter 14). ❖

Independent clause; independent clause.

All changes are not growth; all movement is not forward.   —ELLEN GLASGOW

25b Using a semicolon between related independent clauses that contain commas, even if a coordinating conjunction joins the independent clauses

You will usually use a comma to separate independent clauses linked by a coordinating conjunction (see 7h). When the independent clauses already contain commas, however, use a semicolon instead to separate the clauses.

Independent clause, one that contains commas; coordinating conjunction independent clause.
Independent clause; coordinating conjunction independent clause, one that contains commas.

Aim at the sun, and you may not reach it; but your arrow will fly far higher than if aimed at an object on a level with yourself.   —JOEL HAWES

25c Using a semicolon (or a period) when conjunctive adverbs or other transitional words connect independent clauses

Use a semicolon between two independent clauses when the second clause begins with a conjunctive adverb or other transitional word (4b). ♣ COMMA CAUTION: Do not use only a comma between independent clauses connected by a conjunctive adverb or other words of transition, or you will create a comma splice (see Chapter 14). ♣

Independent clause; conjunctive adverb or other transition, independent clause.

A coelacanth, a supposedly extinct fish, was caught by an African fisherman in 1938; **as a result**, some scientists believe other "extinct" animals may still live in remote parts of the world.

♣ COMMA ALERT: When you place a conjunctive adverb or a transition after the first word in an independent clause, set it off with commas: *This theory may be true; some people, **however**, even suggest the Loch Ness Monster may be a dinosaur.* ♣

25d Using a semicolon between long or comma-containing items in a series.

When a sentence contains a series of words, phrases, or clauses, commas usually separate one item from the next. When the items are long and contain commas for other purposes, you can make your message clearer by separating the items with semicolons instead of commas.

Independent clause that includes a series of items, each or all of which contain commas; another item in the series; another item in the series.

Many are always praising the by-gone time, for it is natural that the old should extol the days of their youth; the weak, the time of their strength; the sick, the season of their vigor; and the disappointed, the spring-tide of their hopes.

—CALEB BINGHAM

25e Avoiding misuse of the semicolon

Don't use a semicolon between a dependent clause and an independent clause: *Because the price of new cars continues to rise, people are keeping their old cars.*

Don't use a semicolon to introduce a list; use a colon: *Keeping these old cars running can be expensive too; rebuilt engines, new transmissions, and replacement tires.*

Using the Semicolon

A: Insert semicolons where needed. They may be placed where there is now no punctuation or they may replace commas. Some sentences may require more than one semicolon. If an item is correct, write *correct* in the left margin.

EXAMPLE   Vision is our most important sense ; we get most of our information about the world by seeing.

1. The sclera is the outer cover of the eye, it helps the eye keep its shape because the sclera is fairly hard.
2. The choroid is just inside the sclera it keeps out unneeded light.
3. The pupil is the opening in the eye this is where the light enters.
4. The cornea is the clear cover of the pupil, therefore, light can enter the eye.
5. The pupil is opened or closed by muscles in the iris, in fact, in bright light the iris closes to decrease the amount of light entering, in low light, it opens to increase the light.
6. After passing through the pupil, light shines on the retina, which sends messages to the brain.
7. The retina contains cells, cones and rods, which are outgrowths of the brain when light strikes them, nerve impulses travel to the brain.
8. The optic nerve connects the eye to the brain, thus any damage to the nerve can cause blindness.
9. Cone cells give us color vision, they are most effective in the day.
10. Rods are sensitive to low light they are involved in night vision.

B: This paragraph is missing seven semicolons. Insert them where needed.

      Hearing is based on sound waves these are pressure changes spreading out from a vibrating source. If we could see sound waves, they might remind us of ripples on water like ripples, sound waves vary in number, size, and speed. When these waves reach us, our ears and brain translate them
5 into pitch, loudness, and timbre. Pitch is the number of wave vibrations per second it determines whether a tone is high or low, whether a singer is a soprano or an alto. Loudness is a measure of the intensity of the waves this is called their amplitude. When we turn up the volume on the stereo, we are raising the amplitude. Sound intensity is measured in decibels. Any sound
10 registering over 130 decibels is painful however, people still listen to loud music or live near railroad tracks. Timbre is hard to describe in everyday language in physics terms, however, timbre is the main wavelength plus any other wavelengths that may come from a particular source. Timbre explains why a note played on a violin sounds different than the same note played

15 on an electric guitar or why two people singing the same note sound different. Physics defines *noise* as too many unrelated frequencies vibrating together nevertheless, people still disagree over whether some sounds are noise or exciting music.

Using the Semicolon and the Comma

Add commas or semicolons as needed to fill in the blanks appropriately.

EXAMPLE   One out of every twenty-five people is colorblind __,__ unable to tell certain colors apart.

1. Colorblindness is inherited _____ it appears more often in men than in women.
2. The most common colorblindness is the inability to tell red from green _____ but more than green and red are involved.
3. Different colors, the result of differences in light wavelengths, create a spectrum _____ the spectrum of colors is red, orange, yellow, green, blue, indigo, and violet.
4. People who are severely red-green colorblind cannot "see" any colors at that end of the spectrum _____ that is _____ they cannot tell the difference between blue-greens, reds, or yellow-greens.
5. Colorblindness varies from person to person _____ people who can distinguish red from green a little are called color-weak.
6. Some people have no cone cells (the cells that send signals about color to the brain) _____ so they are completely colorblind.
7. They have achromatism _____ a rare condition.
8. Such people can see only black, white, and grays _____ what a boring view of the world.
9. However, their problem is much more serious than this _____ they also have trouble focusing on objects.
10. The part of the eye that usually receives images is the fovea, which contains the cone cells _____ achromatics' foveas are blank and cannot receive images.
11. To compensate, they look at objects off center _____ to pick up images with their rod (black and white) cells.
12. It is possible to be colorblind and not know it _____ how can people miss what they have never known?
13. There are several tests for colorblindness _____ most involve seeing (or not seeing) a number or word written on a background of a complementary color _____ for example, a red *48* on a green background.

26 | The Colon

In sentence punctuation, the colon introduces what comes after it: a quotation, a summary or restatement, or a list. The colon also has a few separating functions.

26a | Using a colon to introduce quotations, summaries, and lists

Use a colon at the end of a grammatically complete statement that introduces a formal quotation.

> Francis Bacon was referring to men and women when he wrote of the destructiveness of seeking vengeance: "A man that studieth revenge keeps his own wounds green."

You can use a colon at the end of an independent clause to introduce statements that summarize, restate, or explain what is said in that clause.

> The makers of some movies aimed at teenagers think that their audience is interested in little more than car chases, violence, and nudity: they sadly underestimate young people.

You can use a colon to lead into a final appositive—a word or group of words that renames a noun or pronoun.

> A hot plate can enable any student to become a dormitory chef, preparing simple and satisfying meals: omelets, stir-fried vegetables, even stews.

Use a colon to introduce a list or series of items announced by an independent clause.

> In selecting a major, consider these factors: your talent for the subject, the number of years needed to qualify professionally, and the availability of jobs.

When you use phrases such as *the following* or *as follows*, a colon is usually required. A colon is *not* called for with the words *such as* or *including* (see 26c).

> Woods commonly used in fine furniture include the following: black walnut, mahogany, oak, and pecan.

Independent clause containing words that introduce a quotation: "Quoted words."
Independent clause: summarizing or restating words.
Independent clause: listed items.

26b Using a colon to separate standard material

TITLE AND SUBTITLE
Broca's Brain: Reflections on the Romance of Science

HOURS, MINUTES, AND SECONDS
The lecture began at 9:15 A.M.

CHAPTERS AND VERSES OF THE BIBLE
Ecclesiastes 3:1

LETTER SALUTATION
Dear Ms. Winters:

MEMO FORM

TO: Dean Elliot Gordon
FROM: Professor Steven Wang
RE: Honors and Awards Ceremony

26c Avoiding misuse of the colon

A colon must follow a complete independent clause except when it separates standard material (26b). Lead-in words must make a grammatically complete statement. When they do not, do not use a colon. Also do not use a colon after the words *such as* and *including* or forms of the verb *be*.

No   The shop sold: tee shirts, bumper stickers, posters, and greeting cards.
Yes   The shop sold tee shirts, bumper stickers, posters, and greeting cards.

No   Students work in many of the town's businesses, such as: the diner, the grocery, the laundromat, and the gas station.
Yes   Students work in many of the town's businesses, such as the diner, the grocery, the laundromat, and the gas station.
Yes   Students work in many of the town's businesses: the diner, the grocery, the laundromat, and the gas station.

Do not use a colon to separate a dependent clause from an independent clause.

No   When summer comes: the town is almost deserted.
Yes   When summer comes, the town is almost deserted.

Using the Colon

Rewrite the following sentences, adding colons as needed. If no colon is needed, write *correct* in the left margin.

EXAMPLE   A poll of Philadelphia schoolchildren identified their favorite first
names David and Linda.
A poll of Philadelphia schoolchildren identified their favorite first
names: **David and Linda.**

1. People believe that Napoleon was short, but he was average height 5'6".

2. According to an ABC News-Harris Survey, U.S. males' three favorite free-time activities are as follows eating, watching TV, and fixing things around the house.

3. According to the same survey, females' favorite activities include eating, reading books, and listening to music.

4. In case you were wondering, here are the most common street names in the United States Park, Washington, Maple, Oak, and Lincoln.

5. I plan to call my autobiography *Burrowing The Adventures of a Bookworm.*

6. The train, 20 minutes late, was due at 640.

7. John F. Hylan, mayor of New York in 1922, spoke for all of us "The police are fully able to meet and compete with the criminals."

8. When walking alone at night, remember one thing Be alert!

9. The nineteenth century was a bad time for Turkey it lost three wars to Russia and three to Egypt, and it lost control over Greece.

10. Few animals are man-eaters, but those that are include the following bears, crocodiles, giant squid, leopards, lions, piranhas, sharks, and tigers.

Writing Sentences
with the Colon

Write complete sentences in answer to these questions. Use a colon in each sentence.

EXAMPLE   What time do you wake up?
          I wake up at 5:45.

1. What is the full title and subtitle of one of your textbooks?

2. What are your favorite classes? (Use the expression *as follows*.)

3. What is your advice to someone going to a job interview?

4. Who are the star players on your favorite team?

5. What streets or geographical features mark the borders of your campus?

27 The Apostrophe

The apostrophe plays three major roles: it helps to form the possessive of nouns and a few pronouns, it stands for omitted letters, and it helps to form the plurals of letters and numerals.

27a Using an apostrophe to form the possessive case of nouns and indefinite pronouns

The possessive case shows ownership (*the scientist's invention*) or close relationship (*the governor's policy, the movie's ending*). It indicates the same meaning as phrases beginning *of the* (*the invention of the scientist*).

When nouns and indefinite pronouns do not end in -*s*, add '*s* to show possession.

The **doctor's** diplomas are on her office wall. [singular noun not ending in -*s*]
The class studied the **women's** rights movement. [plural noun not ending in -*s*]
Good health is **everyone's** wish. [indefinite pronoun not ending in -*s*]

When singular nouns end in -*s*, add '*s* to show possession.

The **waitress's** tip was less than she expected.
Les's phone bill was enormous.

When a plural noun ends in -*s*, use only an apostrophe to show possession.

The **workers'** tools were all over the room.
Their **supervisors'** reports were critical of their sloppiness.

In compound words, add '*s* to the last word.

The **police chief's** retirement party was held in the hotel ballroom.
They held their wedding in her **sister-in-law's** backyard.

In individual possession, add '*s* to each noun.

Pat's and Lee's songs are hits. [Pat and Lee each wrote some of the songs; they did not write the songs together.]

Dali's and Turner's paintings were sold for record prices. [Dali and Turner painted different canvasses.]

In joint or group possession, add *'s* to only the last noun.

Pat and Lee's songs are hits. [Pat and Lee wrote the songs together.]

Dali and Turner's show at the art museum was a hit. [Dali and Turner are featured in the same show.]

27b Avoiding use of an apostrophe with the possessive form of personal pronouns

Some pronouns have their own possessive forms. Do not use an apostrophe with these forms: *his, her, hers, its, our, ours, your, yours, their, theirs, whose*. Be especially careful in using *its/it's* and *whose/who's*, which are often confused. *It's* stands for *it is; its* is a personal pronoun showing possession. *Who's* stands for *who is; whose* is a personal pronoun showing possession.

No   The state will elect **it's** governor next week.
Yes   The state will elect **its** governor next week.

No   The candidate **who's** ads appear on television daily expects to win.
Yes   The candidate **whose** ads appear on television daily expects to win.

27c Using an apostrophe to stand for omitted letters, numbers, or words in contractions

In informal English, some words may be combined by omitting one or more letters and inserting apostrophes to signal the omission: *I'm (I am), aren't (are not), he'll (he will)*, and others. These words are called **contractions**.

Apostrophes also indicate the omission of the first two numerals in years: *The professor spoke of the sit-ins of '68*. However, no apostrophe is used when you indicate a span of years: *1948–52*.

27d Using an apostrophe to form plurals of letters, numerals, symbols, and words used as terms

The child practiced writing her **Q's**.
The computer went berserk and printed out pages of **4's**.

In writing the plural form of years, two styles are acceptable: with an apostrophe (1980's) or without (1980s). Whichever form you prefer, use it consistently.

Using the Apostrophe
in Possessive Nouns

Write the possessive forms, singular and plural, for each of the following words. If you are unsure how to form the plural of any word, see your dictionary or section 22d-4.

	Singular Possessive	*Plural Possessive*
EXAMPLE COW	*cow's*	*cows'*
1. sheep		
2. pony		
3. turkey		
4. lion		
5. mouse		
6. she		
7. gorilla		
8. goose		
9. gnu		
10. ox		
11. you		
12. buffalo		
13. zebra		
14. ibex		
15. fly		
16. I		
17. giraffe		
18. dodo		
19. zoo		
20. zoo keeper		
21. he		
22. farm		
23. farmer		
24. ranch		
25. it		

Using the Apostrophe in Possessive Expressions

Rewrite each of these noun phrases as a possessive noun followed by another noun.

EXAMPLE   the schedule of the student
            the student's schedule

1. the pain of the runner

2. the visit of the class

3. the price of the shirt

4. the price of the shirts

5. the wish of everyone

6. the speed of the car

7. the speed of the cars

8. the roar of the ocean

9. the value of something

10. the recipe of my mother-in-law

11. the plan of the committee

12. the results of the competitions

13. the experience of the manager

Using Apostrophes
in Contractions

Write contractions of the following expressions.

EXAMPLE   he + is =   *he's* _____

1. are + not = _____
2. will + not = _____
3. let + us = _____
4. he + had = _____
5. was + not = _____
6. you + would = _____
7. did + not = _____
8. I + will = _____
9. what + is = _____
10. I + am = _____
11. is + not = _____
12. would + not = _____
13. can + not = _____
14. does + not = _____
15. I + have = _____
16. you + are = _____
17. there + is = _____
18. we + would = _____
19. were + not = _____
20. they + are = _____
21. it + is = _____
22. we + have = _____
23. she + will = _____
24. we + are = _____
25. do + not = _____

Using Apostrophes

Insert apostrophes as needed. If no apostrophes are called for in a sentence, write *correct* in the left margin.

EXAMPLE   The detective storys roots go back to at least 1841.

The detective story's roots go back to at least 1841.

1. The modern detective story began with Edgar Allan Poes "The Murders in the Rue Morgue."
2. Its detective reappeared in "The Mystery of Marie Rogêt" in 1842–43.
3. The authors last pure detective story was "The Purloined Letter."
4. The three stories featured amateur detective C. August Dupins ability to solve crimes by using logic.
5. Poe didn't use the word *detective* in the stories.
6. The publics response was not enthusiastic, perhaps because the heros personality was unpleasant.
7. This may explain why there werent any more detective stories by Poe.
8. Twenty years later, in 66, a Frenchman revived the detective story, and this time it was a great success.
9. Soon after, Englishman Wilkie Collins published *The Moonstone.*
10. Collins book was the first full-length detective novel in English.
11. The books hero was a professional detective who grew roses when he wasn't working.
12. *The Moonstone*s hero had a better personality than Dupin, so the publics acceptance of him is understandable.
13. Charles Dickens, Collins friend, was writing a mystery novel when he died.
14. The fragment of *The Mystery of Edwin Drood* has been studied for years, but no ones been able to figure out how Dickens planned to explain the mystery.
15. Its been one of my favorite literary puzzles for years.
16. Arthur Conan Doyles Sherlock Holmes made his debut in "A Study in Scarlet" in 1887.
17. Holmes popularity really dates from July 1891, when "A Scandal in Bohemia" was published.
18. Peoples attention was finally captured, and they demanded more and more stories featuring Holmes.
19. Conan Doyle became so tired of the character that he wrote about Holmes death, killing him in a fall over a waterfall.
20. The readers outcry was so great that Holmes was brought back for more stories in 1902.
21. Then in 1905, Holmes earlier absence was explained.
22. The explanation was weak but the fans couldnt have been happier.

28 | Quotation Marks

Quotation marks most frequently enclose direct quotations—spoken or written words from an outside source. Quotation marks also set off some titles, and they can call attention to words used in special senses. Always use quotation marks in pairs. Be especially careful not to forget the second (closing) quotation mark.

28a | Enclosing direct quotations of not more than four lines in quotation marks

Direct quotations present exact words copied from an original source. Use double quotation marks to enclose short quotations (no more than four lines).

SHORT QUOTATION

According to Marvin Harris in *Cows, Pigs, Wars, and Witches*, "We seem to be more interested in working in order to get people to admire us for our wealth than in the actual wealth itself."

Longer quotations are not enclosed in quotation marks. They are displayed, starting on a new line, and all lines of the quotation are indented ten spaces.

When the words of a short quotation already contain quotation marks, use double quotation marks at the start and end of the directly quoted words. Then substitute single quotation marks (' ') wherever there are double quotation marks in your original source.

Carl Sagan begins his essay called "In Defense of Robots" by telling us, "The word 'Robot,' first introduced by the Czech writer Karl Cāpek, is derived from the Slavic root for 'worker.' "

When the words of a longer quotation already contain quotation marks, display the quotation without enclosing it in quotation marks. Then use quotation marks exactly as they were used in your original source.

Use double quotation marks to enclose a short quotation of poetry (no more than three lines of the poem). If you quote more than one line of poetry, use slashes to show the line divisions (see 29e).

Not everyone would agree with Emily Dickinson's statement: "Success is counted sweetest / By those who ne'er succeed."

Quotation marks most frequently enclose direct quotations—spoken or written words from an outside source. Quotation marks also set off some titles, and they can call attention to words used in special senses. Always use quotation marks in pairs. Be especially careful not to forget the second (closing) quotation mark.

> "The marks were some twenty yards from the body and no one gave them a thought. I don't suppose I should have done so had I not known the legend."
> "There are many sheep dogs on the moor?"
> "No doubt, but this was no sheep dog."
> "You say it was large?"
> "Enormous."
>
> —SIR ARTHUR CONAN DOYLE, *The Hound of the Baskervilles*

In contrast to direct discourse, **indirect discourse** reports only the spirit of what a speaker said. Do not enclose indirect discourse in quotation marks.

DIRECT DISCOURSE   The professor said, "Your midterm is a week from Tuesday."

INDIRECT DISCOURSE   The professor said that our midterm would be a week from Tuesday.

28b Enclosing certain titles in quotation marks

Use quotation marks around the titles of short published works, such as pamphlets and brochures. Also use them around song titles, episodes of television series, and titles of works that are parts of longer works or parts of collected works: poems, short stories, essays, and articles from periodicals.

Stephen Jay Gould examines what we know about dinosaur intelligence in the essay "Were Dinosaurs Dumb?"

Modern readers still enjoy Edgar Allan Poe's short story "The Tell-Tale Heart."

28c Enclosing words used in special senses or for special purposes in quotation marks

Writers sometimes use quotation marks to indicate words or phrases that are not meant to be taken at face value.

The "free" records came with a bill for ten dollars—for postage and handling.

Writers sometimes put technical terms in quotation marks and define them the first time they are used. No quotation marks are used after such terms have been introduced and defined.

"Plagiarism"—the unacknowledged use of another person's words or ideas—can result in expulsion. Plagiarism is a serious offense.

28d

Words being referred to as words can be either enclosed in quotation marks or underlined.

YES   Do not confuse "then" and "than."

YES   Do not confuse *then* and *than*.

28d   Avoiding misuse of quotation marks

Writers sometimes place quotation marks around words they are uncomfortable about using. Instead of resorting to this practice, find appropriate words.

No   Einstein's theory of relativity is very "heavy stuff."

YES   Einstein's theory of relativity is very sophisticated.

Do not enclose a word in quotation marks merely to call attention to it.

No   The report is due on Friday, "or else."

YES   The report is due on Friday, or else.

Do not put quotation marks around the title of your own papers (on a title page or at the top of the first page). The only exception is if your paper's title includes words that require quotation marks for one of the reasons discussed in 28a–c.

28e   Following accepted practices for other punctuation with quotation marks

Place commas and periods inside closing quotation marks.

Besides writing such stories as "The Premature Burial," Edgar Allan Poe was also a respected literary critic and poet.

The bill read, "Registration fees must be paid in full one week before the start of classes."

Place colons and semicolons outside closing quotation marks.

The label on the ketchup said "low salt": it was also low taste.

Some people have trouble singing "The Star-Spangled Banner"; they think the United States should choose a different national anthem.

Place question marks, exclamation points, and dashes inside or outside closing quotation marks, according to the situation. If a question mark, exclamation point, or dash belongs with the words enclosed in quotation marks, put that punctuation mark *inside* the closing quotation mark.

"Where is Andorra?" asked the quiz show host.

Before her signal faded, we heard the CB'er say, "There is a radar trap on Route—"

If a question mark, exclamation point, or dash belongs with words that are *not* included in quotation marks, put the punctuation mark *outside* the closing quotation mark.

Do you know Adrienne Rich's poem "Aunt Jennifer's Tigers"?

Grieving for a dead friend, Tennyson spent seventeen years writing "In Memoriam A. H. H."!

Using Quotation Marks

Insert additional quotation marks as needed. Use double quotation marks unless single quotation marks are specifically needed. Remember to place quotation marks carefully in relation to other marks of punctuation. If a sentence needs no additional quotation marks, write *correct* in the left margin.

EXAMPLE   Speaking of an old friend, Winston Churchill said, In those days he was wiser than he is now; he used frequently to take my advice.

Speaking of an old friend, Winston Churchill said, "In those days he was wiser than he is now; he used frequently to take my advice."

1. According to Chesterfield, Advice is seldom welcome.
2. "If you are looking for trouble, offer some good advice, says Herbert V. Prochnow.
3. Marie Dressler was right: No vice is so bad as advice.
4. Someone once remarked, How we do admire the wisdom of those who come to us for advice!
5. "Free advice, it has been noted, is the kind that costs you nothing unless you act upon it."
6. "The only thing to do with good advice is to pass it on; it is never of any use to oneself," believed Oscar Wilde.
7. I sometimes give myself admirable advice, said Lady Mary Wortley Montagu, but I am incapable of taking it.
8. Says Tom Masson, " 'Be yourself! is the worst advice you can give to some people.
9. The Beatles' song With a Little Help from My Friends contains some good advice.
10. Do you seriously advise me to marry that man?
11. My uncle advised me, The next time you are depressed, read Lewis Carroll's poem Jabberwocky.
12. Do you recall the Beach Boys' words: Be true to your school?
13. Many marriage counselors advise us never to go to sleep angry with our mate.
14. However, comedienne Phyllis Diller suggests, Never go to bed mad. Stay up and fight.
15. Rachel Carson advised, The discipline of the writer is to learn to be still and listen to what his subject has to tell him.
16. If I had to give students advice in choosing a career, I would tell them to select a field that interests them passionately.

Writing Direct Quotations

Rewrite these indirect quotations as direct quotations. You will need to add commas, capitals, and quotation marks. If necessary, change pronouns and verbs to suitable forms.

EXAMPLE   The baseball coach said that the next game was especially important.
          The baseball coach said, "Our next game is especially important."

1. He said that scouts from several professional teams would be watching.

   _____

2. He told the players that big contracts were at stake.

   _____

3. He ended by saying that he was having trouble deciding who should pitch.
   [Make this a split quotation.]

   _____

4. The team manager suggested using the three best pitchers for three innings
   each.

   _____

5. Someone yelled out that that was a good idea.

   _____

6. Everyone agreed, and the coach asked for further ideas about how to give
   every player a chance to impress the scouts.

   _____

Writing Properly Punctuated Dialogue

Write an original dialogue using proper punctuation and appropriate pronouns and verb tenses. Select one of the following situations, letting each person speak at least three times. Remember to start a new paragraph each time the speaker changes. Use your own paper.

1. You are asking your boss for a raise.
2. You are asking one of your parents for advice.
3. You are trying to talk a traffic officer out of giving you a ticket.
4. You and your boyfriend/girlfriend are trying to decide what movie to see.
5. You are trying to convince your younger brother/sister not to drop out of
   high school.

29 Other Marks of Punctuation

29a Using the dash to emphasize interruptions in sentences

The dash, or a pair of dashes, lets you interrupt a sentence to add information. Dashes are like parentheses in that they set off extra material at the beginning, in the middle, or at the end of a sentence. Unlike parentheses, dashes emphasize the interruptions. Use dashes sparingly—so that their dramatic impact is not blunted.

Use a dash or dashes to emphasize explanations, including appositives, examples, and definitions.

APPOSITIVES

Many's the long night I've dreamed of cheese—toasted, mostly.

—ROBERT LOUIS STEVENSON

EXAMPLES

In general, only mute things are eaten alive—plants and invertebrates. If oysters shrieked as they were pried open, or squealed when jabbed with a fork, I doubt whether they would be eaten alive.

—MARSTON BATES

DEFINITIONS

Personal space—"elbow room"—is a vital commodity for the human animal, and one that cannot be ignored without risking serious trouble.

—DESMOND MORRIS, "Territorial Behavior"

Use a dash or dashes to emphasize a contrast.

I know a lot of people didn't expect our relationship to last—but we've just celebrated our two months' anniversary.

—Britt Ekland

Use a dash or dashes to emphasize an "aside." Asides are writers' comments within the structure of a sentence or paragraph.

These five passages have not been picked out because they are especially bad—I could have quoted far worse if I had chosen—but because they illustrate various of the mental vices from which we now suffer.

—George Orwell, "Politics and the English Language"

Commas, semicolons, colons, and periods are not used next to dashes, but if the words you put between a pair of dashes would take a question mark or an exclamation point written as a separate sentence, use that punctuation before the second dash.

The tour guide—do you remember her name?—recommended an excellent restaurant.

Use a dash to show hesitating or broken-off speech.

"Yes," he said. "That is why I am here, you see. They thought we might be interested in that footprint."
"That footprint?" cried Dorothy. "You mean—?"
"No, no; not your footprint, Miss Brant. Another one."

—Carter Dickson, "The Footprint in the Sky"

29b Using parentheses to enclose interrupting material in sentences, as well as for a few special purposes

Parentheses let you interrupt a sentence's structure to add information of many kinds. Parentheses are like dashes in that they set off extra or interrupting words. However, unlike dashes, which make interruptions stand out, parentheses deemphasize what they enclose.

Use parentheses to enclose interrupting words, including explanations, examples, and asides.

EXPLANATIONS

On the second night of his visit, our distinguished guest (Sir Charles Dilke) met Laura in the passage on her way to bed; he said to her: "If you will kiss me, I will give you a signed photograph of myself." To which she answered: "It's awfully good of you, Sir Charles, but I would rather not, for what on earth should I do with the photograph?"

—MARGOT ASQUITH

EXAMPLES

Many books we read as children (*Alice in Wonderland*, for example) are far more enjoyable when we reread them as adults.

ASIDES

I have heard of novelists who say that, while they are creating a novel, the people in it are ever with them, accompanying them on walks, for all I know on drives (though this must be distracting in traffic), to the bath, to bed itself.

—ROSE MACAULAY

Use parentheses for certain numbers and letters of listed items. When you number listed items within a sentence, enclose the numbers (or letters) in parentheses.

I plan to do four things during summer vacation: (1) sleep, (2) work to save money for next semester's tuition, (3) catch up on my reading, and (4) have fun.

In business and legal writing, use parentheses to enclose a numeral repeating a spelled-out number.

The monthly fee to lease a color television is forty dollars ($40).

Never put a comma before an opening parenthesis even if what comes before the parenthetical material requires a comma. Put the parenthetical material in, and then use the comma immediately after the closing parenthesis.

Even though I grew up in a big city (New York), I prefer small-town life.

You can use a question mark or an exclamation point with parenthetical words that occur within the structure of a sentence.

> We entered the old attic (what a mess!) and began the dirty job of organizing the junk of three generations.

Use a period, however, only when you enclose a complete statement in parentheses outside the structure of another sentence. In this case, use a capital letter as well.

> We entered the old attic and began the dirty job of organizing the junk of three generations. (The place was a mess.)

29c Using brackets to enclose insertions into quotations or into parentheses

When you work quoted words into your own sentences, you may have to change a word or two to make the quoted words fit into your structure. You may also want to add explanations to quoted material. Enclose your own words within brackets.

> According to John Ackerman, "He [Dylan Thomas] was aware of the extent to which his temperament and his imagination were the products of his Welsh environment."

When you find a mistake in something you want to quote—for example, a wrong date or a misspelled word—you cannot change another writer's words. So that readers do not think you made the error, insert the Latin word *sic* (meaning "so" or "thus") in brackets next to the error. Doing this indicates that this is exactly what you found in the original.

> The student wrote that, "The Vikings came to North America long before Columbus's arrival in 1942 [sic]."

You can also use brackets to enclose very brief parenthetical material inside parentheses.

> From that point on, Thomas Parker simply disappears. (His death [c. 1441] is unrecorded officially, but a gravestone marker is mentioned in a 1640 parish report.)

29d Using ellipses to signal omissions from quotations as well as hesitating or broken-off speech

An ellipsis is a series of three spaced dots. In quotations, it is used to show that you have left out some of the writer's original words. Ellipses can also show hesitant or broken-off speech.

Ellipses can show that you have omitted words from material you are quoting.

ORIGINAL

My aunt has survived the deaths of her husband and my parents in typical, if I may say so, West Indian fashion. Now in her 70s, and no longer principal of a New York City public school, she rises at 5 A.M. every day to prepare for another day of complicated duties as the volunteer principal of a small black private academy.

—JUNE JORDAN, "Thank You, America"

SOME MATERIAL USED IN A QUOTATION

My aunt has survived the deaths of her husband and my parents. . . . Now in her 70s, and no longer principal of a New York City public school, she rises at 5 A.M. every day to prepare for another day . . . as the volunteer principal of a small black private academy.

If an omission occurs at the beginning of your quoted words, you do not need to use an ellipsis. Also, you do not need to use an ellipsis at the end as long as you end with a complete sentence. If an ellipsis occurs after a complete sentence, use a fourth dot to represent the period of that sentence.

Also, you can use ellipses to show broken-off speech.

"And, anyway, what do you know of him?"
"Nothing. That is why I ask you . . ."
"I would prefer never to speak of him."

—UMBERTO ECO, *The Name of the Rose*

29e

Using the slash correctly for quoting poetry lines, for numerical fractions, and for *and/or* and *he/she*

If you quote more than three lines of a poem in writing, set the poetry off with space and indentations as you would a prose quotation of more than four lines. For three lines or less, quote poetry—enclosed in quotation marks—in sentence format, with a slash to divide one line from the next. Leave a space on each side of the slash.

> Robert Frost makes an important point when he writes, "Before I built a wall I'd want to know/What I was walling in or walling out,/And to whom I was like to give offense."

Capitalize and punctuate each line as it is in the original, with this exception: end your sentence with a period, even if the quoted line of poetry does not have one.

If you have to type numerical fractions, use the slash to separate numerator and denominator and a hyphen to separate a whole number from its fraction: *1/16, 1-2/3, 2/5, 3-7/8.*

You will not use word combinations such as *and/or* often, but where use is acceptable, separate the words with a slash. Leave no space before or after the slash. *He/she* is one option available to you in avoiding sexist language (see 11n and 21a).

Using Dashes, Parentheses, Brackets, Ellipses, and Slashes

Add dashes, parentheses, brackets, ellipses, or slashes as needed. If more than one kind of punctuation is possible, choose the one you think best. Be prepared to explain your decision.

EXAMPLE   "I'll pay by Do you accept checks?"

"I'll pay by—Do you accept checks?"

1. Chicago is not the windiest city in the United States Great Falls, Montana, is.
2. The next windiest cities are 2 Oklahoma City, Oklahoma, 3 Boston, Massachusetts, and 4 Cheyenne, Wyoming.
3. Chicago is relatively calm average wind speed equals 10.4 mph.
4. Greenland the largest island in the world was given its name by Eric the Red in 985.
5. The name was a masterstroke of publicity convincing settlers to come to what was actually an ice-covered wasteland.
6. Let's go to New Orleans for Mardi Oops! I have exams that week.
7. The most expensive part of a trip the airfare can be reduced by careful planning.
8. Contest rules say "The winner must appear to claim his her prize in person."
9. "Broadway my favorite street is a main artery of New York—the hardened artery," claimed Walter Winchell. [Note: *my favorite street* is not part of the quotation.]
10. Punctuate the shortened version of the following quotation: "Too often travel, instead of broadening the mind, merely lengthens the conversation," said Elizabeth Drew. "Too often travel merely lengthens the conversation," said Elizabeth Drew.
11. New Jersy sic has some spectacular parks for camping.
12. Once a camper has been there, he she will always want to return.
13. I can say only one thing about camping I hate it.
14. We leave as soon as Have you seen the bug spray? we finish packing.
15. "Let's take Interstate 80 across" "Are you crazy?"
16. Finding an inexpensive hotel motel isn't always easy.
17. Motels named from a combination of *motorist* and *hotel* are usually cheaper than regular hotels.
18. When traveling, always remember to a leave a schedule with friends, b carry as little cash as possible, and c use the hotel safe for valuables.

Using Assorted Punctuation

A: Add missing punctuation or change mistaken punctuation as needed. There may be more than one choice possible. If so, use the punctuation mark you think best. Be prepared to explain your answers.

The cheetah, is the fastest animal on earth, it can accelerate from one mile an hour to forty miles an hour in under two seconds. Briefly reaching speeds of up to seventy miles an hour. Its stride, may during these bursts of speed, be as much as (23 feet). To help it run at these speeds: the cheetah is built unlike any of the other large cats—powerful heart, oversized liver, long, thin leg bones, relatively small teeth, and a muscular tail (used for balance. Unlike other cats; it cannot pull in its claws. They are blunted by constant contact (with the earth), and so are of little use, in the hunt. The cheetah—instead, makes use of a strong dewclaw on the inside of its front, legs to grab and hold down prey.

B: Add whatever punctuation is needed to this completely unpunctuated paragraph. Be sure to add capital letters as needed too. If more than one kind of punctuation is suitable, select the best one. Be prepared to explain your choices.

Have you ever wondered how instant coffee is made first the coffee beans are prepared as they would be for regular coffee they are roasted blended and ground at the factory workers brew great batches of coffee 1800 to 2000 pounds at a time the coffee is then passed through tubes under great pressure at a high temperature this causes much of the water to boil away creating coffee liquor with a high percentage of solids at this point a decision must be made about what the final product will be powdered instant coffee or freeze dried coffee powdered instant coffee is made by heating the coffee liquor to 500°F in a large drier this boils away the remaining water and the powdered coffee is simply gathered from the bottom of the drier and packed if freeze dried coffee is being made the coffee liquor is frozen into pieces which are then broken into small granules the granules are placed in a vacuum box a box containing no air which turns the frozen water into steam which is removed all that is left are coffee solids some people say they prefer freeze dried coffee because the high temperature used to make regular instant coffee destroys some of the flavor either way the coffee is more convenient than home-brewed coffee

30 Capitals, Italics, Abbreviations, and Numbers

CAPITALS

30a Capitalizing the first word of a sentence

Always capitalize the first letter of the first word in a sentence, a question, or a command.

> Pain is useful because it warns us of danger.
> Does pain serve any purpose?
> Never ignore severe pain.

Whether to capitalize the first letter of a complete sentence enclosed in parentheses depends upon whether that sentence stands alone or falls within the structure of another sentence. Those that stand alone start with a capital letter; those that fall within the structure of another sentence do not start with a capital letter.

> I didn't know till years later that they called it the Cuban Missile Crisis. But I remember Castro. (We called him Castor Oil and were awed by his beard—beards were rare in those days.) We might not have worried so much (what would the Communists want with our small New Hampshire town?) except that we lived 10 miles from an air base.
>
> —JOYCE MAYNARD, "An 18-Year-Old Looks Back on Life"

30b Capitalizing listed items correctly

A **run-in list** works its items into the structure of a sentence. When the items in a run-in list are complete sentences, capitalize the first letter of each item.

> Three groups attended the town meeting on rent control: (1) Landlords brought proof of their expenses. (2) Tenants came to complain about poor maintenance. (3) Real estate agents came to see how the new rules would affect them.

When the items in a run-in list are not complete sentences, do not begin them with capital letters.

> Three groups attended the town meeting on rent control: (1) landlords, (2) tenants, and (3) real estate agents.

30c Capitalizing the first letter of an introduced quotation

When you quote another person's words, do not capitalize the first quoted word if you have made the quoted words part of the structure of your own sentence.

Thomas Henry Huxley called science "trained and organized common sense."

However, if your own words in your sentence serve only to introduce quoted words or if you are directly quoting speech, capitalize the first letter of the quoted words.

According to Thomas Henry Huxley, "Science is nothing but trained and organized common sense."

Do not capitalize a partial quotation or a quotation you resume within a sentence.

"We," said Queen Victoria, "are not amused."

30d Capitalizing the interjection *O* and the pronoun *I*

Temper, **O** fair Love, Love's impetuous rage.   —JOHN DONNE, "On His Mistress"

Once upon a midnight dreary, while **I** pondered, weak and weary, . . .

—EDGAR ALLAN POE, "The Raven"

30e Capitalizing nouns and adjectives according to standard practice

Capitalize proper nouns (7a) and adjectives made from them.

PROPER NOUNS	PROPER ADJECTIVES
Korea	the Korean language
Hollywood	a Hollywood studio

Notice that the articles (*the, a, an*) are not capitalized.

Do not capitalize common nouns (nouns that name general classes of people, places, or things) unless they start a sentence: *a country, the movies, friends, planes*. Many common nouns are capitalized when names or titles are added to them. For example, *lake* is not ordinarily capitalized, but when a specific name is added, it is: *Lake Erie*. Without the specific name, however, even if the specific name is implied, the common noun is not capitalized.

I would like to visit the **Erie Canal** because the **canal** played a big part in opening up the Northeast to trade.

On the next page is a list to help you with capitalization qustions. Although it cannot cover all possibilities, you can apply what you find in the list to similar items.

CAPITALIZATION GUIDE

	CAPITALS	LOWER-CASE LETTERS
Names	Bob Ojeda	
	Mother (name)	my mother (relationship)
Titles	the President (usually reserved for the president in office)	a president
	Professor Edgar Day	the professor
Groups of Humankind	Caucasian (race)	black (*or* Black)
	Negro (race)	white (*or* White)
	Oriental (race)	
Organizations	Congress	congressional
	the Rotary Club	the club
Places	Los Angeles	
	India	
	the South (a region)	turn south (a direction)
	Main Street	the street
Buildings	Carr High School	the high school
	the China Lights	the restaurant
Scientific Terms	Mars, Martian	the moon, the sun
	the Milky Way galaxy	the galaxy
Languages	Portuguese	
School Courses	Chemistry 342	the chemistry course
Names of Things	the *Times-Union*	the newspaper
	Purdue University	the university
	the Dodge Colt	
Time Names	Friday	spring, summer, fall, autumn, winter
	August	
Historical Periods	World War II	the war
	the Great Depression	the depression (any other depression)
Religious Terms	God	a god, a goddess
	Buddhism	
	the Torah	
Letter Parts	Dear Ms. Tauber:	
	Sincerely yours,	
Titles of Works	"The Lottery"	
	Catcher in the Rye	
Acronyms	IRS	
	NATO	
	AFL-CIO	

ITALICS (UNDERLINING)

In printed material, **roman type** is the standard. Type that slants to the right is called **italic**. Words in italics contrast with standard roman type, so italics create an emphasis readers can see. In typewritten and handwritten manuscripts, underline to indicate italics.

30f Following standard practice for underlining titles and other words, letters, or numbers

Some titles require underlining: long written works, names of ships, trains, and some aircraft, film titles, titles of television series. Underlining also calls readers' attention to words in languages other than English and to letters, numbers, and words used in ways other than for their meaning. The list below shows these uses. It also shows (and explains) some titles that call for quotation marks and some names and titles neither underlined nor in quotation marks.

GUIDE TO UNDERLINING

Titles: Underline	Titles: Do Not Underline
The Bell Jar (a novel)	
Death of a Salesman (a play)	
Collected Works of O. Henry (a book)	"The Last Leaf" (one story)
Simon & Schuster Handbook for Writers (a book)	"Writing Argument" (one chapter)
Contexts for Composition (a collection of essays)	"Science and Ethics" (one essay)
The Iliad (a long poem)	"Design" (a short poem)
The African Queen (a film)	
the Los Angeles Times	
Scientific American (a magazine)	"The Molecules of Life" (an article)
Twilight Zone (a television series)	"Terror at 30,000 Feet" (an episode of a television series)
The Best of Bob Dylan (an album)	"Blowin' in the Wind" (one song)

GUIDE TO UNDERLINING *(continued)*

Other Words: Underline

the <u>Intrepid</u> (a ship; don't underline preceding initials like U.S.S.)

<u>Voyager 2</u> (names of specific aircraft, spacecraft, and satellites)

<u>summa cum laude</u> (term in a language other than English)

the plural pronoun <u>they</u> (a word used as a term instead of for the meaning it conveys)

the <u>abc's</u>; confusing <u>3</u>'s *and* <u>8</u>'s (letters and numbers referred to as symbols rather than for the meaning they convey)

Other Words: Do Not Underline

aircraft carrier (a general class of ship)

Boeing 747 (general names shared by classes of aircraft, spacecraft, and satellites)

burrito, chutzpah (widely used and commonly understood words from languages other than English)

30g Underlining sparingly for special emphasis

Instead of counting on underlining to deliver impact, try to make word choices and sentence structures convey emphasis. Reserve underlining for special situations.

ABBREVIATIONS

30h Using abbreviations in the body of a paper according to standard practice

What you are writing and who will read that writing should help you to determine whether to use an abbreviation or a spelled-out word. A few abbreviations are standard in any writing circumstance.

A.M. AND P.M. WITH SPECIFIC TIMES

8:20 A.M. or 8:20 a.m.   9:35 P.M. or 9:35 p.m.

A.D. AND B.C. WITH SPECIFIC YEARS

A.D. 576 [A.D. precedes the year.]   33 B.C. [B.C. follows the year.]

TITLES OF ADDRESS BEFORE NAMES

Dr. P. C. Smith

Ms. Rachel Wang

Mr. Scott Kamiel

Mrs. Ann Wenter

ACADEMIC DEGREES AFTER NAMES

Jean Loft, Ph.D.

Asha Rohra, M.D.

Peter Kim, J.D.

Verna Johnson, D.D.

♣ ABBREVIATION CAUTION: Don't use a title of address before a name *and* an academic degree after a name. Use one or the other. ♣

If you use a long name or term often in a paper, you can abbreviate it. The first time you use it, give the full term, with the abbreviation in parentheses right after the spelled-out form. After that you can use the abbreviation alone.

Volunteers in Service to America (VISTA) began at about the same time as the Peace Corps, but VISTA participants do not go to exotic foreign countries.

You can use *USSR* without giving the spelled-out form first. You can abbreviate *U.S.* as a modifier (*the U.S. economy*), but spell out *United States* when you use it as a noun.

If you include a full address—street, city, and state—in the body of a paper, you can use the postal abbreviation for the state name, but spell out any other combination of a city and a state.

No   **Miami, FL**, is very different from the city on *Miami Vice*.

YES   **Miami, Florida**, is very different from the city on *Miami Vice*.

Symbols are seldom used in the body of papers written for courses in the humanities. You can use a percent symbol (%) or a cent sign (¢), for example, in a table, graph, or other illustration, but in the body of the paper spell out *percent* and *cent*. You can, however, use a dollar sign with specific dollar amounts: *$1.29, $10 million*.

Let common sense and your readers' needs guide you. If you mention temperatures once or twice in a paper, spell them out: *ninety degrees, minus twenty-six degrees*. If you mention temperatures throughout a paper, use figures (see 30i) and symbols: *90°, −26°*.

NUMBERS

30i Using figures and spelled-out numbers according to standard practice

Depending on how often numbers appear in a paper and what they refer to, you will sometimes express numbers in words and sometimes in figures. The guidelines here are those used in the humanities. For the guidelines that other disciplines follow, ask your instructor or consult style manuals written for specific fields.

If numerical exactness is not a prime purpose in your paper and you mention numbers only a few times, spell out numbers that can be expressed in one or two words.

> Most people need to take the road test for their driver's license **two or three** times.

> Eating **one** extra slice of bread a day can lead to a weight gain of about **seven** pounds per year.

♣ HYPHENATION ALERT: Use a hyphen between spelled-out two-word numbers from *twenty-one* through *ninety-nine*. ♣

If you use numbers frequently in a paper, spell out numbers from *one* to *nine* and use figures for numbers *10* and above.

| two shirts | 12 blocks |
| third base | 21st year |

Never start a sentence with a figure. If a sentence starts with a number, spell it out or revise so that the number does not come first.

> Thirteen is known as a baker's dozen because bakers used to give an extra roll or pastry to customers who placed large orders.
> Nineteen fifty saw the start of the Korean War.
> The Korean War started in 1950.

Give specific numbers—dates, addresses, measurements, identification numbers—in figures.

GUIDE FOR USING SPECIFIC NUMBERS

Dates	August 6, 1941 1732–1845 34 B.C. to A.D. 230
Addresses	10 Downing Street 237 North 8th Street (*or* 237 North Eighth Street) Export Falls, MN 92025
Times	8:09 A.M.; 3:30 (*but* half past three, quarter of seven, six o'clock)
Decimals and Fractions	5.55; 98.6; 3.1415; 7/8; 12-1/4 (*but* one quarter, one half, two thirds)
Chapters and Pages	Chapter 27; page 245
Scores and Statistics	a 6–0 score; a 5 to 3 ratio; 29 percent
Identification Numbers	94.4 on the FM dial; call 1-212-555-0000
Measurements	2 feet; 67.8 miles per hour; 1.5 gallons; 2 level teaspoons; 3 liters; 8½″ × 11″ paper or 8½ × 11-inch paper
Act, Scene, and Line Numbers	act II, scene 2, lines 75–79
Temperatures	43°F; −4° Celsius
Money	$1.2 billion; $3.41; 25 cents

Using Capital Letters

A: Select the passage in each pair that needs capital letters. Then rewrite the passage correctly on the line provided.

EXAMPLE   (a) going to the city next summer

           (b) going to milwaukee in june

           (b) going to Milwaukee in June

1. (a) president truman
   (b) the next president

   _____

2. (a) the ancient gods
   (b) god's love

   _____

3. (a) the federal communication
       commission
   (b) a government agency

   _____

4. (a) a meeting in the afternoon
   (b) a meeting on friday

   _____

5. (a) my favorite aunt
   (b) my aunt clara

   _____

6. (a) when i graduate
   (b) when we graduate

   _____

7. (a) the rising sun
   (b) the sun is rising

   _____

8. (a) mother teresa
   (b) my mother

   _____

9. (a) dinner at a fine restaurant
   (b) dinner at the steak
       palace

   _____

10. (a) english 202
    (b) a literature course

    _____

11. (a) across the main street
    (b) across main street

    _____

12. (a) the los angeles lakers
    (b) a basketball team

    _____

13. (a) the election officials
    (b) election day

    _____

14. (a) northeast of town
    (b) a town in the northeast

    _____

15. (a) a college in florida
    (b) a college on the coast

    _____

16. (a) ''the gift of the magi''
    (b) a story about sacrifice

    _____

17. (a) learning a second
       language
    (b) learning french

    _____

18. (a) getting a job at nassau
       county medical center
    (b) getting a job at a hospital

    _____

19. (a) stars shining in the sky
    (b) the moon and venus
       shining in the sky

    _____

20. (a) the hudson river
    (b) the polluted river

    _____

B: Rewrite these sentences on the lines provided, adding or deleting capital letters as needed. If no changes are needed, write *correct* on the line.

EXAMPLE   My uncle Peter and my Aunt are visiting.
          My Uncle Peter and my aunt are visiting.

1. The Mississippi river empties into the gulf of Mexico.

   _____

2. The Restaurant rents its back room for Private Parties.

   _____

3. He just moved two blocks South of the Railroad tracks.

   _____

4. The Semester ends in may.

   _____

5. He is saving his money to buy a Camaro or another Sports Car.

   _____

6. John Gavin, the former Ambassador to Mexico, used to be an Actor and even had his own Television Series.

   _____

7. We took a Cruise along the pacific coast all the way to alaska.

   _____

8. Madison high school graduates often choose to go to State Schools rather than Private Universities.

   _____

9. The famous race car driver made a commercial for a motor oil company.

   _____

10. The local baptist and lutheran churches joined together to open a Food Bank just North of the Park.

_____

11. The woman donated her recipe for french bread to the Cookbook the pta was selling to raise money for a new Gym.

_____

12. The bible is shared by jews and christians.

_____

13. Tickets to the Play-offs were available at the houston astrodome box office.

_____

14. At the Brookhaven national laboratory in upton, New York, visitors can see a de-activated Nuclear Reactor.

_____

15. The beatles' "I want to hold your hand" helped gain them an american audience.

_____

| EXERCISE **30-2** |
| **(30f)** |

Using Italics

A: Select the passage in each of these pairs that needs italics added. Then rewrite the passage correctly on the line provided, using underlining to indicate italics.

EXAMPLE   (a) My favorite movie is a mystery.
(b) My favorite movie is Citizen Kane.
My favorite movie is Citizen Kane. _____

1. (a) a book about war and peace
   (b) War and Peace

_____

2. (a) the humor of Bill Cosby
   (b) The Bill Cosby Show

_____

3. (a) The Washington Post
   (b) a Washington newspaper

   _____

4. (a) a cruise ship
   (b) The Queen Elizabeth II

   _____

5. (a) a space ship
   (b) the U.S.S. Enterprise

   _____

6. (a) We are homo sapiens.
   (b) We are human beings.

   _____

7. (a) pay particular attention
   (b) nota bene

   _____

8. (a) Many words have the common root, cycle.
   (b) Many words come from the same source.

   _____

9. (a) Don't tease your pets.
   (b) Never tease a hungry crocodile.

   _____

10. (a) The Orient Express was the setting of a famous mystery novel.
    (b) Amtrak goes all over the United States.

    _____

B: Rewrite these sentences on the lines provided, adding italics (underlining) as needed. If no italics are needed, write *correct* on the line.

EXAMPLE   How do you pronounce chamois?
          How do you pronounce chamois? [sham'ē]
          _____

1. The word cool has many meanings.

   _____

2. The new hospital is shaped like the letter H.

   _____

3. Scientifically the chimpanzee is called Pan troglodytes and the gorilla is Gorilla gorilla.

_____

4. I'm feeling muy bien after seeing the play Man of La Mancha.

_____

5. The H.M.S. Bounty was a real ship.

_____

6. The troubles of its crew are told in the book Mutiny on the Bounty.

_____

7. I subscribe to a Memphis newspaper.

_____

8. William Randolph Hearst began his career in journalism in 1887 running his father's paper, the San Francisco Examiner.

_____

9. By the end of his career, he had a nationwide chain of papers, and his policies had given rise to the term "yellow journalism."

_____

10. The movie Citizen Kane (1941) was an unflattering portrait of a thinly disguised Hearst.

_____

EXERCISE **30-3**
(30g)

Using Abbreviations

A. Rewrite each of these sentences, replacing inappropriate abbreviations with their full forms. If a sentence is correct as given, write *correct* on the line.

EXAMPLE   It takes years to become a dr.
          It takes years to become a doctor. _____

1. The Chang bros. are opening a fishing charter co.

_____

2. It will be off pier no. 17, not far from L.A., Calif.

   _____

3. They plan to go after game fish, e.g., shark, some of which are as much as 45 ft. long.

   _____

4. Election Day is always the 2nd Tues. in Nov.

   _____

5. What did you get for Xmas?

   _____

6. Everyone ought to know the story of Wm. Henry Harrison, 9th pres. of the U.S.

   _____

7. He is mentioned in my textbook on the hist. of poli. sci. and philo.

   _____

8. The prof. says the midterm will cover chaps. 1–5.

   _____

9. The midterm & final each count 40%.

   _____

10. The body contains about 10 pts. of blood.

    _____

11. Some people sell their blood for a few $'s.

    _____

12. A kilo. equals 2.2 lbs.

    _____

13. The counselor had an MSW degree from NYU.

    _____

14. She had put herself through school working as an assist. mgr. in a fast food rest.

    _____

15. Mr. and Mrs. McDonald live on Maple Ave. in Duluth, Minn.

    _____

B: Rewrite each of these sentences, replacing inappropriate full forms with standard abbreviations. It may be necessary to slightly rearrange some sentences.

EXAMPLE   Americans celebrate independence on the fourth day of July.
          Americans celebrate independence on July 4th. _____

1. The bank's loan officer awoke at 2:00 *ante meridiem.*

   _____

2. He was thinking about the family that had applied for a loan of thirty thousand dollars.

   _____

3. Doctor Jones had given them a letter of reference.

   _____

4. Bill Smith, a Certified Public Accountant, had also sent a letter.

   _____

5. For collateral, they offered a Spanish doubloon dated 1642 *Anno Domini.*

   _____

6. The doubloon had been in the family since nineteen nineteen.

   _____

7. Mister and Missus Grossman wanted to use the money to set up a company to make precision measuring devices.

   _____

8. They already had a contract with the National Aeronautics and Space Administration.

   _____

9. The banker wanted to give his okay, but loans this big had to be co-authorized by the bank president.

   _____

10. However, the president had taken her Self-Contained-Underwater-Breathing-Apparatus and gone on a vacation.

    _____

Using Figures

Rewrite each of these sentences, replacing inappropriate figures with words or inappropriate words with figures. If a sentence is correct as given, write *correct* on the line.

EXAMPLE   He is six feet four and a half inches.
          He is 6'4½".

1. There are a hundred and seven women in the freshman class at the law school this year.

   _____

2. Ten years ago there were only 47.

   _____

3. ⅓ the faculty is female now compared with ⅟₁₀ then.

   _____

4. Many students share apartments in a building that charges six hundred dollars for two rooms, $700 for three rooms, and $775 for 4 rooms.

   _____

5. The semester begins on September fourteenth.

   _____

6. The entering class will graduate on June first, nineteen ninety-three.

   _____

7. Entrance requirements are on pages thirty to thirty-five.

   _____

8. The average law student is expected to drink 1½ gallons of coffee a day over the next 3 years.

   _____

9. The drop-out rate is about twenty-nine percent.

   _____

10. The law school is located at Fifteen Clark Street.

    _____

31 Paraphrasing, Summarizing, and Quoting Sources

For many writing assignments, you are expected to draw upon outside sources—such as books, articles, films, and interviews—to explain and support your ideas. **Paraphrasing, summarizing**, and **quoting** are three techniques that writers use (1) to take notes from sources and (2) to incorporate into their own writing the ideas and sometimes the words of sources.

CORRECT PRACTICE FOR USING OUTSIDE SOURCES IN YOUR WRITING

1. Avoid plagiarism by always giving credit for ideas and words not originally yours.
2. Document sources accurately and completely.
3. Know how and when to use the techniques of paraphrase, summary, and quotation.

31a Avoiding plagiarism

To plagiarize is to present another person's words or ideas as if they were your own. Plagiarism is stealing. It is a serious offense that can be grounds for failure of a course or expulsion from a college. Plagiarism can be intentional, as when you deliberately copy or borrow from the work of other people in your writing without mentioning and documenting the source. Plagiarism can be unintentional—but no less serious an offense—if you are unaware of what must be acknowledged and how to go about documenting. In college, all students are expected to know what plagiarism is and how to avoid it. If you are not absolutely clear about what is involved, take time *now* to learn the rules so that you never expose yourself to charges of plagiarism.

You are not expected to document (give the source of) *common knowledge*—for example, that Columbus's ships landed in America in 1492. You might have to look up the date on which Neil Armstrong walked on the moon, but such material is common knowledge nevertheless. Similarly, you should not document *personal knowledge*—for example, that your grandmother was born June 6, 1916.

What should you document? You must acknowledge the source of any words you quote. Along with your documentation, you must always use quotation marks or, if the material is more than three lines, an indented format. In addition, you must give your source when you present someone else's ideas in your own words.

31b Understanding the concept of documentation

Basic to paraphrasing, summarizing, and quoting is documentation—acknowledging your sources by giving full and accurate information about the author, title, and date of publication, and related facts. For information about how to document properly in a particular discipline, ask your instructor or refer to the *Simon & Schuster Handbook for Writers.*

31c Paraphrasing accurately

When you **paraphrase**, you recreate in your own words a passage written by another author. Your paraphrasings offer an account of what various authorities have to say, not in their words but in yours. These ideas give substance and believability to your message. Also, paraphrasing forces you to read closely and to get the words' precise meaning into your notes. To do so, use words that come naturally to you, even if it means using more words than the author does. Use synonyms for the author's words wherever you can, but make sure that the sentences in your paraphrase make sense.

GUIDELINES FOR WRITING A PARAPHRASE

1. Say what the source says, but no more.
2. Reproduce the source's order of ideas and emphases.
3. Use your own words and phrasing to restate the message. If certain synonyms are awkward, quote the material—but do this very sparingly.
4. Read over your sentences to make sure that they make sense and do not distort the source's meaning.
5. Expect your material to be as long as, and possibly longer than, the original.
6. Avoid plagiarism.
7. Write down all documentation facts so that you can document your source when you use it in your writing.

31d Summarizing accurately

Summary reviews the main points of a passage. A summary gives you a written overview of what you have read. It is probably the most frequently used device in note-taking for papers.

To summarize a paragraph, a passage, or a chapter, you isolate its main points and write a general statement about each topic. A formal summary is composed of these sentences tied together with appropriate transitions. In an informal summary for your notes, you can worry less about transitions because the notes are meant only to give you the essence of the source.

GUIDELINES FOR WRITING A SUMMARY

1. Identify the main points.
2. Condense the main points without losing the essence of the material.
3. Use your own words to condense the message. If words have been coined by the source or if certain synonyms are awkward, quote the words—but do this very sparingly.
4. Keep your summary short.
5. Avoid plagiarism.
6. Write down all documentation facts so that you can document your source when you use it in your writing.

31e Using quotations effectively

Quotations have special impact in your writing. While paraphrase and summary put one step between your source and your readers, quotations give your readers the chance to encounter directly the words of your source. A carefully chosen, brief quotation from an expert can establish the validity of what you say.

GUIDELINES FOR WORKING QUOTATIONS INTO YOUR WRITING

1. Set off quotations with quotation marks; otherwise you will be plagiarizing.
2. Do not use quotations in more than a third of your paper; rely mostly on paraphrase and summary to report information from sources.
3. Use quotations to *support* what you say, not to present your thesis and main points.
4. Choose a quotation if
   a. its language is particularly appropriate.
   b. its thought is particularly difficult to rephrase accurately.
   c. the authority of the source is especially important as support for your thesis and main ideas.
   d. the source's words are open to interpretation.
5. Quote accurately.
6. Select quotations from authorities in your subject.
7. Select quotations that fit your meaning.
8. Keep long quotations to a minimum.
9. Work quotations smoothly into your writing.
10. Document your source.

Paraphrasing

A. Paraphrase the following paragraph.

The years between 18 and 50 are the center of life, the unfolding of maximum opportunity and capacity. But without any guide to the inner changes on the way to full adulthood, we are swimming blind. When we don't "fit in," we are likely to think of our behavior as evidence of our inadequacies, rather than as a valid stage unfolding in a sequence of growth, something we all accept when applied to childhood. It is even easier to blame our periods of disequilibrium on the closest person or institution: our mother, our marriage, our work, the nuclear family, the system. We seize on the cop-out.

—GAIL SHEEHY, *Passages*

B. Select any sample paragraph in Chapter 4 and paraphrase it.

C. Select a paragraph from one of your textbooks or any other nonfiction work and paraphrase it.

Summarizing

A. Summarize the following paragraph.

For as long as there has been adolescence, we belonging to its self-conscious legions have had the problem of hiding our gruesome little secret (inadequacy) while trying to appear as the attractive, confident, convivial persons we all want to be all the time. How do we humor ourselves through this contradiction between the ages of 18 and 22? We seek an idea to believe in, heroes and heroines to copy, and we begin to rule out what we don't want to do with our lives.

—GAIL SHEEHY, *Passages*

B. Select any sample paragraph in Chapter 4 and summarize it.

C. Select a paragraph from one of your textbooks or any other nonfiction work and summarize it.

Quoting

A. Select the portion of this passage that could be usefully quoted in a report. Carefully and accurately copy that portion of the passage. Be prepared to explain why quoting, rather than summarizing or paraphrasing, is called for.

> Studies record a dramatic climb in satisfaction with marriage in the mid-forties for those couples who have survived the passage into midlife together. What this finding reflects is not that our mate miraculously improves but that tolerance can become spontaneous once we stop displacing our inner contradictions on our spouse. The steep rise of contentment levels off after 50 at a higher plateau.
>
> Partners know each other pretty well by this time (although there is, and always should be, room for surprise). Middle age presents many couples with the opportunity for true companionship, for by now it is clear that shared interests and a healthy respect for privacy are not mutually exclusive. There is a good chance of having someone to grow old with, to share friends and memories and walks in the rain with, someone to absorb the hush of a household where children no longer reside and to make it resonate with the joys of recaptured time together.

—GAIL SHEEHY, *Passages*

B. Select any sample paragraph in Chapter 4 and write a paraphrase which includes the most important passages as quotations.

C. Select a paragraph from one of your textbooks or any other nonfiction work, and take notes that combine paraphrase with careful, selective quotation.

Index

Section numbers are in boldface type and page numbers in regular type. The listing **7a**: 61 thus refers you to page 61, which is in section 7a.

Emily R. Gordon (right) received her M.A. from Queens College of the City University of New York (CUNY) in 1978. Involved in teaching since 1971, she currently holds joint appointments at Queensborough Community College of CUNY and Hofstra University.

She brings a varied teaching background to her writing, having taught on many skills levels: Basic Writing, Freshman Composition, English as a Second Language, and Advanced Composition. She has also served as a supervisor and trainer of writing lab tutors. She has many years' experience with holistic scoring, having served locally as Chief Reader and on the national level participating at readings of the English Composition Test of the College Boards and the Advanced Placement Examination in English for the Educational Testing Service. She is author of *Diagnostic and Competency Tests to Accompany the Simon & Schuster Handbook for Writers* (Prentice Hall). She has served as guest editor of the *Queensborough Review* (1986) and is a member of the Editorial Board of the *Journal of Basic Writing* (1987–).

Lynn Quitman Troyka (left) received her Ph.D. from New York University in 1973. She joined the faculty of Queensborough Community College of the City University of New York (CUNY) in 1967 where she became a Professor (specializing in writing) in 1976.

She is author of the *Simon & Schuster Handbook for Writers*, the companion volume to this workbook. She is also co-author of *Steps in Composition*, Fifth Edition (Prentice Hall), and author of *Structured Reading*, Third Edition (Prentice Hall). She is a past chair (1981) of the Conference on College Composition and Communication, and is currently Chair of both the College Section of NCTE and the Division on the Teaching of Writing of the Modern Language Association.